CULTURE AND CATASTROPHE

Also by Steven E. Aschheim

BROTHERS AND STRANGERS: The East European Jew in German and German-Jewish
  Consciousness, 1800–1923
THE NIETZSCHE LEGACY IN GERMANY, 1890–1990

Culture and Catastrophe

German and Jewish Confrontations with National Socialism and Other Crises

Steven E. Aschheim

MACMILLAN

First published 1996 by
MACMILLAN PRESS LTD
Houndmills, Basingstoke, Hampshire RG21 6XS
and London
Companies and representatives
throughout the world

ISBN 0–333–62312–6 hardcover
ISBN 0–333–62313–4 paperback

A catalogue record for this book is available
from the British Library.

10   9   8   7   6   5   4   3   2   1
05   04   03   02   01   00   99   98   97   96

Printed and bound in Great Britain by
Biddles Ltd
Guildford and Kings Lynn

For Hannah . . . with love

Contents

Preface

The present collection of essays revolves around the intricate interplay between culture and catastrophe. It seeks to engage the various permutations, the complexity and unresolved dimensions of this connection especially as it relates to the origins, disposition and aftermath of National Socialism. Chapter 2, the focus of which is upon the Weimar Republic, does not touch upon the National Socialist experience but as it analyzes the relation between Jewish intellectuals, German culture and the emergence of a novel consciousness of catastrophe (or apocalypse) and redemption it merits inclusion here.

About two years ago the always-encouraging George Mosse suggested that I publish some of my articles in book form. I was flattered by his confidence in me but kept in mind my friend Ezra Mendelsohn's admonitions that only great historians had a right to re-publish their work! I took his advice to heart and so, with the exception of Chapter 3, all the essays in this collection are new (some will appear simultaneously in other places and languages). I hope that they constitute something of a meaningful and coherent unity.

If they do, this will be due to the help and sagacious advice of many friends and colleagues. I have already mentioned Ezra Mendelsohn (my inspirational conversation-partner at the Hebrew University) and George Mosse's counsel and friendship. My critical dialogue with him reflects the central relevance and continuing influence of his work on my own. John Landau, as always, was the great sounding-board, prepared to put up with my crises and meanderings at any ungodly time of the morning and gently intent – though not always successful – on deepening my thought. I had many interesting conversations with Martin Bauer, Jonathan Frankel, Jerrold Kessel, Jerry Muller and Dan Pekarsky. They all showed real interest in the project and tried their utmost to save me from embarassing errors. My thanks to Niko Pfund and T.M.Farmiloe for their helpfulness and willingness to publish this book, and to Keith Povey for his helpful yet unobtrusive editorial work.

I have left the most delightful part for the end. Nothing could give me more pleasure than to dedicate this book to my beautiful and wise wife Hannah. I cannot imagine my life without her. Only within the confines of a warm, boisterous home do I find it possible to do any work. My lovely children Ariella, Yoni and Daniel make sure that such conditions apply all the time. It is a family that makes it all worthwhile.

STEVEN E. ASCHHEIM

Acknowledgements

We wish to thank the following publishers for permission to reprint from the following articles upon which Chapters 3 and 7 of this book are based (note that the author has taken the opportunity to make changes to the original published work):

Chapter 3, '"The Jew Within": The Myth of Judaization in Germany', first appeared in *The Jewish Response to German Culture*, ed. Jehuda Reinharz and Walter Schatzberg © 1985 by the University Press of New England.

Chapter 7, 'Small Forays, Grand Theories and Deep Origins: Current Trends in the Historiography of the Holocaust', is taken from *Studies in Contemporary Jewry, Vol. 10, Reshaping the Past: Jewish History and the Historians,* ed. Jonathan Frankel (New York/Oxford: Oxford University Press, 1994).

1 Culture and Catastrophe

As the years go by, the relations between 'culture' (however defined) and the 'catastrophe' unleashed by National Socialism (from whatever perspective) becomes more and more complex and multi-faceted. What remains consistent – and this in itself is perhaps a source of ongoing astonishment – is the degree to which the two have always been regarded as in some (however elusive) way co-implicated. At all kinds of levels, the diverse articulations, the multiple permutations and ever-renewed elaborations – as well as the heated denials – of these connections have themselves become an integral part of the web of Western sensibility, built into the framework of its ethical, political and theoretical self-consciousness.

This chapter seeks to explore some of these manifold connections in preliminary and suggestive rather than systematic fashion. Indeed, it will have to omit entirely some important twists of this complicated relationship. The ways in which the National Socialists themselves related to culture, for instance, lies beyond the purview of this essay[1]. Suffice it to say that it is not sufficient to dismiss this issue by recalling Goebbels' (apocryphal?) statement that 'Every time I hear the word "culture" I reach for my revolver'. For all its brutality (perhaps because of it) Nazism always spoke in the name of the great German cultural tradition, annexed its pantheon of heroes and bent their fame and thought to its own purposes. Such 'high culture' not only lent an aura of much-needed respectability to Nazism on public occasions. It also was used to justify the atrocities they committed. Were not such actions necessary for the defence of clean classical cultural values and ideal images against those polluted, degenerate groups who sought to sully and defile them?[2]

What is more germane here, however, is the degree to which some of National Socialism's – more intellectual – victims *confronted and interpreted their experiences precisely through this prism of culture and catastrophe* (though they underwent quite different experiences and often reached divergent conclusions). The poignant cultural irony of Nazi atrocities becomes sharply apparent when one recalls the degree to which many of its victims had traditionally regarded Germany as a major civilising force. Generations of modernizing East European Jews had looked admiringly towards Germany as the most prominent avenue to *Bildung* and Enlightenment.[3] Even more painful was the fact that from the late eighteenth century on, German Jews had constructed themselves in that culture's image – indeed, in crucial ways were to become partially constitutive of it (a perception which in turn aroused the vehement indignation of their anti-semitic opponents).[4]

1

It is only within this context that the remarkable memoirs of Jean Amery (1912–1978) become comprehensible. Amery was born and raised in Vienna where he thoroughly absorbed the European – especially the German – humanistic tradition. When he became a victim of National Socialism he did so as a secular, German-speaking Jewish intellectual whose entire being was steeped in, and dependent upon, its values and associations. For Amery, perhaps the most stark existential fact he confronted in the camps was the stripping away of this spiritual inheritance, the experience of expropriation from his own culture. 'No matter to what he turned, it did not belong to him, but to the enemy ... In Auschwitz the isolated individual had to relinquish all of German culture ... to even the lowest SS man.'[5]

Amery's reflections uniquely recount not only this involuntary relinquishment but also the breakdown of culture as such in the face of catastrophe, the radically unsuccessful confrontation of the rational intellect with ultimate horror. Here was an inheritance, he writes, that was not only 'of no help, but ... led straight into a tragic dialectic of self-destruction.' For, unlike political or religious prisoners who were sustained by their beliefs and convictions, borne by a spiritual continuity that not even Auschwitz could interrupt, for Amery, the literary, philosophical and aesthetic arsenal available to the unbelieving intellectual was hopelessly inadequate. While theological or ideological faith placed the reality of horror within the frame of a transcendent, unalterable idea, the intellectual – used, as Amery cynically put it, to subjecting power to a critical analysis while at the same time capitulating to it – finally faced 'a reality that could not be escaped and that therefore finally seemed *reasonable*.' Thinking – and the cultural tools and substance that informed it – was nullified when its associations seemed to have lost all relevance and power of explanation, 'when at almost every step it ran into uncrossable borders. The axes of its traditional frames of reference then shattered.'[6]

But if for Amery culture and intellect were rendered dysfunctional, its tropes and metaphors unable to account for, or console in the face of, this unimaginable catastrophe, for some it was a key to bearing it. The title of the camp diary of the Dutch critic and translator Nico Rost (1898–1967), *Goethe in Dachau*, was not ironically intended (nor did it imply a prevalent thesis of the 1940s and 1950s that somehow there was a direct line from Luther – or Goethe – to Hitler).[7] The diary is filled with descriptions of Rost's daily consolatory immersions into the great works and his re-readings of the tradition deepened by his camp experiences.[8] Rost describes his period in Dachau as essentially made endurable, lightened, by this passionate re-exposure to and reaffirmation of the great Western philosophical and literary works and German classical culture in particular. Amery, reflecting on the diary, locates Rost's admirable, almost uncanny, ability to substitute 'classical literature for Red Cross packages' in the decisive distinction between Dachau – which possessed a library and where the intellect could still possess a social function – and Auschwitz where 'a book was something hardly still imaginable' and where 'the intellect was nothing more than itself and there was no chance to apply it to a social structure, no matter how insufficient, no matter how concealed it may have been.'[9]

Yet, as the recollections of yet another famous Auschwitz inmate, Primo Levi (1919–1987), reveal there were – even in *anus mundi* – other possibilities of experiencing this relationship. Perhaps the most memorable chapter of his *Survival in Auschwitz* revolves around – and is entitled – 'The Canto of Ulysses.' There Levi relates how, in the midst of the daily round of the camp, he sought to remember canto 26 of Dante's *Inferno* ('The canto of Ulysses. Who knows how or why it comes into my mind ... .Who is Dante? What is the *Comedy*?')[10] in order to explain its beauty and significance to his young friend, Jean Samuel, the messenger of the work *Kommando*. Levi's act of Dante remembrance, far from demonstrating the bankruptcy of culture, uncovers the layers of its explanatory power, its continuing relevance and radiant humanising capacity.[11] Levi's Ulysses is available as a vital link with tradition, experientially resonant, a Catholic hell excruciatingly revelatory of its secular equivalent designed to degrade human beings and burn their flesh.

Although, as Zvi Jagendorf has pointed out, there is no salvation in Levi's narrative, there is the secular freedom of cultural remembrance and analogy. And, for all the despair, his partial recovery of an incomplete quotation – 'I would give today's soup to know how to connect "the like on any day" to the last lines' – is testament to the fact that the *Lager* has not obliterated all civilized tradition. Cultural remembrance becomes both a form of consolation and a token of opposition, 'the mind's resistance to the methodical brutality of the Lager. For the struggle to reconstruct the text and speak the quotation correctly, even if unsuccessful, affirms the existence of a kind of causality which is strong enough to rival the enforced cruelty of the camp regime.'[12] The 'Canto of Ulysses' recounts an actual moment at Auschwitz where culture affirmed its majestic capacity for both making sense of and – in a limited but deeply human way – overcoming the meaninglessness and reality of the inferno.

Years later, Levi verified the authenticity of this incident, its many details confirmed by his still surviving friend, Jean Samuel. Dante's verses, Levi retrospectively insisted, 'had great value. They made it possible for me to re-establish a link with the past, saving it from oblivion and reinforcing my identity. They convinced me that my mind, though besieged by everyday necessities, had not ceased to function.' It is significant that Levi's comments were couched in the context of his dissent from Amery insisting that: 'Culture could be useful: not often, not everywhere, not for everyone, but sometimes, on rare occasions, precious as a precious stone, it was actually useful, and one felt almost lifted up from the ground – with the danger of crashing back down again, the pain being all the greater the higher and longer the exaltation had lasted.'[13]

Levi intuitively linked Dante's portrayal of Hell with the camp experience. Not all of his readers were happy with this way of thinking. For certain Jews – made deeply suspicious of the classical Western inheritance – it was precisely the Canto chapter that roused their ire. Dante, they objected, was central to a wider anti-Semitic culture that had culminated in the camps. To invoke him – in such a setting – was evidence of Levi's Jewish alienation that was so 'complete that even Auschwitz could not teach him the futility of assimilation.'[14] But (this dubious assimilationist lesson apart) in the absence of cognitive tools commensurable with the enormity of the event, it was quite natural for Levi's 'imagination' of the catastrophe to turn in this direction. This was true even when the camps ceased to be a reality. Later critics have similarly sought analogous – if not explanatory – orientation within the matrix of precisely these traditional cultural associations. 'The reality of concentration camps', Hannah Arendt wrote in *The Origins of Totalitarianism*, 'resembles nothing so much as medieval pictures of Hell. The one thing that cannot be reproduced is what made the traditional conceptions of Hell tolerable to man: the Last Judgement, the idea of an absolute standard of justice combined with the infinite possibility of grace.'[15] George Steiner (who himself has been instrumental in opening up the question of, and investigating the links between, culture and catastrophe) has put it even more graphically:

L'univers concentrationnaire has no true counterpart in the secular mode. Its analogue is Hell. The camp embodies, often down to minutiae, the images and chronicles of Hell in European art and thought from the twelfth to the eighteenth centuries. It is these representations which gave to the deranged horrors of Belsen a kind of 'expected logic' ... .The concentration and death camps of the twentieth century, wherever they exist, under whatever regime, are *Hell made immanent*. They are the transference of Hell from below the earth to its surface. Because it imagined more fully than any other text, because it argued the centrality of Hell in the Western order, the *Commedia* remains our literal guide-book – to the flames, to the ice-fields, to the meat-hooks. In the camps the millenary pornography of fear and vengeance cultivated in the Western mind by the Christian doctrines of damnation, was realized.[16]

At any rate, if for Amery the humanist inheritance was rendered dysfunctional and for Rost and Levi culture played a clarificatory, consolatory and humanising role ('perhaps' wrote Levi, 'it saved me'[17]), for many of those who did not experience the event at first hand, those critics and intellectuals who produced what today must be considered the key texts of the immediate post-war period, those beginning to more reflectively assimilate and think through the catastrophe, culture, far from being represented as the simple antithesis of Nazism, was regarded as *essentially complicit in the disaster*. This, of course, was understood in various, even contradictory, ways but nevertheless informed a whole slew of works that sought to grasp the event and place it into some kind of comprehensible perspective.

Most famously, in his post-war essays and novels, Thomas Mann gave classical and complex expression to the *Sonderweg* view, the notion of a specifically *German* cultural connection to National Socialism. What endowed this reading with peculiar persuasive force was Mann's refusal to exempt himself from complicity, insisting that it was all 'part of my inner experience': 'Not a word of all that I have told you about Germany ... came out of alien, cool, objective knowledge, it is all within me, I have been through it all.'[18] (We should not forget that Mann's earlier works – most notoriously the 1918 *Reflections of a Nonpolitical Man*[19] – apotheosized many of the tendencies he now excoriated. Arguably, the idealist style and mythical categories that he now criticised, informed his thought throughout: only now the priorities were inverted.[20]) To Western ears, it was comforting too that Mann refused – what he took to be – the facile distinction between 'good' and 'bad' Germans, insisting on the interconnections between the (many) noble and evil aspects of German history and psychology. There was an inner dialectic at work within German culture; 'wicked Germany is merely good Germany gone astray, good Germany in misfortune, in guilt, and ruin.'[21]

There is no point rehearsing in detail the multiple facets of Mann's analysis of German culture. The ambiguous effects of Luther and his reformation, Germany's peculiar apolitical tradition, its provincial cosmpolitanism and so on – all are portrayed as endowed with positive, ennobling dimensions that are simultaneously implicated in the 'secret union of the German spirit with the Demonic', linked to the metamorphosis – or degeneration – of good into evil. This, for example, Mann argues was the precise fate of German romanticism with its predeliction (to which Mann, as his description indicates, was still attracted) towards 'a certain dark richness ... .of soul that feels very close to the chthonian, irrational, and demonic forces of life, that is the true sources of life', a predeliction destined to lead to the brink. Romanticism's grand qualities – consciousness of depth, strength and fullness – provided the potential for its breaking out 'into hysterical barbarism, into a spree and a paroxysm of arrogance and crime, which now finds its horrible end in a national catastrophe, a physical and psychical collapse without parallel.'[22]

In Mann's literary masterwork anatomizing the German catastrophe, *Dr. Faustus* (1947), it is precisely that which is most *creative* in the German soul, and above all its essential Dionysian musicality – music which was at once 'calculated order and chaos-breeding irrationality'[23] – that is indicted as the demonic core. Here, National Socialist barbarism is conceived not as antithetical to the highest in German culture but rather as standing in direct – if parodistic and degenerated – relation to it, its (distorted) meaning and essence disclosed only by reference to Germany's traditional cultural order.

What Mann did in literary and essayistic fashion his great Marxist admirer Georg Lukács[24] attempted to do in historico-philosophic form. He too found the essential explanation for – and meaning of – 'German Fascism' as peculiarly disclosed in a specific culture, in the manifold post-Hegelian manifestations of what he termed 'irrationalism.'[25] However, *The Destruction of Reason* (1952) simply dispensed with Mann's insistence upon the ironic complexities of 'irrationalism.' Virtually all post-1848, and especially post-1871, German cultural developments – after which, according to Lukács, bourgeois thought lost its universal and progressive Hegelian thrust and became the retarded ideational reflection of a peculiarly delayed, increasingly brutalized capitalism – are undifferentiatedly presented as forms of ever-more radical, anti-objectivist, progress-denying, mythologizing irrationalism.[26] Nazism was merely the natural culmination, the most brutal and virulent expression of this development. 'In Hitler's politics', Lukács insisted, 'we can see the translation of irrationalist philosophy into practice.'[27]

Max Horkheimer and Theodor Adorno's by-now classic attempt to account for Nazism, *Dialectic of Enlightenment* (1947), adopted a quite different tack.[28] Unlike Mann, they did not relate barbarism to the particular cultural modalities of a *German Sonderweg*, nor, à la Lukács, to an autonomous irrationalism that had become unhinged from its essentially progressive, rational moorings, but rather to a much broader frame, to what had traditionally been regarded as the ultimate civilising and culturally refined agent of the West – Enlightenment itself (conceived not only in terms of the eighteenth century movement of that name but as the very project of 'rational' thought and instrumental action characteristic of all of Western civilisation). Modern barbarism and totalitarianism, far from being the enemies of classical liberalism, were in effect one of its logical offshoots. The structures of 'domination' and exploitation – the general instrumentalization of man as well as nature – were implicit in the whole Enlightenment project and, carried to its logical extreme, responsible for the horrors of the twentieth century.[29]

This work, to be sure, proferred a *dialectic* of enlightenment – enlightenment both as a demystifying expression of antipathy to domination and as a tool for such domination (a dialectic best recognized by Hegel and Nietzsche)[30] – yet by the end the reader could have been forgiven for missing the other side of the dialectic and being left with an overwhelming impression of reason as almost entirely a force making for barbarism and repression rather than overcoming it.

That this work has become perhaps the most definitive contemporary statement of the intimate nexus between culture, barbarism and catastrophe may perhaps tell us less about the subject at hand than about our own sensitivities and predilections. It has spawned a whole genre of works of indictment that – with scant attention to the tangible, mediating historical links – causally relate (often poorly defined and ideologically loaded) conceptions of the culture of 'modernity' or 'Enlightenment'[32] to National Socialism and genocide. In its most recent manifestations there is no longer even the pretence of a *dialectic* of Enlightenment. Thus, for Berel Lang, whose *bête noire* in this respect is none other than Immanuel Kant, the very preconditions *required* for Nazi genocide emanate almost entirely from the Enlightenment. The *Aufklaerung*'s totalizing and universalizing impulses, its non-allowance for particularity and rationalist concept of humanity in which those deemed not to possess the appropriate characteristics are excluded from the human family, make genocide a thinkable proposition and opens the way to extermination.[33] (In an argument that presents Nazism as the incarnation of a world-view it utterly despised and openly opposed, there is precious little attempt to establish the concrete connections linking these two movements.[34])

The *Dialectic of Enlightenment* – and the other works that stand in this tradition – is clearly 'dominated by the question of Nazism'[35] yet because it collapses distinctive developments into ahistorical generalisations, it is difficult to separate the phenomenon of National Socialism from a far wider and ongoing (mass-cultural) barbarism of what is held to be characteristic of the entire capitalist West.

It is the generalized critique of instrumental rationality as the hallmark of modern civilization as such, and the disinclination to engage in concrete historical particularities that ironically renders this neo-Marxist reading uncomfortably parallel to its apparently diametrically opposed Heideggerian elision. To be sure, the differences are obvious (quite apart from the glaring fact that Heidegger had been a Nazi party member and ideologist): the *Dialectic of Enlightenment* included, albeit in highly abstract form, an analysis of the elements of anti-semitism; it was Adorno who was clearly concerned with the implications of the post-Holocaust era[36] and proclaimed that 'after Auschwitz no poetry is possible'[37] and another member of the Frankfurt School, Herbert

Marcuse, who explicitly challenged Heidegger to specifically address and condemn the extermination of the Jews.[38]

Yet in their concern for the wider picture and the meaning – as well as the critique – of the overall pattern of modern developments and in their disregard for historical contingency a certain commonality pertains. For Heidegger, of course, the overwhelming issue was nothing less than the 'history of Being' in the West. Virtually all modern cultural and political barbarities are reduced to undifferentiated manifestations of 'nihilism', the 'will to power' and technological domination, symptoms of the demise of Being and the growth of an unrelieved wasteland.[39] (This universalising technique for evading the particularities of German crimes became a staple diet of the German radical right after the war.[40]) At the time of his denazification proceedings, Heidegger proclaimed nothing less than the 'universal rule of the will to power within history, now understood to embrace the planet. Today everything stands in this historical reality, no matter whether it is called communism, or fascism, or world democracy.'[41] This was the basis of his notorious equation of motorized agriculture with the gas chambers, his levelling of the genocide of the Jews with Allied treatment of East Germans.[42] As Juergen Habermas caustically summed it up 'under the levelling gaze of the philosopher of Being even the extermination of the Jews seems merely an event equivalent to many others.'[43]

It is true that another post-war masterwork, Hannah Arendt's *The Origins of Totalitarianism* (1951), did not regard either the specifically German or, indeed, the Western (rationalist or otherwise) cultural tradition as complicit in the catastrophe. There were no mainstream connections, Arendt maintained, between Hitler and the themes and predispositions of European thought. She went out of her way to argue that totalitarianism – and the camps that incarnated its essence – was a radical *novum* marking a decisive break with, indeed a fundamental negation of, all previously known culture and tradition. Indeed, for Arendt the emergence of the Nazi type actually 'replaced *the German*.' This 'type, who in sensing the danger of utter destruction decides to turn himself into a destroying force', she insisted, 'is not confined to Germany alone. The Nothing from which Nazism sprang could be defined in less mystical terms as the vacuum resulting from an almost simultaneous breakdown of Europe's social and political structures.'[44] Arendt, in effect, rested her analysis upon a widespread, but highly problematic and vaguely conceptualised, theory of mass society – an analysis shared, in one way or another, by Heidegger, Adorno and the conservative German historians, Friedrich Meinecke and Gerhard Ritter, alike.[45]

In Arendt's case, the theory of mass society enabled her to cling onto the belief in the essentially humanising qualities of Western culture and tradition. The roots of barbarism, she suggested, were to be found in processes of uprooting and atomization and had no cultural history in any conventional sense of the term (perhaps obscuring the fact, as one critic has recently argued, 'that Hitler's New Order was indeed an Order, which as long as it was victorious, was acceptable to many, without the sanction of terror, and which could be justified in terms of themes that had been long present' and that were a recognizable part of the historical European inheritance[46]).

In all these works then, their many differences notwithstanding, there lay a common denominator. Whether one approached National Socialism as in some way an outgrowth of, or standing in dialectical relation to, 'history' and 'culture', or, indeed, utterly denied such connections, all these theories were occasioned by essentially the same sense of outrage, the shock that such events could issue from within a modern, civilised society, and in particular be perpetrated by *the* most Enlightened *Kulturnation*. The enduring fascination with (and deep need to account for) National Socialism and the atrocities it committed – the rich multiplicity of ruminations it has produced and its accumulative imprint on our political and intellectual discourse (as well as the accompanying, ubiquitous attempts to relativise or neutralize or elide and displace its significance and impact) – resides precisely in this, rather ethnocentric, sense of scandal and riddle, *the abiding astonishment that a modern allegedly cultured society could thus deport itself*: 'The cry of the murdered sounded in the earshot of the universities; the sadism went on a street away from the theaters and museums ... the high places of literacy, of philosophy, of artistic expression, became the setting for Belsen ... We know now', writes George Steiner, 'that a man can read Goethe or Rilke in the evening, that he can play Bach and Schubert, and go to his day's work at Auschwitz in the morning.'[47]

In these insights lies a (Central and West) Euro-centrism, a certain implied superiority that goes together with a refreshingly self-critical posture, a self-interrogatory attitude itself also definitive of the culture under question. The blackness of such atrocities, Steiner continues, 'did not spring up in the Gobi desert or the rain forests of the Amazon'. By extension, if and when it does in places removed from the European center – such as Rwanda – one is (tragically) likely to be less appalled, less able to empathically connect.[48] It is precisely the enduring outrage, and the ongoing fascination,[49] generated by the penetration of the barbarous within the allegedly cultured, the transgression of basic taboos within the framework of advanced civilisation, that has endowed Nazism with its distinctive status within Western sensibility.[50]

Since World War II, Treblinka and Auschwitz have evolved into what Jean Amery has called 'symbolic code words.'[51] They have come to function as a kind of outermost metaphysical norm but also as tangible shorthand, the culture's repository for, and embodiment of, 'radical evil'[52] (or the 'demonic' to use a favourite epithet of the 1940s and 1950s), encoded into consciousness as *the* measure of absolute inhumanity.[53] This was so even in the face of the worst excesses of the Stalinist regime (and not only because of the obvious differences between the two cases). Nor was it fully explicable in terms of Russia's slight, but significant, distance from the geographical and spiritual center of European gravity and its image as a 'half-Asian' power characterised by a continuous tradition of despotism. Above all, for countless intellectuals and supporters, the redemptive promise, the universalist, utopian strain of Communism – so obviously lacking in Nazism – rendered possible a mode of justificatory thinking they would never have dreamed of applying to Nazism. At the end of 1994(!) a shockingly unrepentant Eric Hobsbawm, one of the century's great historians and a lifelong member of the Communist party, could still argue that the elimination of millions of people in the Soviet experiment was still justifiable in these terms: 'Because in a period in which, as you might say, mass murder and mass suffering are absolutely universal, the chance of a new world being born in great suffering would still have been worth backing.'[54]

In a quite distinctive way, then, 'Nazism' has developed into a dense, available paradigm, serving manifold purposes of discourse, a figural commodity whose powerful, putatively 'absolute' associations have necessarily interacted with – and continue to be influenced and re-channeled by – changing modes of self-understanding and mobilised and manipulated by divergent political and psychological needs and interests. The resulting inscriptions of the National Socialist catastrophe – as well as the ensuing attempts to challenge and unravel them – must therefore be understood in terms of essentially dynamic and complex processes, reflective of shifting intellectual sensibilities and the changing perspectives of those interested parties and institutions most central to the mediation of this event. *'Culture' – including changing conceptions as to what constitutes culture, canonical authority and modes of transmission – itself has thus always impinged on and redefined the catastrophe, absorbing and reshaping it.* For our purposes all reflections surrounding the National Socialist experience become grist for the mill. Adorno-like ruminations proclaiming the radical failure, 'untruth' and ensuing paradoxes of culture – 'All post-Auschwitz culture, including its urgent critique, is garbage. Whoever pleads for the maintenance of this radically culpable and shabby culture becomes its accomplice, while the man who says no to culture is directly furthering the barbarism which our culture showed itself to be'[55] – will themselves be treated as cultural documents, absorbed into an ongoing discourse (a process against which Adorno himself warned), symptomatic of a whole genre of – an often flattening, melodramatic – *Kulturkritik* produced in the aftermath of the catastrophe.

The rest of this exploratory essay will, then, begin to trace the dynamics of this emotionally charged limit-case within post-World War II Western discourse, examine the major strategies of its commemoration and canonization (or repression and displacement), and analyze some of the consequences, shifting functions and ambiguities tied to its representation.[56] Its peculiar location and loading – the central metaphorical and symbolic functions it has come to assume (especially as it impinges on German and Jewish identity) – has always generated certain tensions tending either to reinforce or undermine the prevailing paradigm. More than ever, however, that paradigm is presently beset by pressures towards redefinition, challenges to its status and quite striking processes of ironic self-subversion.

Here we can point to only a few, divergent examples of the tensions induced by this potent symbolism and the resulting drive to exploit, problematise or undermine it. In the first place, it is only because of Nazism's peculiar emplacement, the insistence upon the radical uniqueness and incomparability of its more extreme criminal acts, that many of the present stormy academic debates and challenges concerning this status, most recently and extremely exemplified in the German *Historikerstreit*, take on their peculiar salience.[57] The *Historikerstreit*, I would suggest, makes sense only within the context of this aura. The demand to 'historicise' the narrative around National Socialism and its defining atrocities could only arouse the indignation and heated debate that ensued because of the metahistorical dimensions with which it has been so regularly endowed.

'Auschwitz', Dan Diner has written, 'is a no-man's land of understanding, a black box of explanation, a vacuum of extrahistorical singificance, which sucks in attempts at historiographic interpretation ... As the ultimate extreme case, and thus as an absolute standard of history, this event can hardly be historicized.'[58] This assumption of metahistoricity applies equally to those who, like Werner Hamacher, argue that Auschwitz, far from acting as an absolute standard of history, destroys its very possibility: 'This "history" cannot enter into history. It deranges all dates and destroys the ways to understand them.'[59]

But, by training, historians 'historicize' and with most other historical events – the French Revolution, the decline of the British Empire and so on – they do so as a matter of course. Historians operate on the assumption that historical events and phenomena are, by definition, unique (thereby rendering insistence on 'uniqueness' as relatively superfluous) while at the same time possessing both general and distinguishing features. Indeed, to a large extent, the singularity of any particular event becomes assertable and comprehensible only within a comparative historical perspective.

In this respect, the *Historikerstreit* did not raise a genuinely historical question but highlighted the extra-historical functions and place of National

Socialism within various national moral economies and identities. It was precisely because Nazism and its genocidal impulses possess a moral, trans-historical status that the question could arise at all. (It was not the issues of 'historisation' or the question of singularity that were so disturbing in this debate. The genuinely pernicious ingredient was Ernst Nolte's depiction of the Holocaust as an act of anticipatory self-defence in which the Nazis took preventive action against their Jewish [Bolshevik] enemies because 'they regarded themselves and their ilk as potential or real victims of an "Asiatic" deed.'[60])

Although they are entirely differently motivated, there is an interesting, perhaps ironic, convergence between various German and Jewish perceptions as to the extra-historical status of the various components of this event. For many Germans, especially in the immediate post-war period, the Third Reich and World War II was portrayed literally as a kind of 'natural' catastrophe, a disaster that was somehow above and beyond the work of ordinary human agents or any normal pattern of history.[61] This fed into later representations of the Holocaust as a kind of metaphysical, trans-historical event, inaccessible and radically inexplicable.[62]

Elisabeth Domansky has recently uncovered some of the needs this mystifying construction satisfies and the delicious and unexpected functional ironies that accompany it within the German context:

> The unwritten constitution of West Germany rested not so much on 'remembering' the Holocaust as on remembering its 'uniqueness' and 'inexplicability'. ... [This] allowed the West Germans to see the Holocaust as something that could not be explained even in the context of the Third Reich. The Holocaust thus lost all characteristics of a historical event and was transferred to the realm of the ahistorical that defies explanation and renders the question of responsibility obsolete. This maneuver enabled West Germany to remember the Holocaust without remembering the Third Reich.[63]

The effects of, and challenges to, the prevailing paradigm are, of course, manifold. It is largely within its terms – and the need to somehow weaken, if not entirely unravel, it – that the very emergence of 'Holocaust denial' should be understood.[64] On the surface, this is an almost incomprehensible project. It begins to be a little more understandable (though no more legitimate) if one grasps that, because the extermination of European Jewry acts as a kind of morally negative absolute within post World II sensibility, any attempt to re-legitimize anti-Semitism within Western society will have to seek to undermine and subvert that code at its very core.

To be sure, whatever plausibility Holocaust-denial may possess is in part related to the very enormity of the event itself and a general incapacity to absorb its dimensions.[65] Moreover, those involved in this exercise have demonstrated an ability to capitalize on certain serious errors of fact replicated in official circles and intellectual proclamations.[66] Most importantly and in the broadest terms, although there is clearly no direct link between them, this kind of so-called 'revisionism' is nourished by the intellectual atmosphere attendant upon elements of a post-modernist sensibility and its perception of the radically self-referential (well-nigh arbitrary) nature and equal validity of almost all competing historical narratives.[67]

That post-modernism betokens a crisis in the representation of Nazism and the Holocaust must, at least on the surface, be regarded as a paradox. For its very genesis has often been described as a reaction and antidote to modern mass murder: as Jean Paul Lyotard has put it, the 'nineteenth and twentieth centuries have given us as much terror as we can take.'[68] Viewed thus, Auschwitz stands as the ultimate revelation of the bankruptcy of the grand, metanarratives of the Enlightenment and their accompanying belief in progress and reason. In a post-Auschwitz world, it is argued, such homogenizing and manipulating modes must give way to (non-privileging) heterogenous and paradoxical narrative strategies. 'Let us wage a war on totality', Lyotard proclaims, 'let us be witnesses to the unpresentable; let us activate the differences and save the honour of the name.'[69]

This may appear unexceptionable. Yet it depends upon an internally reductive view of the Enlightenment project as well as a quite unpersuasive – because never historically demonstrated – assertion as to its causal links with the Shoah. This is an argument in which, as Terry Eagleton notes, 'all narratives suffer a certain spurious homogenizing: "modernity" for Lyotard would seem *nothing* but a tale of terroristic Reason and Nazism little more than the lethal terminus of totalizing thought. This reckless travesty ignores the fact that the death camps were among other things the upshot of a barbarous irrationalism which, like some aspects of post-modernism itself, junked history, refused argumentation, aestheticized politics and staked all on the charisma of those who told the stories.'[70] Too often, post-modernists commit the very 'metaphysics' and 'essentialization' they berate, constructing their own metanarrative whereby all others are flattened into the same suspect 'metaphysical' category. This effectively blocks any possibility of differentiated judgement and rational choice between the various narratives. Ironically post-modernity as reaction and antidote to Auschwitz – its role as the great divide, the irreparable rupture rendering 'history' itself as suspect – has made the writing of its own object a veritable impossibility.

By reducing history in general to an aesthetic choice between narrative strategies, and by its dissolution of traditional criteria of historical reality, validation and truth – 'it must be clear', writes Lyotard, 'that it is our business not to supply reality but to invent allusions to the conceivable which cannot be presented'[71] – post-modernism specifically tends to undermine the 'monumental-didactic' narrative structure of the paradigm and erode the previously consensual and virtually unassailable moral and symbolic status of Nazism within our culture.[72]

In the claim as to the basic inaccesibility and inamenability of this event to accurate or reliable historical representation, its emphasis upon prooflessness, there is a paradoxical meeting between those who regard the code as paradigmatic and those who seek to radically undermine it. Some of the current convolutions of intellectuals committed to both the privileged status of these events *and* a radical post-modernist posture may be found in the recent, brilliant and very problematic work of Shoshana Felman. Felman highlights, in salutary fashion, the complexity contained in strategies of representation, the concealments and displacements entailed in witnessing and the re-negotiations inherent in the cultural inscription of such an event (issues to which historians, I am convinced, will henceforth have to demonstrate more sensitivity.) But beyond this Felman argues that the very consciousness of the crisis, and the sharp limits (as well as, perhaps, the unexplored potentialities), of representation itself derive from the experience of Nazism and the impossibility of 'getting inside' the *Shoah*. It is not merely the supreme example and test case of the difficulties of historical representation, but also the dominant reason for our disbelief in its very possibility. 'The Holocaust in Western history', she writes, 'functions ... in much the same way as a *primal scene* functions in psychoanalysis. It is a witnessing that cannot be made present to itself, present to consciousness.'[73]

Felman's Holocaust, moreover, is the source of a distinctive contemporary sensibility. 'The cryptic forms of modern narrative and modern art', she claims in sweepingly ahistorical fashion (is 'modernity' a post-Holocaust phenomenon?)

> – whether consciously or not – partake of that historical impossibility of writing a historical narration of the Holocaust, by bearing testimony, through their very cryptic form, to *the radical historical crisis in witnessing* the Holocaust has opened up. ... This is why contemporary narrative – the narrative of that which, in the Holocaust, cannot be witnessed – has by necessity inaugurated a contemporary Age of Testimony, and why the age of testimony has also turned out to be, paradoxically enough, the somewhat unique *age of historical prooflessness*.[74]

More specifically, Felman argues that in the post-Holocaust age of incommensurable testimony, of historical prooflessness, the critical activites of translation and deconstruction – 'the undoing of an illusory historical perception or understanding by bearing witness to what the "perception" or the "understanding" precisely fails to see or fails to witness'[75] – must be employed in order to be faithful to the richly complex (almost ineffable) nature of the event (exemplified by Claude Lanzmann's method in his film *Shoah*, the most insightful chapter in Felman's work).

Felman's problematizing intent is impeccable insofar as it seeks to prevent ossification of the subject through either triumphalist canonization or deadening academicism. Yet to the degree that the Holocaust serves as a deconstructionist paradigm for the inexplicability and incommensurability of human experience in general (and thus the virtual impossibility of writing 'history' as such) the de-essentializing impulse ends up by creating its own mystificatory and essentialized – mythological – opposite (and places Felman perilously close to ideological bedfellows she would not deem in the least desirable).

Need one repeat that the 'Final Solution' was a secular, human event that occurred at a particular, identifiable time and place and that – while always keeping the radical and unprecedented dimensions of the event clearly in mind[76] – it should be equally amenable to the rules and methods that govern the (still defensible) practice of historiography in general. Most historians would agree that no event can ever be fully grasped from 'within'; they have never claimed the ability to arrive at 'ultimate' knowledge. By and large, the craft is animated by the conviction that comprehensibility is a finite, changing and plural, rather than a single, final state.[77] Nevertheless, it demands certain demonstrable criteria as to what constitutes evidence and how to evaluate it and insists upon the practice of critical and situational distinctions. It is in their sophistic collapse that the danger of such deconstructionist analyses lie. There is no point rehearsing here the notorious Paul de Man case and his wartime Nazi and anti-Jewish sympathies.[78] What does merit attention, however, is the nature of Felman's disingenuous argument on his behalf – an argument that highlights the dangers contained in certain inscriptive deconstructionist practices (we shall turn presently to some of its potentially more positive uses and possibilities).

Felman insists upon transforming de Man's complete silence about his stained past into evidence for its determinative centrality, rendering it as the governing moral and creative force informing his subsequent thought and sensibility, indeed, all his work:

Incorporating the silence of the witness who has returned mute into his very writing, de Man's entire work and his later theories bear implicit witness to the Holocaust, not as its (impossible and failed) narrator (a narrator-journalist whom the war had dispossessed of his own voice) but as a witness to the very blindness of his own, and others' witness, a firsthand witness to the Holocaust's disintegration of the witness.[79]

The most questionable aspect of de Man's later comportment – his muteness, his silence – is endowed with a certain grace, interpreted as the genesis of his deconstructionism and casuistically converted into a purported capacity to transmute the catastrophe into an entire system of thought in which witnessing and testimony itself is problematized. Indeed, de Man's 'complex articulation of the impossibility of confession embodies, paradoxically enough, not a denial of the author's guilt but, on the contrary, the most radical and irrevocable assumption of historical responsibility.'[80]

Another defender of de Man, Geoffrey H. Hartman – who also posits a connection between the theoretician's earlier attitudes and his later work arguing that the mature thought represents a critique of the youthful attraction to the rhetoric of organicity – gets to the simple nub of the question when he comments, albeit parenthetically, that a disavowal of his earlier ideology 'would have been simple enough, and the question stands why de Man did not *also* take that path.'[81] More pungently, Dominick LaCapra writes that

even if one fully agrees with Felman about the nature of the the silent inscription of historicity and the Holocaust in de Man's later texts, one may yet argue that this procedure is not sufficient to explain the absence of an explicit attempt to come to terms with the early articles. (One may also object to a reduction of alternatives to an extreme binary opposition between silence and a finalized, 'totalizing overview.') A conception of the workings of the later texts in terms of silent traces, mute omniprescences and allegorical allusions is too general to account for a specific lack, notably when the conception is prompted by a specific desire to justify that lack. Indeed, if de Man believed that silence was the only acceptable response to the Holocaust or his own relation to it, he might at the very least have said as much.[82]

If de Man's Holocaust is indeed his primal scene, it rests upon a notion of repression caustically analysed by Frederick Crews in another context as 'inaccessible and possibly nonexistent psychic material to which the theorist or therapist is nevertheless determined to assign explanatory power.'[83]

But beyond the evidentiary problem, in this resacralized miasma of ineffability, there occurs a veritable collapse of historical judgement and the possibility of establishing any meaningful distinctions. Victims, perpetrators and bystanders become cognitively and morally almost interchangeable. There is a certain scandal here. Felman portrays de Man – certainly no survivor of the *Shoah* – as a kind of victim and on a par with Primo Levi (whose texts are quoted as if his ideas and situation and de Man's were meaningfully interchangeable). If the event thus created quite unexpected victims, it also, Felman argues in her reading of Camus, supports the notion of a universal, and thus radically undifferentiated, guilt: 'But the Holocaust has not left innocence – the witness' innocence – intact. On the site of "one of the greatest crimes in history" innocence can only mean lack of awareness of one's participation in the crime.'[84]

Translation and problematization are indeed inherent in the tough and never-ending labour of historical reconstruction, of establishing the complex grounds of its possibility, but such activities should serve as aids in reinforcing critical distinctions rather than displacing them into an obscurantist realm where not only the history of the *Shoah* but history itself – history *as* Holocaust – is well-nigh dissolved.

This does not mean that in many of her observations Felman has not drawn our attention to crucial issues in the cultural representation of catastrophe. Whatever one's position on such matters it is important to note that postmodernist intellectual and cultural sensibilities will, in all probability, continue to both inform – and be informed by – our shifting perceptions of Nazism and its atrocities and our ability to creatively assimilate and respond to it. The degree to which discussions of both topics have become bound up with each other is itself quite remarkable.[85] While we cannot pursue this matter in any detail here, it is essential to note that important aspects of the post-modernist sensibility, especially its overall problematization of memory, is willy-nilly being drawn into – and perhaps now even defines – the active task of cultural inscription. With the passing of time, such critical problematization will probably itself increasingly constitute a crucial – and potentially positive – mode of keeping memory of the catastrophe alive.[86] In order to understand the ways in which this is developing we need to examine the construction of historical memories of National Socialism where the issues have been, and continue to be, most deeply relevant and existentially crucial.

In Germany and Israel, for obvious historical reasons, the inscription of both Nazism and the Final Solution has always been integrally linked to core questions of national identity and negotiated – in some way or another – into the respective prevailing national ideologies and self-definitions. After the initial exposure of the horrors of the camps, when the immediate shock began to wear off, the question of *Vergangenheitsbewaeltigung*, of effectively 'working through', 'coming to terms' with – or eliding – this immediate past, of collectively and individually assimilating and commemorating (or alternatively deflecting, neutralizing or repressing) it, came unavoidably to the fore. It is a process that in constantly changing form continues to this day.

To some degree, of course, the very definition of the issue – 'Whose cat-astrophe? What catastrophe?' – has always been a question of perspective.[87] In the earliest reflections of historians such as Friedrich Meinecke and Gerhard Ritter (who likewise regarded National Socialism as a kind of demonic force), Nazism and the Third Reich was viewed almost completely as a *German* cat-astrophe. Analysis of the Jewish Question was, to say the least, skimpy, and the policy of genocide (at best) relegated to the margins.[88] In his classic *Die Schuldfrage* (1946) Karl Jaspers noted that under National Socialism – includ-ing amongst Germans themselves – spheres of experience had been extra-ordinarily diverse and fragmented. There was an immense difference, he wrote, whether one sustained suffering and losses 'in combat at the front, at home, or in a concentration camp; whether he was a hunted Gestapo victim or one of those who, even though in fear, profited by the regime. Virtually every one has lost close relatives and friends, but how he lost them – in front-line combat, in bombings, in concentration camps or in the mass murders of the regime – results in greatly divergent attitudes.'[89]

If there were obvious and enormous differences in the respective German and Jewish and Israeli situations and interpretations – involving nothing less than the distinction between the perpetrators and victims of genocide – there were, nevertheless, certain structural parallels at work. Both countries were immediately confronted with perplexing questions of comprehension and remembrance. In both cases there were clearly discernible, and significant, distinctions between public and private responses. Moreover, until the mid-1960s – albeit for entirely different reasons – the respective *public* com-memorations and explanations assumed a rather formulaic character, inserted into compensatory, meaning-bestowing narratives that conformed to the pre-vailing ideologies of the time.

In the case of Germany, this was done largely by emphasising 'resistance', adopting an explicitly anti-Fascist liberal-democratic creed, stressing the qualitative gulf between the post-war condition of the country and its 1933–1945 history while at the same time proclaiming official 'repentance' and accepting responsibility for the past (concretised ultimately by the pol-icy of reparations). At least on the public level – as part of its formal identi-ty and 'official' collective memory – this indicated, as various commentators have recently remarked, a rather unique acceptance of a nation to incorpo-rate recognition of and responsibility for the horrendous crimes it had com-mitted.[90] As James Young, reminds us,

> ... while the victors of history have long erected monuments to their tri-
> umphs and victims have built memorials to their martyrdom, only rarely
> does a nation call upon itself to remember the victims of crimes it has per-

petrated. Where are the national monuments to the genocide of American Indians, to the millions of Africans enslaved and murdered, to the Russian kulaks and peasants starved to death by the millions?[91]

But official recognition of German criminality carried with it inbuilt tensions and resistances: in the light of this what would constitute acceptable self-definitions? If ritual enactment at Bitburg explicitly revealed a certain sense of resentment and longing for 'normalization' these underlying emotions long predated that particular event.[92] It is not, however, at all clear what the effects of the many commemorative exercises were and in what directions they chanelled these complex emotions. Paradoxically, according to some analysts, they may have served less as a form of public mourning and genuine engagement than as a means for exorcistic displacement, a kind of ritual absolution from guilt.[93] (Moreover, one should not exaggerate the degree of such commemoration. To date no 'central' national memorial for victims of the Holocaust and Nazism in general has been constructed.)

What is known of the less formalized, private responses tends – in very general terms, of course – to support the notion that serious confrontation with the past, genuine *Trauerarbeit*, was very much the exception than the rule. This, at any rate, is what was indicated in the work of the pioneers in the study of the post-war German psychic economy, Alexander and Margarete Mitscherlich, and their identification in 1967 of a generalised 'inability to mourn.'[94] The preconditions for experiencing guilt and remorse, they argued, entailed a 'working through' of the past and its losses. But the traumatic experiences of the Third Reich, they argued, were bound to elude consciousness because they were associated with experiences that were unendurably painful and shattering to self-esteem. As a result little, if any, such 'working through' took place (and 'blanks' developed in the autobiography of the individual). Projective and denial mechanisms operated to mask this unmanageable reality and, in so doing, resulted in only a sporadic comprehension of the evil of German war-aims and the destruction it had wrought.

In our context what needs to be stressed is that the very 'need' to mobilise these psychological mechanisms was generated by repeated internal and external allegations of personal and collective German evil and guilt.

The imperatives towards blunting, rationalizing or repressing the event or, at least, one's own relationship to it, again underlined the fact that the worst excesses of the Nazi regime were inescapably implicated in post-war German self-definitions. Very early on – I discuss a particular case in Chapter 5 – there was a German tendency either to blame or to claim parity with (or even greater suffering than) the classic victims of Nazism. As Moses Moskowitz, a US officer, noted in 1946: 'Perhaps the most common mechanism by which the German masses avoid a sense of guilt for the fate of the ... six million Jewish dead, is to convince themselves that they too, have been victims of Nazism, and possibly in greater measure than any other people.'[95]

To be sure, the 'competition' as to who constituted the greater, the most 'authentic' victim began within the specific context of the Third Reich and the devastations of World War II. But precisely the rapid bestowing of paradigmatic status upon Nazism ensured that its uses and applications would reach far beyond its original historical occasion, producing 'extra-historical' responses and agendas that tended to operate in conflicting directions. On the one hand, given its symbolic and emotional force as a guiding moral metaphor, the 'Holocaust' and the language of genocide was used to characterise any number of historical and contemporary persecutions and atrocities (ranging from the mediaeval witch-craze through black slavery to Vietnam). The differences in origin, scope and consequences were usually rather significant and the analogies did not necessarily illuminate either the *Shoah* or the comparative historical case in question.[96]

On the other hand, over the years the insistence upon the uniqueness of the Holocaust assumed the form of an extrahistorical and political vested interest, becoming a crucial means of defining the particularity of Jewish identity. The rhetoric – and elevation – of singular Jewish victimization inevitably produced a certain resentment and initiated a kind of fruitless competition in historical – but also ongoing – victimization (informing even current Black–Jewish tensions).[97] Michael Bernstein has elegantly formulated the problem: 'once victimhood is understood to endow one with special claims and rights, the scramble to attain that designation for one's own interest group is heated as any other for legitimacy and power.'[98]

The 'uniqueness' that is built into the paradigm – a paradigm that from its beginnings has satisfied multiple 'extra-historical' cultural and political functions – has thus itself become a site of conflict. The Holocaust was certainly singular, unique, but given the fact that (for historians) historical events are such by definition this may be a rather prosaic observation. As David Biale has recently pointed out, 'the very discourse of uniqueness is ... meaningful only either when history is invoked in political debate (as in the German historians' controversy) or in theological speculation; for historians concerned with understanding the past for its own sake, "uniqueness" is either trivial, meaningless or a code word for an extra-historical agenda. ... the best medicine for the vulgar exercise of comparative victimization is not the copious assertion of Jewish uniqueness, but an end to the fruitless debate between the uniqueness and universality of suffering in the first place.'[99] In an acute and unresolved way the legacy of the catastrophe has opened up ultimate questions relating to the possibilities and limits of human empathy and solidarity, of blocking out or recognizing the suffering of others. It has raised the delicate problem of balancing, as Biale puts it, historically meaningful distinctions between atrocities with the commonalities of experience that allow for some kind of common ground and solidarity. These dilemmas and tensions are now, more than ever, tending to define Israeli (and Jewish) cultural responses to the catastrophe. It is to their historical development that we must now turn.

The centrality of the Nazi trauma within Israeli life needs little elaboration. But there too its inscriptive meanderings have been complicated, dynamic and ambiguous. There too, at least in the initial stages, a deep divide pertained between public commemoration and private experience. In the early years of Statehood, the *Churban* (destruction) as it was initially called, was made manageable by digesting it – as the extreme edge, to be sure – into the traditional, Zionist narrative of the transition from a powerless Diaspora to potent sovereignty, a saga that moved from exile and catastrophe to resistance and, ultimately, collective national deliverance. But because this version more or less locked the event into conventional ideological categories of martyrdom and redemption (laden as it also always was with the equalizing heroic motifs taken from the uprising of the Warsaw Ghetto) this somehow lessened the need for a differentiated, direct confrontation with the horrific specificities of the event.

Symptomatically, the thousands of survivors who came into the country were often looked upon with a mixture of awe, pity and scorn; a rather alien species, set aside and branded (in a literal double sense) by their special experience. Long before the 'Holocaust' emerged as a crystallised historical construct, before it began to be articulated in explicit theoretical and ideological terms, it possessed a kind of shadowy mythic status, an event from a different world populated more by archetypes than by real people; victims as well as perpetrators assumed superhuman proportions, characterised more often than not as angels, scholars and saints, monsters, demons and satans respectively.

Perhaps the first overt, national confrontation with the traumatic recent past took place in the 1954 Kastner libel case where the Hungarian Zionist leader, in charge of negotiations with Eichmann and other Nazi figures, was found guilty of collaboration with the enemy (and murdered after his trial). The terms of the trial remained fixedly archetypical – Jews were either heroic resisters or hapless victims who went like sheep to the slaughter (or, like Kastner, hopelessly corrupt traitors). For instance, the presiding judge, Binyamin Halevi, invoked Faust and pontificated that Kastner had 'sold his soul to the devil.' No intermediate categories, no more subtle shades of behaviour induced by complex, tragic circumstances, seemed psychologically permissible.

But these were public responses. No one has better depicted the essentially subliminal, subterranenan individual paths pursued in the psychic internalisation of this trauma than the novelist David Grossman. In his portrait of a child (of survivors) growing up in the early years of Israeli Statehood, the uncanny power of the Jewish experience under Nazism becomes frighteningly and palpably real. Through his protagonist Momik, Grossman captures the repressed yet radically determinative nature of the event recounting, in graphic detail, the child's relentless grappling with the mysterious 'Nazi Beast', that dark but absolutely omnipresent force: 'Whatever it was that happened Over There', Momik muses, 'must have really been something for everyone to try so hard not to talk about it.'

It is precisely because the family transmits what happened 'over there' as a kind of shame, in impenenetrably coded and convoluted ways, that renders it constitutive. It is the pervasive but unacknowledged nature of the family's traumas that provide them with their foundational role: 'Sometimes they come in to his room at night and stand next to his bed. They just wait to take one last look at him before they start with the nightmares. That's when Momik strains every muscle to look as if he's asleep, to look like a healthy, happy boy, just as cheerful as he can be ...'[100]

We must, however, return to the public realm and the changes that Israeli political culture registered in its appropriation of the *Churban*. Beginning in 1961 with the Eichmann trial, and accelerating after the high point of June 1967, a particular constellation of events produced paradigmatic shifts in Israeli (and general Jewish) representations of the catastrophe and placed what had been latent at the very defining center of consciousness.

The outlines of these developments are familiar enough. In the days and weeks immediately preceding the Six Day War, a feeling of utter isolation and vulnerability, indeed, the fear of possible extermination, permeated the country. As the most obvious available existential and historical analogy, the *Shoah* suddenly assumed a central experiential relevance. No longer remote exilic history but a perceived imminent prospect, its meaning and salience underwent dramatic transformation. The prevailing wisdom and governing ideology were metamorphosised. The predicament of the Jewish state and the powerless Diaspora were now no longer antithetical; Jewish fate was existentially and politically one. The uniqueness of Jewish continuity, fate and victimhood – with the Holocaust as its measure and standard – was now, more than ever, underlined.

While Diaspora Jewish self-definition was more and more tied to identification with the Holocaust, Israeli political culture increasingly invoked it as the crucial legitimizing force behind the State's existence. In both cases the – quite accurate – historical perception of the 'uniqueness' of the Holocaust assumed extrahistorical, ideological functions.

Despite the insistence of many uncomfortable intellectuals at the time that Jerusalem was not Auschwitz, that the fact of sovereignty made all the difference[101] and that the structure of the Arab–Israeli conflict was not analogical to the anti-Semitic Nazi project, the *Shoah* was continually invoked as part of a continuing Jewish historical isolation – 'the whole world was and is against us' – and made into the governing metaphor of the Arab–Israeli conflict. Menachem Begin's famous reference to Yassir Arafat in Beirut during the Lebanon war as 'Hitler in his bunker' is only the most well known of an ongoing tendency. But if Yitzhak Shamir described Israel's pre–1967 geography as 'the borders of Auschwitz' we should note that such rhetoric of extermination was not limited to the right: Begin liked to note that the liberal foreign minister Abba Eban had also described the pre–1967 map of Israel as 'Auschwitz lines.'[102] The contemporary Israeli radical right derives its sustenance from this generalised – but now possibly waning – perception and takes it to an extreme. The world is depicted in terms of the murderous enemies and destroyers of the Jewish people and the Arabs portrayed as a mix of the Nazi and Amalek metaphors. The general phenomenon of Kahanism – and indeed the particular act of Baruch Goldstein and his multiple murder of Arabs at the Tomb of the Fathers in Hebron in 1994 – is incomprehensible outside of this mind-set.

At any rate, a new ideology, finely – if ephemerally – generated by and tuned to the events, fears and accomplishments of the historical moment was born after June 1967. The *Shoah*, especially the scandal of its radical singularity, was now represented as the bedrock of Jewish identity (whether religious or secular, Israeli or Diaspora). In this new 'epoch', in the post-Holocaust era, a new set of 'imperatives' had emerged. In the words of Emil L. Fackenheim, perhaps the key exponent of this viewpoint, (authentic) Jewish existence had to be radically affirmed and grounded in an 'absolute commandment: *Jews are forbidden to grant posthumous victories to Hitler.*'[103] (The presumptive, coercive tone of this injunction apart, few noted at the time that the contrary option – assimilation – was not exactly a racist Hitlerian ideal!)[104]

The *Shoah*, as it now increasingly became to be known, exploded into public consciousness and political discourse. The thinking of men like Fackenheim and Elie Wiesel provided articulation to sentiments that were previously mute, inchoate and touched on deep-seated popular attitudes and feelings (and to that extent, no doubt, captured a compelling necessity in the collective psyche). Placing the *Shoah* at the center of events, making it an explanatory key and moral arbiter of Jewish identity made it 'respectable', brought it out of the dark, vaguely obscene recesses that it had inhabited before. Previously quite unintegrable, unamenable to conventional frameworks, it was now able to find eloquent, unashamed, indeed triumphalist, public relevance and expression. Given the staggering enormity of the event and its impression on the victims some kind of transformation in official collective memory was bound to occur.

In numerous ways, this assumed the form of a secular religion. At the deepest level, precisely because they were the locus of desecration, of obscene violations of basic taboos, the sites of obscenity came to possess an aura of untouchability and sanctity: Auschwitz and Treblinka took on the aura of 'holy' places[105] and the central memorial to the catastrophe – Yad Vashem – became its shrine (a visit to which is obligatory for all foreign dignitaries). Quite unlike earlier times a veritable celebratory mystique of the survivor emerged.

These developments are too familiar to require any further elaboration. They inevitably carried with them the danger of banalization and what Robert Alter has called 'deformations.'[106] Perhaps the most striking recent example would be the emotive trips of youth to the death-camps in Poland functioning, in effect, as a means of identity-affirmation and a way of validating both the realities of Jewish victimization and the redemptive functions of Jewish sovereignty. For participants the experience is, no doubt, a deeply moving one, yet the exploitative elements have been extensively noted and criticised. The cynical expression 'Shoah-business' reflected these developments which have, in turn, enabled many West Germans – and others – to accuse Jewish circles of adopting an exploitative attitude to the Holocaust.[107]

Indeed, it is as much these annexations as the inherent tendencies to revise historical narratives that have led to a serious questioning of the very notion 'the Holocaust' as essentially ideological. It is, Arno Mayer argues, a religiously freighted term resonant with sacrifice by fire in exaltation of God, linked to a cult of remembrance that tends to disconnect the Jewish catastrophe from its secular historical setting 'while placing it within the providential history of the Jewish people to be commemorated, lamented and restrictively interpreted. ... A central premise is that the victimization of the Jews at the hands of Nazi Germany and its collaborators is absolutely unprecedented, completely *sui generis*, and thus beyond historical reimagining.'[108] (Whether or not this was correct, Mayer's own attempt at historical reimagining, was itself – as I try to show in Chapter 7 – hopelessly ideological.)

If the 1967 War produced this new ideology, the political conditions it brought about almost immediately threatened its consensual possibilities. For the unleashing of Holocaust rhetoric (that most immediately accessible emotional shorthand), the incessant appeal to the *Shoah* (that most resonantly evocative – but variously interpretable – absolute metaphor) entailed its inevitable engagement in the political and cultural conflicts that have char-acterised the country since then. Mobilised and brandished as a weapon in the ongoing political divide (for and against the occupation and annexation of the territories acquired during the June War), no side developed a dis-course in which the Holocaust was (or could be) left honourably above and beyond the battle. The imperative to invoke the analogies (or lack of them) and draw the appropriate – always problematic and ideologically loaded – 'lessons' became irresistible. Far from being statically and uniformly inscribed the catastophe has been constantly re-applied and reworked becoming, in the words of Sidra de Koven-Ezrachi, a dynamic 'prism of the ambiguities and contradictions that inhere in the society itself.'[109]

The Israeli liberal-left, for instance, has increasingly been critical of this 'secular religion' and what it holds to be its politically manipulative func-tions.[110] In so doing it has sought to de-particularize and universalize the 'lessons' of the Holocaust. Insisting that dehumanisation and murder were not peculiarly German but universal human possibilities they invoked the most sensitive point of the code challenging its most ultimate premise: that Jews – as ultimate victims – could never be victimizers and were indeed inca-pable of oppression and cruelty[111] The Jewish experience of ultimate vic-timization, they argued, should act as a spur for long-delayed (but presently slowly unfolding) fully-realised recognition of the humanity of the Palestinian 'Other.' Instead of positing an unbreachable ideology of incomparability that acted as a block on the empathic capacity of the suffering of others, the Left's 'imperative' posited that one's own historical experience could provide the necessary qualities for a sympathetic imagination of the catastrophe of oth-ers, even, perhaps especially, one's own victims (without fudging necessary and important distinctions). It argued that the very enormity and uniqueness of the event was being employed as a pretext, a means of soothing the con-science of those involved in perpetrating present – if obviously lesser – injus-tices and wrong-doing.

But such delicate comparative distinctions were not always possible. Precisely because of the Holocaust's status as a governing metaphor and symbol, Palestinians and Arab Israeli's sought to turn this ubiquitous didac-tic tool against those who brandished it (and, incidentally, demonstrated the perceptual limits and selective strategies that inform empathic capacities in general). In their view this was not an obviously different, incomparable and lesser event; for them the archetypes of the Nazi and the Israeli occupier melded and were, indeed, often made interchangeable. Zionism in general was depicted as a genocidal force that systematically destroyed the fabric of

Palestinian society. Indeed, for some Palestinians (however unbelievably) the fate of those under occupation was regarded as infinitely worse than those who perished in Treblinka and Auschwitz. In the camps, they exclaimed, death was instant and the suffering over in one day, whereas the occupation was enduring, the pain, suffering and killing unending.[112]

Indeed, what this illustrates is a process in which Holocaust discourse, precisely because it has so pervasively penetrated the cultural and political marketplace, has increasingly ricocheted and in multi-faceted (often contradictory) directions become unhinged from its official versions, transmuted, in de Koven-Ezrachi's words, into 'radical and subversive symbols. The images themselves, the emblems of Nazism, now seem to be released from social taboo ...'[113]

This anti-canonic alteration of the context and the banalization of Holocaust rhetoric has occurred at any number of – more or less trivial – levels. Here only one or two examples – taken from the Israel of 1994 – must suffice. Perhaps the most bizarre instance that sought to invoke – but sensationally redirect – the code is the case of the Sephardi rabbi Uzi Meshulam and his band of religious followers (who in their zeal against the governing powers fortressed themselves and engaged in a prolonged gun-battle with the police). Meshulam and his group have consistently branded the white, Israeli establishment as 'Ashke-Nazi', and accused it of abducting Yemenite children during the early years of statehood and even conducting medical experiments upon them. Perhaps even more paradoxically, the same right-wing settlers who most dramatically annexed the Nazi analogy in the struggle against the Arabs, hurled that very accusation against their own army and the Israeli soldiers sent to control their demonstrations and illegal activities in the occupied territories. They have not as yet noticed the irony of the similarity betwen their nationalist rhetoric and similar Palestinian claims.[114]

Perhaps more of a challenge to, and revelatory of, the normative ways in which the code has been integrated into Israeli society was the recent gay commemoration at Jerusalem's Yad Vashem of the Nazi murder of homosexuals. For many this was experienced as dramatically anomalous, a kind of violation and 'contamination' of a previously unstated sense of the 'purity' of such commemorations. (Supporters of the ceremony pointed out that this kind of thinking replicated Nazi logic – indicating again the ubiquitous temptation of such normative analogies.)[115]

We cannot go into the details of the debate that flared up nor are we competent to to adjudicate the rights and wrongs of the matter. (The differences between the Nazi persecution of homosexuals and the extermination of the Jews have been clearly established[116] and obviously Jews, including Jewish homosexuals, were killed not on account of their sexual proclivities but on the basis of their 'racial' definition.) What we need to account for here, however, is the source of the tension and outrage this demonstration occasioned amongst various, especially but not exclusively religious,[117] sectors. It was entirely inappropriate, as one indignant observer noted, to use Yad Vashem to make a political statement, not about the *Shoah* but about 'Gay Pride'. It constituted an act of 'desecration': in the name of 'the heterosexual, "normal" Jewish world', homosexuality was a 'sin' in need of 'destruction.'[118] The sense of anomaly, I would suggest, is explicable only if we note that the ceremony simultaneously highlighted and problematized the previously rather hidden ways in which the code was comfortably tied into traditional religious assumptions, a normative healthy masculine nationalist ethos and, more generally, a respectable bourgeois morality.[119]

Numerous commentators have observed that the various cultural inscriptions of catastophe – canonization, commemoration, monumentalization or even a 'certain noisiness' – may block as much as facilitate access to the object, may unwittingly function to conceal the nature and memory of events rather than illuminate and recapture them. Encrusted within the frameworks of interested national and collective representations, 'finished products' unresponsive to changing circumstances and sensibilities may coarsen as much as generate historical understanding; through emotional routinization and cliche-ridden thoughtlessness they may even relieve the burden of reflection and *replace* memory.[120]

Yet, it is not possible to proceed without such forms of commemoration even if, as James Young puts it, 'at some point, it may . ... be the activity of remembering together that becomes the shared memory.'[121] Given its inherent vagaries, Young has persuasively argued, 'the surest engagement with memory lies in its perpetual irresolution.' While Young is specifically referring to the German case his argument is surely generally valid: the best memorial, the most serious confrontation will consist in 'the never-to-be-resolved debate over which kind of memory to preserve, how to do it, in whose name, and to what end.'[122] There is a creative paradox at work here. In conjunction with the foundational (if always changing) role that National Socialism plays – and I believe will continue to play – within Western sensibility, the very instability of interpretation and the controversies around its appropriate commemoration and proper historical representation will itself also act as the generator, if not the guarantor, of its future vital cultural centrality.

Perhaps nothing better illustrates this process and its possibilities than the various – groping, fringe and quite uncoordinated – attempts to engage memory and known cultural inscriptions in dynamic, consciously problematizing and personalizing ways, tearing them out of known, predictable contexts and radically defamiliarizing them. Some of Germany's participatory and self-destructing 'counter-monuments' must be regarded in this light.[123]

For obvious reasons, Israeli political culture in general (and obviously its relationship to its greatest trauma, the *Shoah*) has not – could not have been – been characterised by irony. It is only now that a process of reflexive re-examination and demythologization (for better or for worse) on any number of subjects has begun to set in. (The recent televised docudrama of the Kastner case questioning older stereotypical Israeli attitudes is only the most obvious example.) By no means yet the conventional wisdom, these critical incursions are receiving more and more attention.

In our context perhaps the most telling example is to be found in the work of the avant-garde Acco Theatre Group. The title of a recent film documenting their activities – 'Don't Touch My Holocaust' – points to their explicit highlighting and challenging of what they take to be the self-righteous, sacrosanct, indeed, taboo status of the *Shoah* within Israeli society.[124] They have done this in a remarkable 'living' theatrical experience (set in the city of Acco) entitled 'Arbeit Macht Frei.' A group of players (given the extra-theatrical setting, the audience is never sure whether or not it is being engaged by 'real' people or actors) puts the participating viewer through an extraordinary emotional roller-coaster, exposing the omnipresent uses, exploitation and cliches of Holocaust appropriation within Israeli society and the Israeli psyche. 'Arbeit Macht Frei' is an exercise in defamiliarization, explicitly designed to desacrate and radically shift and challenge everyday encrusted perceptions, attitudes and reflexes. Thus, the audience is taken to the nearby memorial site, the Ghetto Fighter's Museum (*Lochamei Haghetto'ot*). There the guide leads and instructs the group – as if it had never heard of these events – and talks in terms of 'his' experience. But, it turns out, the guide is an Arab. The radically 'Other' has now appropriated one's own experience and it is through him that one hear's one's own clichés incanted. The squirming discomfort it produces in its Jewish audiences is intense. Yet another shocking scene depicts a survivor's positive nurturing of, almost erotic satisfaction in, the experience. The survivor derives enormous pride in having her child recite in detail the horrors she has undergone – while the role of the Arab servant is to wipe her tattooed number and keep it constantly clean.

For all that 'Arbeit Macht Frei' taps into a a highly differentiated and wide range of emotions and exhibits a complex engagement towards its subject. Indeed, in the very act of desacralization it maintains a degree of sympathy for the objects of its satire and a certain resistance to its own debunking.[125]

The future modes of culturally inscribing the catastrophe cannot be predicted. What is certain is that they will be crucially affected by changing political and cultural constellations. This applies – each in their own way – to both Germany and Israel. In Germany, with its increased political and economic power, unification will no doubt constitute a spur to reconsider and rewrite national history. The impulse to repress the past may, as so many observers fear, overcome the drive to honestly engage and come to terms with what has once again become a common German history. If Bitburg presented an indication, the process of unification will certainly push in the – always existing but now even greater – impulse towards 'normalization.' (Some of the ironies of unification have already begun to assume grotesque proportions. Thus, on the basis of compensatory laws enacted after 1990 regarding previously owned private property in what became the DDR, the successors of Topf und Soehne, the concern that designed and built the incinerators for Auschwitz and other camps, have recently demanded the return of the site of the factory and other holdings that were situated in East Germany and were expropriated by the Communists! Although the Thuringian government rejected this demand, it did hold under advisement the demand for financial compensation![126])

Germany, as James Young has suggested, may indeed feel the impulse to 'become a little more like other nations; its national institutions will recall primarily its own martyrs and triumphs. These include civilian victims of Allied bombings, dutiful soldiers killed on the front, and members of the wartime resistance to Hitler.'[127] The commemorations in February 1995 of the Dresden bombings by the Allies worked dramatically in this direction. Side by side with previous assertions insisting upon the radical incomparability of the 'Final Solution' with other wartime atrocities, these ceremonies, both implicitly and explicitly, underlined the 'equivalence' of German victimization and the indivisibility of the deaths of all victims. Nevertheless, I would suggest, the coded power and symbolism of the Nazi experience has not been expunged precisely because of the very tensions and ambiguities and problematization that come with remembrance and which will continue to serve as a means of somehow perpetuating it.

In Israel, to be sure, there is of course no prospect of the Jewish experience under National Socialism 'disappearing' from memory. Still, well before the Oslo agreement was signed, Yitzhak Rabin insisted on challenging the old rhetoric, arguing that not victimization but prudent power and self-reliance were the significant achievements of Zionism. The horizons that the peace process have opened up may point to its perhaps assuming different symbolic functions and occupying a less central mobilizing role in a more secure political culture whose future outlines are as yet unclear.[128]

At any rate, in both the German and Israeli cases, as we move further and further away from the National Socialist period, it is only within these new political contexts and in the participatory, reinterpetive and problematizing modes that a living collective memory – especially for new generations that had no personal experience of the event – stands the best chance of being perpetuated. The temptation to draw (alternative) 'lessons' will, of course, continue unabated. But would it be too much to hope that they will all encompass, as Primo Levi phrased it already in 1947, 'the shame that the Germans never knew, the shame which the just man experiences when confronted by a crime committed by another, and he feels remorse because of its existence, because of its having been irrevocably introduced into the world of existing things, and because his will has proven nonexistent or feeble and was incapable of putting up a good defence.'[129]

2 German Jews beyond *Bildung* and Liberalism: The Radical Jewish Revival in the Weimar Republic

> The liberal German-Jewish position, which has been meeting ground to almost the whole of German Jewry for nearly a century, has obviously dwindled to the size of a pin-point. ...
>
> Franz Rosenzweig (1924)[1]

> Today, as at the very beginning, my work lives in this paradox, in the hope of a true communication from the mountain, of that most invisible, smallest fluctuation of history which causes truth to break forth from the illusions of 'development'.
>
> Gershom Scholem (1937)[2]

> Only the Messiah himself consummates all history, in the sense that he alone redeems, completes, creates its relation to the Messianic. For this reason nothing historical can relate itself on its own account to anything Messianic.
>
> Walter Benjamin (1940)[3]

> Finally the pride of being Jewish has awoken. It stirs within us restlessly ...
>
> Ernst Bloch (1918)[4]

Over the past few years there has emerged a rather persuasive paradigm delineating the distinctive qualities of the modern German-Jewish experience. As expounded by David Sorkin[5] and especially George Mosse in his *German Jews Beyond Judaism*,[6] it holds that in the course of the special protracted circumstances underlying their emancipation and acculturation German Jewry forged what has to be understood as an essentially new (and indeed unique) form of Jewish identity and culture. The timing of German-Jewish emancipation, they argue, determined the definition and content of this new 'Jewishness'. For its beginings – the first decade of the nineteenth century – coincided with the autumn of the German Enlightenment. From that time on Jewish self-definitions and hopes were shaped in its image. Its accompany-

31

ing postulates – liberalism, the notions of progress and gradual perfectibility, the optimistic belief in a humanity making its way from darkness to light – became deeply ingrained within German Jewry.

But beyond that, according to this paradigm, it was the peculiar nature and ideals of German culture in the age of emancipation that provided the substance of this German-Jewish identity (p. ix). For Enlightenment in Germany was accompanied by that unique construct known as *Bildung* (a notion so bound to its native context that no precise English or Hebrew equivalent exists[7]). *Bildung* – or self-cultivation – combined what we conventionally understand as formal education' with that of character-formation and moral and aesthetic refinement. To be sure the idea of *Bildung* underwent various transformations in the course of modern German cultural history, but Jews internalised and (even after 1933) tenaciously clung on to its original classic meaning as formulated by giants such as Goethe and Wilhelm von Humboldt.[8]

What was the inner content of this ideal? *Bildung* referred to a continuous process of self-formation, the gradual unfolding of the harmonious, autonomous personality through the cultivation of reason, aesthetic taste and the moral imperative. Jews found this ideal so congenial and adopted it so quickly because it held that potentially *everyone* could attain it. *Bildung*, as Mosse puts it (pp. 3–4) 'transcended all differences of nationality and religion through the unfolding of the individual personality'. It was thus an ideal perfectly suited to the requirements of Jewish integration and acculturation (especially into the middle-class) rendering it the animating ideal of modern German Jewry, 'basic to [the] Jewish engagement with liberalism and socialism, fundamental to the search for a new Jewish identity after emancipation.' Over the years, so this argument goes, Jewishness and the classical notion of *Bildung* became more and more synonymous. 'Above all', Ludwig Strauss once said, 'in a study of Goethe one finds one's Jewish substance'; Kurt Blumenfeld defined himself as 'a Zionist by the grace of Goethe.'[9]

The connection between *Bildung* and Jewishness was never stronger, Mosse claims than during the Weimar Republic when 'most Germans themselves had distorted the original concept beyond recognition.' During this polarized period when more and more segments of German society (especially its originators, the bourgeoisie) were jettisoning the ideal, the Jews, so goes the argument, most stubbornly clung on to its liberal-humanist precepts: the belief in the progressive powers of reason, the (perhaps politically naïve) insistence upon the primacy of culture, self-cultivation and the critical mind.[10] Jewish intellectuals, Mosse holds, had always been the primary advocates of these values within German society. But it epitomised their role in Weimar culture even more acutely. In a society engulfed by waves of extreme nationalism and confrontation politics, Jewish intellectuals more than ever sought to perpetuate and transmit this classical ideal of *Bildung* and 'to exorcise the irrational by examining it rationally and dissecting it in the rational mind' (p. 19).

Mosse is here seeking to distill a fundamental impulse, to capture that which was most characteristic of the German-Jewish psyche and to discern its enduring legacy. He does not claim that all Jews necessarily partook of the *Bildungs* sensibility in equal measure – there were clearly illiberal, narrow-minded, even 'reactionary' Jews; city dwellers internalised it more than those who lived in small towns and it was most clearly expressed by an articulate, educated minority. Nevertheless, he insists, 'most were touched by its ideal of self-cultivation and liberal outlook on society and politics', an ideal that became 'a part of German-Jewish identity, infiltrating to some extent most aspects of Jewish life in Germany' (pp. 1–2) (including Orthodoxy and the Zionist fringe.)

To be sure, critics have directly challenged the validity of this paradigm as *the* key to German Jewish identity. Shulamit Volkov has argued for a more heterogenous notion of *Bildung*. Volkov reminds us that the 'autumn of the Enlightenment' was also the beginning of romanticism and points to the attraction that less 'rational', morally elevated aspects of German culture possessed for Jews throughout the post-Enlightenment period.[11] 'Jewishness', Paul Mendes-Flohr has argued from another point of view, 'is more than a mere sensibility or even an identity in the existential and psychological sense'; a sociologically meaningful identity requires a shared community, culture and sense of solidarity with other Jews.[12] It may also be that more of the tradition may have lingered on in German-Jewish lives than Mosse is prepared to allow. Nevertheless I believe that it does at least capture something essential about the impulses and assumptions that German-Jewish intellectuals[13] and the educated bourgeoisie (liberal, socialist, even religious and Zionist) lastingly brought to bear: the belief in the primacy of culture, the humanizing emphasis on 'the autonomy of personal relationships' (p. 11) and so on.

Many of these insights I thus take to be essentially valid. Nevertheless to argue, as Mosse does, that it was the *Bildungs* German-Jewish tradition that largely determined what today we take to be the essence of 'Weimar culture' (p. 1) in some critical respects obscures more than it illuminates. Indeed, it is my contention that Weimar culture's most vital impulses were informed by an explicit suspicion, even outright negation, of many of the essential postulates that made up the *Bildungs* tradition and that it was not only the increasingly brutalized nationalist camp that jettisoned the notion, as Mosse would have it. In some important ways it also characterised the projects of a remarkable generation[14] of intellectuals like Walter Benjamin, Ernst Bloch, Franz

Rosenzweig and Gershom Scholem who formulated novel – and at times astonishing – fusions of radical and Jewish thematics. Each of their endeavours was distinctive and merits separate, detailed study. But they were linked by a thick network of personal (not always harmonious) relationships and a common set of concerns and dispositions.[15] Each, in their own distinctive way, has taken on almost paradigmatic status as embodiments of an emergent Jewish and Weimarian sensibility that has become part of the overall cultural and intellectual legacy of the twentieth century.[16]

We shall presently examine these projects in greater detail. But it is necessary first to recognise that – for all its many distinguishing qualities – this manifold Jewish renaissance was of a piece with some of the fundamental animating themes characteristic of the Weimar Republic and an age that had just experienced a war of unprecedented upheaval and dislocation. The figures to which we refer all defined themselves as in opposition to mainstream liberal, 'bourgeois' Jewry. Certainly none of them were representative of official communal positions. In that sense they may have been 'marginal'. But, quite contrary to what Mosse holds, their thought was quintessentially stamped by the times in which they lived. Far from being isolated remnants of a classical tradition rendered irrelevant by contemporary events they were very much in touch with contemporary currents, their projects resonant with the characteristic concerns, categories and assumptions of a restless and radical age. For the purposes of this paper, it is important to stress that their thought was animated by explicitly anti-bourgeois and post-liberal impulses. Here was a revival dependent upon, and made possible by, the construction of what can only be described as post-*Bildung* conceptual frameworks. The guiding themes of this renaissance – and its respective emphases on cataclysm, apocalypse and redemption, on radical anti-evolutionary Utopian modes and the rediscovery of (Jewish) mystic and messianic materials[17] – must be understood as particular expressions of concerns that today are, by and large, regarded as most novel and characteristic of the Weimar intellectual enterprise.

It is of course no easy task defining the distinctive signature of a culture.[18] 'Pure' distillations are seldom to be found. In the Weimar Republic, as elsewhere, older patterns of thought and behaviour persisted and existed side by side with newer creations. Moreover, much that then came to fruition originated in the pre-War *Kaiserreich*. Nevertheless, despite an admittedly highly complex, plural constellation, I do think it useful to try and identify those core creative – spiritual, intellectual and artistic – features that most decisively seemed to capture what was most epochally peculiar. I am clearly rejecting as too partial (and obvious) the argument that attitudes and perceptions in the Republic were so deeply fragmented and contradictory, the right–left cleavages so great, that no common parameters whatsoever may be found:[19] 'German culture at the time of the Weimar Republic', writes Eberhard Kolb, 'was a deeply divided culture – we may even say that there were two cultures which had scarcely anything to say to each other and were mutually alien and hostile, each denying (though with different degrees of justification) that the other was a culture at all.'[20]

At one level this is, of course, indisputable. But beyond the obvious differences the notion of a hopelessly riven culture diverts attention from the common inheritance and predicament that constituted the transformed post-World War I German reality. In this common informing context articulate elites of very different intellectual stripes shared more in sensibility and ways of thinking than they would have cared to admit.[21] What we take to be quintessentially Weimarian intellectual projects are, I submit, those essentially post-liberal ruminations, posited on the ruins of a destroyed political and cultural order, that sought novel – and usually radical – answers to the problems of a fundamentally transformed European civilization. Intellectuals of both the left and the right (especially those who, for whatever reason, find the most echo in our own late twentieth century) shared the desire for a kind of 'root' re-thinking. The coherence lay less in the various preferred solutions than in the modes of conceptualisation – the drive to think everything anew – and, above all, in a certain messianic or even apocalytpic temper.[22] It is common knowledge that the right, given its post-War dislocation and disempowerment, became increasingly radical, revolutionary, even apocalyptic. Precisely because it too felt dislocated and disempowered it now adopted such radical stances.[23] What Karl Loewith has written about its conceptual armory – the perception of decline and impending European catastrophe and the concomitant radical 'will to rupture, revolution, and awakening'[24] – was, however, by no means limited to the right. Many of the same strains animated much of what was new on the intellectual left and, often in interdependent ways, the Jewish radical revival. As George Steiner has remarked[25] the representative 'master' texts of Weimar culture – Martin Heidegger's *Being and Time* (1927), Ernst Bloch's *Spirit of Utopia* (1918) and Oswald Spengler's *Decline of the West* (1918 and 1922) – were all characterized by an acute sense of rupture and nihilistic breakdown and all explored novel and radical ways in which to both comprehend and address this new predicament. He could as easily have added to this list, perhaps as the master text of the Weimar Jewish renaissance, Franz Rosenzweig's similarly motivated *The Star of Redemption*.

These kinds of texts have a bearing on our central theme for they were expressions of an overall sensibility that either explicitly challenged, opposed or jettisoned many of the most cherished presuppositions inherent in classical *Bildung* (and in so doing formulated significantly revised conceptions of both Jewishness and general culture.) For what underlay the notion of *Bildung* and gave it plausibility was the essentially liberal-Enlightenment belief in notions of totality and the gradual evolution of humankind,[26] in 'progress'. *Bildung* envisaged a gradual, unfolding process of self-formation that applied not only to the life of individuals but eventually to its realization for all of humanity. As one historian of *Bildung*, Rudolf Vierhaus, has shown, the notion was predicated upon the concepts of individuality and 'development'. *Bildung*, defined as 'inner self-contained development leading outwards' (*'selbstaendige Entwicklung von innen heraus'*) presupposed rational Enlightenment ideas of gradual historical progress, development and *process*.[27] Moreover, as Mosse himself stresses, the substance and style of *'Bildung* was not chaotic or experimental but disciplined and self-controlled'.[28] It also, I should add, took for granted what modernists later would seriously doubt: the assumption of the unity and continuity of the self.

The Weimar Jewish revival was based on rejecting virtually every one of these presuppositions (although it is worth noting that the intellectuals who articulated it were also the inheritors of this tradition and their sophisticated ruminations were in part made possible by it.) The rejection can be clarified by contrasting it to what Martin Buber later wrote. A Jewish revival that was solely future-oriented, he argued, should not be satisfactory; just as important as the quest for arrival was consciousness of the point of departures.[29] But this is not what I have in mind. As Mosse argues, the varieties of modern German Judaism from Orthodoxy to Zionism (including the *Voelkish* nationalism of Buber[30]) definitionally integrated Jewish origins into some kind of a forward-looking, humanising *Bildungs* outlook. Indeed, Buber cannot be considered a part of this kind of Weimar radicalism because his vision of Jewish renewal was predicated upon a typically *Bildungs* basis – the radical self re-formation of the individual Jew and his *inner* world.[31] The Weimar Jewish revivalists recognised this and, in part, modelled their renaissance on explicitly anti-Buberian premises, rejecting Buber's pre–1914 call for a return to a personal Judaism of renewal and pure *Erlebnis*.[32]

This revival, it is true, shared some of the convictions that young radicals were already voicing in the years immediately prior to 1914. The revolt against bourgeois elders, the rejection of assimilation, doubts about the *Deutschtum–Judentum* synthesis[33] all preceded the war. But now, under the vastly changed conditions of war and a polarised Republic, they not only adopted new critical perspectives and novel ways of casting the problems but also of answering them. Theirs was an eclectic radicalism that characteristically fused Messianic, utopian and modernist modes of thought. The period abounds with numerous examples of its experimental (often esoteric) character. It was expressed atmospherically in such diverse institutions as the famous *Juedisches Lehrhaus* in Frankfurt, the *Juedische Volksheim* and the utopian socialist Safed society in Berlin, the Heidelberg sanitorium (1924–1928) that combined Judaism with psychoanalysis (the 'Thorapeutikum' as it was known!) and the 'metaphysical magicians' in Oskar Goldberg's circle.[34] Although this paper concentrates on four of the most significant embodiments of this new radicalism, historians have included other such diverse figures as Georg Lukács, Gustav Landauer, Kurt Hiller, Salomo Friedlaender,[35] Erich Fromm and Leo Loewenthal within its contours. (Characteristically, the young Loewenthal's Zionism had little to do with Palestine. It was rather, as he wrote to Ernst Simon in 1920, a mode of consciousness, the most appropriate way in which Jews could realise Bloch's *Spirit of Utopia*![36])

Bloch, Scholem, Rosenzweig and Benjamin knew each other – or, at the very least, about each other – and the critical, highly complex perspectives they developed about each other's work and person[37] is testimony to the separate nature of their undertakings, their divergent conceptions of Judaism and varying degrees of committment to it. Yet all – Scholem and Rosenzweig in their respective reconceptualisations of Judaism and Benjamin and Bloch as they appropriated Judaic ingredients into their eclectic recasting of Marxism – nevertheless rejected crucial ingredients of the *Bildungs* inheritance. They did so because the quasi-messianic, utopian and apocalyptic temper, those critical and prophetic tools, which so widely pervaded the Weimar Republic (and which, at least in part, prompted these thinkers to turn to the Jewish messianic and mystic traditions for inspiration[38]) subverted many of the foundations of the *Bildungs* world. They all questioned the very idea of gradual historical progress and emphasised in its place the importance of historical cataclysm, caesurae and rupture. Small wonder that in 1919 a shocked (and politically very conservative[39]) Franz Rosenzweig – faced with the magnitude of the European catastrophe – said of Oswald Spengler, author of that right-wing, apocalyptic work *The Decline of the West*, that he was 'objectively probably the greatest philosopher of history that has appeared since Hegel.'[40] (Bloch, incidentally, originally envisaged calling what became known as *Spirit of Utopia*, '*Music and Apocalypse.*'[41])

For all these men it was no longer the rational process of 'self-formation' and 'development' that would ultimately bring salvation but rather epiphanic events, flashing moments that by disrupting the flow of history would provide intimations of redemption or, as in the case of Rosenzweig, conceive of redemption entirely outside of history.[42] (For Rosenzweig, precisely because the Jews constituted a metahistorical community – a nation beyond history – they were the realization of the future Redemption within pre-Messianic time and could act as custodians of human eschatological hope.[43])

While the notion of *Bildung* may have had pietistic roots, its centrality to German culture from the second half of the eighteenth century epitomized its secular, entirely self-referential nature, denoting 'a process of integral self-development ... that was an inherent part of the individual..'[44] What could have been further away from this world than the quasi-theological (almost heteronomous) categories of the Weimar Jewish revival? In Rosenzweig's case this requires no illustration. But it was similarly the Marxist Benjamin who wrote: 'My thinking relates to theology the way a blotter does to ink. It is soaked through with it.'[45] Benjamin's thought is so idiosyncratic precisely because it is permeated by this sensibility, creating a historical materialism that, as he put it, 'establishes a conception of the present which is shot through with the chips of Messianic time.'[46] In ways similarly alien to mainstream Marxism, Bloch was fascinated with subterranean religious phenomena, his explosive utopian project nurtured by the religious imagination. His *Spirit of Utopia* ends with the words 'truth as prayer' ('*Wahrheit als Gebet*').[47] He was certainly perceived in the theological mode. Emil Lask asked: 'Who are the four evangelicals? Matthew, Mark, Lukacs and Bloch.'[48] And careful philological scholar and critical historian though he may have been, Scholem's language and writings were throughout laden with the theological dimension, the 'hope', as he put it, 'of a true communication from the mountain.'[49]

This theological sensibility was animated by an acute consciousness of messianic themes. Benjamin's Marxism is unthinkable without it. Which other historical materialist could have written that 'the Messiah comes not only as the redeemer, he comes as the subduer of the Antichrist'?[50] Bloch's entire *oeuvre* can be regarded as a sustained meditation on the vibrant and radiant possibilities of an 'atheistic messianism'[51] and eschatological hope as an *a priori* of human existence, culture and politics.[52] As we have seen, Rosenzweig was also acutely aware of the messianic dimension, rendering the Jews its realization within premessianic historical time.[53] Scholem's brilliant sensitivity to its internal dynamics is well-known. He did, after all, later become the primary incisive analyst of the paradoxical dialectics inherent in the messianic – and related apocalyptic – idea.[54] But it was not merely as analyst that Scholem approached the matter. To be sure, he was as aware of the dangers of messianism as he was fascinated by to it. Yet, throughout, it provided him with a (critical-redemptive) perspective that rendered it more than a simple historical category.[55] Its normative role in his thought was most clearly expressed in his 1931 critique of what he perceived to be Rosenzweig's neutralization of the apocalyptic strain in Jewish messianism. This neutralization undermined what Scholem regarded to be the profound truth of apocalyptic messianism: the 'recognition of the catastrophic potential of all historical order in an unredeemed world ... the truth that redemption possesses not only a liberating but also a destructive force.'[56]

This messianic mode of thinking and its variegated thematics – the dismissal of gradual change, the emphasis on origins and restoration to a golden age, a radical utopianism (in which salvation appears either at the end of history or as an event within history but never produced by it) and the apocalyptic–catastrophic dimension in which a qualitative rent utterly divides the Messianic age from the past[57] – operates with a notion of 'redemption' that is diametrically opposed to the optimistic notions of progress and process inherent in the liberal Enlightenment notion of *Bildung*.

One look, for instance, at the structure of restorative messianism and its notion of origin as goal[58] – traces of which can be found in the thought of all these thinkers – demonstrates an overturning of the insistence upon growth and development that lay at the heart of *Bildung*. Paradoxically, the idea of return to an original, paradisical state lies both in the past *and* the future. As Bloch put it: 'The world is not true, but it will successfully return home through human beings and through truth.'[59]

More importantly, restorative messianism entailed a curious view of language as the most powerful, almost magical, key to – and medium of – redemption. We must be careful to identify what was new here. German-speaking Jewish intellectuals had always been sensitive to the shaping powers of language.[60] But prior to 1914 – in keeping with the activities of rational *Bildung* intellectuals – they were prone to stress its duplicities and dangers. Men like Karl Kraus and Felix Mauthner were the most penetrating *critics* of language, unmasking its limits and untruths (a tradition later radicalised by Ludwig Wittgenstein).[61] At that time (in an astonishing 1911 diary entry) no one pointed more tellingly to its deficiencies and limits than did Franz Kafka:

> Yesterday it occurred to me that I did not always love my mother as she deserved and as I could, only because the German language prevented it. The Jewish mother is no 'Mutter', to call her 'Mutter' makes her a little comic ... 'Mutter' is peculiarly German for the Jew, it unconsciously contains, together with the Christian splendor Christian coldness also. ...[62]

With their messianic and modernist predispositions the Weimar Jewish revivalist intellectuals now *went beyond critique and sought the ultimate redemptive possibilities of language*. Emphasis on origins focussed thought on the recovery of lost meanings, on truth as hidden, part of a primal, esoteric structure waiting to be revealed. The many differences in the conceptions of these Weimar intellectuals notwithstanding there were important underlying commonalities (although these were not always perceived as

such).[63] Thus, strikingly, Rosenzweig believed in a human *Ursprache*, a kind
of pre-Babel speech in which he posited a primordial unity between name
and thing. (One need only mention the similarity to Heidegger in this context.[64]) Rosenzweig's view of the redemptive powers of language,[65] the belief
that, given God's eternal presence, the lost *Ursprache* could be reconstitut-
ed, rendered translation a peculiarly potent medium:[66] 'Every translation is
a messianic act, which brings redemption nearer.'[67] Similarly, Walter
Benjamin, that materialist metaphysician, proclaimed the existence of a paradisical linguistic condition in which, as he put it, 'language and revelation
are one without any tension'.[68] Despite the differences – Benjamin posited
an archaic-mythical 'language of revelation', while Rosenzweig regarded it
as eternally present, 'language as revelation'[69] – their conceptions of the role
of origins and revelation clearly undercut the secular, unfolding and self-
forming idea of *Bildung*.

Scholem too imbibed this view of the potency of original language – especially the holy tongue. This is most remarkably illustrated in his letter to
Rosenzweig (on the occasion of the latter's fortieth birthday in 1926). In this
'Confession on our Language' ('Bekenntnis ueber unsere Sprache')[70] Hebrew,
as Robert Alter puts it, 'is imagined as a system of deep taps into the abyss
... which, once having been activated, will open up an irresistible resurgence
of the depths'.[71] 'This land', wrote Scholem of what was then Palestine, 'is
a volcano: It inhabits the language. ... People here actually do not realize
what they are doing. They think they have turned Hebrew into a secular language, that they have pulled out its apocalyptic sting. But that is untrue. The
secularization of a language is a mere phrase, no more than a slogan. ... A
language is composed of names. The power of the language is bound up in
the name, and its abyss is sealed within the name. Having conjured up the
ancient names day after day, we can no longer suppress their potencies. We
roused them, and they will manifest themselves, for we have conjured them
up with very great power.'[72]

I concede that Scholem's relationship to my general argument here is a
complex one. Still I would take issue with Mosse's paper on Scholem – an
extension and application of his overall thesis – which renders Scholem's
project (though centred upon the quest for Jewish nationhood rather than
integration into Germany) comprehensible only in terms of its *Bildungs* base:
the moral, humanist posture, never at ease with normative nationalism; the
insistence on the primacy of culture; the perception of the historical process
as an open, not a finished, product.[73]

These elements are certainly there. But the interpretation is strained because
it is unable to comfortably incorporate the many essentially post-liberal, even
anarchistic, ingredients of Scholem's thought that Mosse himself emphasis-

es: the profound anti-bourgeois convictions, the irrepressible attraction to the unconventional and even the bizarre, the notion of Zionism as a highly experimental wager and so on.[74] Classical *Bildung*, Mosse stresses elsewhere, 'was not chaotic or experimental but disciplined and self-controlled'. That may have characterised Scholem's method of work but it did not fit his anarchistic predilections nor the way he believed history operated. Indeed as early as 1916 in a fashion quite antithetical to the philosophy of *Bildung* he dismissed outright 'the illusions of "development"' as an obstacle to truth (see the opening motto).

I would like to suggest that the discourse of this Jewish renaissance, like that of the Weimar radical right (Ernst Juenger, Martin Heidegger, Oswald Spengler and so on),[75] was couched in clearly post-Nietzschean terms. It is not surprising that, in the post-war Weimar context, far removed from the refined, cultivated world of *Bildung*, they all took as their starting point a heightened awareness of the nihilistic predicament and its simultaneously destructive and liberating possibilities. Unlike Bloch, Rosenzweig and Benjamin who, albeit in complex ways, admired Nietzsche,[76] Scholem consistently denied any such affinity. Yet the tonal resonance and thematic resemblance is obvious: the notions of abyss, immoralism, catastrophe and apocalypse, nihilism and antinomianism inform his conceptual universe and everywhere permeate his writings. Moreover, I would argue, it was precisely these contemporaneously familiar and radical categories (whether they were also mined from the Jewish tradition is here not relevant) which rendered his presentation of the most esoteric byways of Jewish history immediately accessible and exciting to the modern reader.

The years 1916–18, Scholem has testified, were decisive in the making of this kind of thinking and lay behind his startling and original application of these categories to the world of Kabbalah where, as he stated, he found 'intuitive affirmation of mystical theses which walked the fine line between religion and nihilism ... [and] courage to venture out into an abyss, which one day could end up in us ourselves ...'[77]

Contemporaries were aware of this very un-*Bildung* like fascination: in 1922 Rosenzweig labelled Scholem simply as a 'nihilist'.[78] He wrote the following in 1960 but its animating spirit and categories derived from his formative World War I and Weimar years: 'Every acute and radical Messianism that is taken seriously tears open an abyss in which by inner necessity antinomian tendencies and libertine moral conceptions gain strength.'[79] His preoccupation with and fascination for nihilism and the radical transgression of limits, the connections between nihilistic powers of destruction and vital powers of national renewal – most classically expressed in his 1937 Hebrew essay – *'Mitzsva haba'ah ba'averah'* ('Redemption Through Sin' in English) exploring how 'Messianism was transformed into nihilism'[80] – could not have been further away from the ways in which *Bildungs* intellectuals regarded the world and its potential.[81] To be sure, as David Biale has persuasively demonstrated, Scholem was 'at once the child of the vitalistic counter-culture of turn of the century Europe, but also its critic, a kind of anti-Nietzschean Nietzschean' whose attraction to the irrational and the demonic was tempered by an awareness of its catatrophic potentialities.[82]

Scholem's acute, life-long awareness of what he called the 'abyss', provides an even deeper insight into the ways in which he and this generation left the *Bildungs* inheritance far behind.[83] It reflected a basic assumption concerning the ultimate nature of reality. The stability of the world is illusory and potentially filled with terror: 'reassuring orderliness and coherence [were] not intrinsic to it'.[84] Scholem's historical world is characterized by a deep grasp of its interrelated destructive and radiant possibilities. To be sure, classical *Bildung* stressed a certain open-endedness but this was always predicated upon the belief in progressive development, in a civilizing and humanising process far removed from Benjamin's (now-famous) dictum that there 'is no document of civilization which is not at the same time a document of barbarism.'[85]

Our Jewish Weimarians could no longer automatically accept these progressive, civilizing propositions which had been deeply punctured by the traumatising experience of World War I. In his diary of 1916 the young Scholem already registered the death and burial of Europe.[86] In November 1918 Rosenzweig wrote: 'The 'culture' that was ours will be destroyed even in our lifetime ... Something new will take its place, of course. But it will not be ours.'[87] He now regarded history as a purely destructive force and it was to Jewish eternality that he turned for redemption. At any rate, a progressive philosophy of history – an assumption that had provided *Bildung* with its ontological and epistemological underpinnings – was no longer viable for any of these thinkers. Ernst Bloch, with all of his visions of future hope, nowhere posits a system of historical development; he explicitly opposes the notion of 'progress'. There is no continuum. True humanity, rather, can emerge at any time, at flashing, chosen moments and ultimate realization is pushed into the never realizable future.[88] While humanization remains the goal it is far removed from the liberal-Enlightenment model: 'History', he wrote, 'is no entity advancing along a single line. ... it is a polyrhythmic and multi-spacial entity with enough unmastered and as yet by no means revealed and resolved corners ...'[89]

These thinkers shared a kind of neo-eschatological bias characterised by the conviction that there was a radical disjunction between history and redemption.[90] Rosenzweig, the anti-Hegelian, dismissed history as an endless cycle of wars and revolution in principle unable to redeem itself. As Stéphane Moses has demonstrated, historical reason and the notion of historical telos were rejected and a new conception of time developed.[91] *Bildung*'s twins – growth and self-formative progress – were dismissed.[92] Rifts, ruptures and revolutions took precedence over the continuum of homogeneous time. But this was not, as we have seen, a merely negative critique for a redemptive alternative – surprisingly similar in structure despite the obvious differences separating these thinkers – was offered.[93]

This consisted of the notion of actualisation, redemption as a constant immanent possibility, now or at any given time (*Jetztzeit*). In place of an uninterrupted progressive totality, time is now conceived in terms of qualitative moments. Thus Rosenzweig replaced the conventional Enlightenment notion of time with the eternal Jewish cycle and linked it to *Jetztzeit* where redemption was possible at all times. The Marxist Benjamin (and similarly Bloch) no longer regarded revolution as the culmination of a progressive process but as the sudden eruption of a deeper truth that exploded the continuity of history. Here the rents and fractures are what counts for continuity, according to Benjamin, was a category of the victors while discontinuity represented the realm of the oppressed and their uprisings.[94] History was thus a non-linear process fuelled by the possibilities of new beginnings. If Scholem did not subscribe to Benjamin's view he certainly understood its inner structure describing it as 'the secularization of Jewish apocalyptic doctrine', where 'the noble and positive power of destruction ... now becomes an aspect of redemption, related to the immanence of the world, acted out in the history of human labor.'[95]

It must be noted that this post-*Bildung* sensibility typically went together with what I can only call a 'modernist' cast of thought. This was manifested in numerous ways.[96] It characterised the stylistic tendencies attendant upon the breakdown of a causal, linear sense of time and development.[97] It had much to do with the self-conscious montage form in which Bloch constructed much of his work (most famously in *Heritage of Our Times*). As he wrote there: 'the combinations of manifold montage hold no expired totalities, no fraudulently idolized "eternal values", but rather interrupted ruins, in new figurations' which possessed redemptive potential.[99] It also accounts for much of Benjamin's mode of writing, epitomised in his 'One- Way Street' that densely personal record combining observations, dreams, aphorisms and prose epigrams. Modernism in general challenged those narrative modes, tellingly known as the *Bildungs*roman, that endorsed a life of continuity or growth within a single biography or even across generations.[100] Bloch made it clear that the times had rendered this an impossibility. 'When the bourgeois world was still revolutionary ... the path was still from the *Sturm und*

Drang period to [Goethe's] *Wilhelm Meister* as the bourgeois *Bildungs*roman through the "world"; the imagined balance culminated ... as Hegel's "reconciliation of the subject with necessity" ... today ... in the perfect non-world, anti-world or even ruin-world of the upper middle-class hollow space, "reconciliation" is neither a danger nor possible for concrete writers.'[101]

But there is a deeper point here, integrally related to the theme of our paper. This (once again post-Nietzschean) modernist consciousness challenged perhaps the most fundamental presupposition underlying *Bildung* – the notion of a unified, continuous self. As Bloch admiringly wrote of Benjamin's work: 'It's "I" is very near, but variable, indeed there are very many 'I's ... Constantly new "I"s'. ... extinguish one another.'[102] Benjamin's brilliant study of surrealism not only explicitly addresses this problem but demonstrates how, in Charles Taylor's words, the modernist quest for 'the liberation of experience can seem to require that we step outside the circle of the single, unitary identity, and that we open ourselves to the flux which moves beyond the scope of control or integration ... the epiphanic centre of gravity begins to be displaced from the self to the flow of experience, to new forms of unity, to language conceived in a variety of ways.'[103] Whereas in *Bildung* it is the formative powers of the self that are redemptive they are now to be found without. 'Language takes precedence', wrote Benjamin. 'Not only before meaning. Also before the self. In the world's structure dream loosens individuality like a bad tooth.'[104]

The Weimar Jewish revival, we must conclude, provides a paradoxical challenge to the *Bildungs*paradigm and its conception of the intellectual substance and legacy of German Jewry.[105] Its makers defined their Jewishness not, as Mosse would have it, in terms of an ongoing *Bildungs* view of the world but rather by exploding many of its most cherished assumptions (and, perhaps, hanging on to selected others such as the ongoing belief in the humanizing capacities of culture and the personalizing of relationships). This was a renaissance whose predispositions, sensibility and categories were not isolated from but linked to many of the most definitive currents of the time, currents which also helped to determine which (usually neglected and esoteric) Jewish sources and materials would be integrated into the respective visions. Indelibly stamped by contemporary circumstances, their novel reconceptualisations of Judaism and affirmations of Jewishness were rendered possible, assumed their peculiar vitality and found their resonance precisely by proceeding well beyond the calmer worlds of classical liberalism and *Bildung*.

3 'The Jew Within': The Myth of 'Judaization' in Germany

The history of the strange doctrine of 'Judaization' has gone relatively unremarked. Yet this idea in its various permutations was an integral part of the discourse surrounding the modern *Judenfrage*. In Germany, where the debate on the Jewish Question was particularly protracted, programmatic, and philosophically oriented, the notion took on special salience. The idea became a sort of reference point, and most parties were impelled to employ it and bend it to their own purposes (whether in advocatory, oppositional, or deflective ways).

At its most elementary level, the term 'Judaization' (or 'Jewification' – I shall use the terms interchangeably) simply reflected the belief that Jews wielded disproportionate influence and occupied (or were about to occupy) pivotal positions of inordinate economic, political, and cultural power. This was its most obvious and familiar meaning. But it often went beyond this to refer to a more subtle, deeper danger: *Verjudung* connoted a condition in which the 'Jewish spirit' had somehow permeated society and its key institutions, one in which Jewish *Geist* had seeped through the spiritual pores of the nation to penetrate and undermine the German psyche itself. Toward the end of the nineteenth century this theme had become an ideological reflex of the political antisemites, but in terms of its genesis and development, the sensibility it conveyed and the functions it fulfilled, the idea was not limited to such circles. For here was a powerful, polyvalent myth with a life of its own, one that was able to provide comforting explanations for a variety of crises and unfamiliar situations. Elastic in application, easily adapted to different interest groups and ideological orientations, its strength lay precisely in its indeterminate symbolic allusiveness.

The question of Jewish emancipation in Germany was often accompanied by fears of the debilitating effects Jewish integration would have on the larger body politic. Critics of emancipation regarded Jewish assimilation as a potentially corrupting agent, dissolutive of society itself.[1] Already at the beginning of the nineteenth century, however, Jakob Fries argued that it was not Jews as such but Judaism and the 'Jewish spirit' which constituted the problem: 'We declare war not against the Jews, our brothers, but against Judaism. Should one we love be stricken by the plague, is it not proper that we wish him deliverance from it? Should we abuse those who, stricken by the plague, lament its horrors and conjecture how to free themselves from it? . . . In fact, improving the condition of the Jews in society means rooting out Judaism.'[2]

This claim, that the attack upon Judaism was based upon a humanist, even redemptive concern for the Jew, later became, as we shall see, a *leitmotif* of many antisemites. But from the beginning there was agreement that some form of 'de-Judaization' (vague as the demand may have been) was the precondition for emancipation. Defenders and opponents of the Jews alike shared this view. In this way the difficulties of *Entjudung* became part of the problematic of the modernizing, intellectual German Jew. Judaism was increasingly 'psychologized', experienced, in the words of Hannah Arendt, as a kind of character trait, a personal defect. In his deeply ironic yet compassionate way, Heinrich Heine depicted it as an 'Incurable deep ill! defying treatment ... Will Time, the eternal goddess, in compassion/ Root out this dark calamity transmitted from sire to son?'[3]

The frustrations of de-Judaization were not only felt by Jewish *literati*, for the apparent failure of the *Entjudung* project also became an obsessive ingredient of nineteenth-century anti-Jewish mythology. But here it was not so much the intractibility of Jewishness that was held to be alarming. It was, rather, the claim that the assimilation process had been reversed: instead of Jews being absorbed into German life, Germany itself was being 'Judaized'. That the notion of *Verjudung* achieved its greatest popularity and plausibility in the post-emancipation period is not surprising. The full myth of a 'Jewified' society was dependent upon the perception that Jews had access to the levers of power, a state of affairs that had been facilitated by the abolition of previous disabilities. It reflected anxieties that accompanied the introduction of legal equality and the dismantling of traditional protective barriers separating Christians from Jews. It provided a theory to explain the process and fact of newly acquired Jewish 'dominance' over national institutions.[4] This myth was essentially one of social and ideological contagion. Not Jewish purification but German pollution and powerlessness, it held, was the outcome of emancipation.

I am concerned in this chapter with some of the *modern* manifestations of the theme of 'Judaization'. This does not imply, of course, that such a notion was limited to the modern period. Indeed, people have been labelled as 'Judaizers' almost from the inception of Christian theology itself (and it is this that perhaps provides its modern incarnation with greater depth). The original Judaizers, for example, were St Peter's followers who urged conformity to Jewish ritual law against St Paul. Since then the accusation of 'Judaization' was pinned on to all manner of challenge against Christian

Orthodoxy.[5] Heresy and 'Judaization' became virtually synonymous activities. Given the historic Jewish–Christian tension, it was easy for Christians to regard Jews in terms of the theological abomination of dissent. But the myth of 'Judaization' went further than this: the Jew not only embodied dissent, he also became a metaphor for heresy itself, symbol of subversion whether or not its agents were themselves Jewish. All signs of heresy, any kind of dissent, could be labelled as 'Judaizing' activities.[6]

A similar generalizing, symbolizing function attended the traditional association between Jews and moneylending. Indeed, these medieval roots lent resonance to the myth in its later modern garb. Words like *judeln* (1522)[7] and *mauscheln* (1680)[8] entered into general German usage as pejorative terms indicating distasteful (Jewish) ways of thinking, talking, and economic dealing. Christians, too, could be said to indulge in *judeln*. Indeed, those who engaged in usury were often themselves labelled as *Kristenjuden*. In fifteenth-century Germany, Christian usury was termed the *Judenspiess*, or 'Jews' spear'. (Such symbolic equations were, of course, not limited to Germany. Even though Jews had been officially absent from England for many years, in his 1612 essay *Of Usury* Sir Francis Bacon recommended that all usurers 'should have tawny orange bonnets, because they do Judaize'. And, in words strikingly close to later nineteenth-century rhetoric, we find Bernard of Clairvaux, who preached the Second Crusade, commenting, 'I keep silence on the point that we regret to see Christian usurers judaizing worse than Jews.'[9])

There are striking continuities between the medieval and modern versions of the myth: the attribution of great Jewish power and subversive intention; the combined use of the Jew as concrete embodiment *and* symbol; the detachable nature of the 'Jewish spirit' and its ability to penetrate non-Jews in thought and behaviour; the obvious secularization of religious heresy into the appropriate political ideology of which Jews were presumed to be both the carriers and symbols (liberalism, Marxism, etc.).

The subject of usury and moneylending, however, was not so much secularized as extended and elaborated to fit the new socioeconomic circumstances of the nineteenth century. The association with money, the equation of Judaism with egoism and materialism, persisted and was reinforced. Regardless of its other variations, no version of the 'Jewification' myth was without this dimension. Thus Jakob Fries, whom we have already mentioned and whose arguments were not untypical, identified Judaism with 'the whole lot of deceitful, second-hand pedlars and hawkers'. Unless their social structure and mental constitution were revolutionized, they would not be able to give up old economic habits. They would 'acquire power through money wherever despotism or distress engenders oppressive taxation . . . wherever the well-being of the citizen is so endangered that indebtedness on a small scale grows ever worse'. Like later commentators, Fries linked the rise of Jewish power to faults within the host society. 'Judaization' was the consequence of local wastefulness and sloth: 'The idle, stagnant capital of these countries is devoured by the Jews like worms gnawing on rotting matter.'[10]

In the late eighteenth and early nineteenth centuries, however, there was still no developed theory as to the overall *Verjudung* of German society and its collective soul. For contemporaries in this preemancipation phase, the problem was not so much the 'Judaization' of Germans as skepticism concerning either the Germanization or Christianization of the Jew. As Friedrich Buchholz wrote in 1803, even if the Jewish youth was raised and educated in a Christian home he 'would return to huckstering [*Schacher*] and again become a Jew'. Baptism, too, would be ineffective, for instead of renouncing *Schacher* the Jew was 'bound to transform the sacrament itself into the object of huckstering.' The only effective path to Jewish reform, Buchholz concluded, was participation in military life.[11] Only as Jewish incorporation into German society and culture increased did a more inclusive notion emerge. The theory of *Verjudung* was the negative mirror image of assimilation.

It is perhaps no accident that the first clearly secular and more systematic idea of 'Judaization' was formulated and circulated, in the main, by estranged Jewish intellectuals of the radical neo-Hegelian school. It was these men who were groping toward the articulation of an incipient socialist theory. In psychological terms the struggle involved in this 'breakthrough', in the early critique of bourgeois society, entailed not only Jewish self-criticism but the compulsion to self-immolation as they increasingly identified bourgeois society with Jewish principles.[12] Regardless of the psychological wellsprings of socialist ideology in Germany, in the present context what counts is the fact that these intellectuals invented a kind of 'theory' that was applied to society as a whole and employed socioeconomic rather than theologically informed categories; ironically, the medieval tradition of depicting even certain Christian economic practices as 'Jewish' was revived.

The young Heinrich Heine, for instance, did not merely associate Jews with philistine wealth; he categorized the obsession with moneymaking as such as a Jewish activity. In an early letter (1816) he wrote, 'I call all Hamburgers Jews, and those I call baptized Jews in order to distinguish them from the circumcised are called *vulgo*' Christians.'[13] The radical attack on wealth, its identification with Jewry, and the gradual 'Jewification' of Christian society as it transformed itself into a capitalist one were captured in vignette rather than systematic form by Heine. Baron James de Rothschild he termed 'Herr von Shylock in Paris, the mightiest Baron of Christendom.'[14] In an unpublished passage from the *Baths of Lucca* (1829) he wrote that finance capital had become the new religion, and, as a result, Rome was dying from the 'Jewish poison'.[15]

But these were the rather inchoate sentiments of a Jew always profoundly ambivalent toward his own Jewishness. They were never articulated into a general theory. Indeed the more mature Heine did an about-turn and proposed a positive and quite different understanding of 'Judaization':

In Northern Europe and in America, especially in the Scandinavian and Anglo-Saxon countries, among the Germanic peoples, and partly among the Celtic ones, the Palestinian way of life has prevailed to such a marked degree that we seem to be living among Jews ... The genuine, the ageless, the true – the morality of ancient Judaism – will bloom in these countries just as acceptably to God as once in the lands by the Jordan and the heights of Lebanon. One needs neither palm-trees nor camels to be good; and goodness is better than beauty.

The readiness with which these nations adopted Jewish life, customs and modes of thought may not be altogether due to their susceptibility to culture. The cause of this phenomenon should always be sought in the character of the Jewish people, who have had a great affinity with the Germans ... Judea has always seemed to me a fragment of the West which has somewhere gotten lost in the East.[16]

It should be noted that the priority of ethics over aesthetics reflected the change in Heine's previous preference of Hellenism over Nazarenism. The broader relevance here lies, however, in the fact that Heine, like many German Jews before and after him, sought in the Bible, in ethics, in Jewish rationalism, and in other elements of Jewish life areas where it could be argued that Judaism had had a beneficial, shaping, even osmotic effect, on the course of Western civilization. There is a long and interesting history of such countermodels of 'Judaization' worth exploring. Suffice it to say that the attempts to give the matter a more positive valence did not usually prevail; from its earliest beginnings the notion was overdetermined, saturated with negative connotations.

It is with Moses Hess and especially Karl Marx that 'Judaization' was placed within a clearly theoretical framework.[17] In Hess's moralistic essay 'On Money' (1845), the Feuerbachian critique of religion was located squarely within the socioeconomic sphere and the language of theologico-anthropological projection applied to the relationship between capital, Judaism, and Christianity. 'Money', wrote the impassioned Hess, 'was alienated spilt blood', and the modern commercial state, which was based upon the worship of money, was based upon the deepest denial of the species-essence of man as a social being. Hess argued that Christianity represented the logic of egoism, the belief that isolated individual existence was a desirable state. As the egoistic man externalized himself theoretically in God, in the real world man externalized himself through money. The world had been transformed into a vast stock exchange that Hess identified as the 'Jewish–Christian peddler world':

> The Jews, who in the natural history of the social animal world had the world-historical mission to elicit the predator in humanity, have now at last completed their task. The mystery of Judaism and Christianity has been revealed in the modern Jewish–Christian peddler world. The mystery of the blood of Christ, like the mystery of the ancient Jewish blood worship, finally appears undisguised as the mystery of the predator. In ancient Judaism the blood cult was only prototypical, in medieval Christendom it was theoretically, ideally, logically realised . . . but only in the imagination. In the modern Jewish-Christian peddler world it is no longer symbolic or mystical but a daily, prosaic matter.[18]

Hess's later conversion to Jewish nationalism obviously entailed a repudiation of such views. But even in this essay the theme of 'Judaization' was mentioned merely in passing. It is only with Marx's essay *On the Jewish Question* (1844) that it becomes the central informing category, that the analysis is invested with apparently more theoretical and socio-historical sophistication. Few essays have been more thoroughly analyzed than this one: here only its relation to the theme of 'Judaization' will be discussed.

A polemic against his fellow Young Hegelian Bruno Bauer's opposition to Jewish emancipation,[19] Marx's advocacy of Jewish civil rights in bourgeois society was ambiguous in the extreme. That one could not deny *political* emancipation to the Jew, Marx argued, was somehow beside the point, for it was political emancipation itself that was the object of criticism. For Marx, political emancipation, which Bauer had identified with emancipation of the state from religion, had to be radically distinguished from its final and absolute form, *human* emancipation. Precisely because Jews could be emancipated politically without renouncing Judaism completely, it was necessary to keep in mind the goal of human emancipation and locate the problem 'in the *nature* and *category* of political emancipation.'[20]

All these reflections were prompted by Marx's exceedingly negative conception of Judaism. Historical progress required its complete renunciation: 'What is the profane basis of Judaism? *Practical* need, *self-interest*. What is the worldly cult of the Jew? Huckstering. What is his god? *Money*. ... What was, in itself, the basis of the Jewish religion? Practical need, egoism. ... Money is the jealous god of Israel, beside which no other god may exist. ...

The bill of exchange is the real god of the Jew. His god is only an illusory bill of exchange.'

It is, however, Marx's rendering of the 'Judaizing' process as a definitive force in modern society that, in the present context, is crucial: 'The Jew has emancipated himself in a Jewish manner, not only by acquiring the power of money, but also because *money* had become through him and also apart from him, a world power, while the practical Jewish spirit had become the practical spirit of the Christian nations. The Jews have emancipated themselves in so far as the Christians have become Jews.'[21]

It is noteworthy that Christianity was regarded here as a kind of vehicle through which Judaism could realize itself. This perception – that Christianity had been infected by Judaism and was never really able to overcome it – was later to obsess many anti-Semites (racist and otherwise):

> From the beginning, the Christian was the theorizing Jew; consequently the Jew is the practical Christian. And the practical Christian has become a Jew again. It was only in appearance that Christianity overcame real Judaism. ... Christianity is the sublime thought of Judaism; Judaism is the vulgar practical application of Christianity. But this practical application could only become universal when Christianity as perfected religion had accomplished, in a *theoretical* fashion, the alienation of man from himself and nature. It was only then Judaism could attain universal domination and could turn alienated man and alienated nature into *alienable*, saleable objects, in thrall to egoistic need and huckstering.[22]

The world had internalized and 'become' the Jew. In the age of 'species-being', human emancipation was therefore conditional upon emanciption from Judaism.

Despite its familiarity, Marx's *On the Jewish Question* remains an extraordinary document. While the conceptual garb is secular, apparently sociological, its content is decidely mythological in nature.[23] The transformation of the Jew into a collective symbol (in this case, into a metaphor for the evils of bourgeois society) was present in all versions of the *Verjudung* myth. The 'Jewish spirit', moreover, could encompass a wide, and often contradictory, range of human qualities. How were such attributes discovered? The specific characteristics of Jewish *Geist* were always deduced from the nature of the object under criticism – liberalism, capitalism, secularism or whatever – and then identified as such. With Marx, as with others, these qualities were then posited as virtually immutable, incorrigible. The 'Jewish spirit' was inevitably dehistoricized, hypostatized into static, eternal qualities.

Beyond this, however, Marx's analysis contained a thrust that other, later doctrines of 'Judaization' would also emphasize: the contention that unchanging Jewish *Geist* possessed immense power and was capable of penetrating all of society, permeating even those who seemed as far away from Judaism as possible. The notion of *Verjudung* could work in this way because it posited a 'spirit' that was a part of, and yet at the same time disengaged from, its original carriers. The medieval identification of non-Jewish usurers as *Kristenjuden* was one indication of such an infection. What was new with Marx was the generalization of this principle into one of total social change. If in the medieval version Christian usurers were an indication of such a 'Jewish' infection, they were stigmatized as such and held in contempt. In all modern versions of the myth such containment was impossible. This reflected obvious social changes: Jewish penetrability was facilitated because the dividing walls of the ghetto had crumbled, traditional boundaries had eroded, and the secularization of general and Jewish life had proceeded apace. Consequently, society as a whole could be infected and the Jewish principle more plausibly represented as universally operative.

Marx's apologists usually contend that Marx did not attack Jews as such but only the 'spirit of Judaism', which, in turn, was symbolic shorthand for the 'spirit of capitalism.'[24] But this kind of distinction, one that as we shall see was constantly invoked during the nineteenth and early part of the twentieth centuries, was always exceedingly problematic. Marx's crude equation of the Jew and his religion with money, huckstering, and materialist egoism could not but reinforce anti-Jewish stereotypes at the most basic level.

Jewish participation and visibility in the cultural, economic, and political life of nineteenth-century Germany provided the myth with the necessary generating fuel. Such myths assume plausibility only if they contain some relation, however tenuous, to social reality. And *Verjudung*, in its many variations, was never an entirely arbitrary myth: the 'Jewish spirit' always transmitted a corrupting materialist message. The traditional stereotype, perpetuated in much of nineteenth-century German philosophy and popular literature, hypostatized the Jew as exclusivist, egoistic, and materialistic. This was a convenient foil on which to displace the distaste and anxieties that accompanied the transformation of Germany into a modern, capitalist society, a transformation in which the post-ghetto Jewish presence seemed to visibly increase. The myth of 'Judaization' helped to simplify considerably the analysis of essentially complex abstract processes: the sociological was transformed into the metaphysical, the institutional into the religioeth(n)ic or racial, cause and effect inverted. Moreover, the myth melded with a new, peculiarly modern consciousness of the role of 'material' forces in moulding culture, with a heightened awareness of the 'economic' as an autonomous factor in social and political affairs.[25]

Marx, it should be noted, never resorted to biological or racist conceptions. Moreover, this essay was written when he was twenty-six years old,
and he never again wrote on the 'Jewish Question'. Whether or not he privately clung to these early convictions, the more mature Marx employed only
impeccably 'impersonal' categories such as class, means and relations of
production, and so forth. Materialist method replaced the original idealism,
and the sociological prevailed over the religioethnic. What, however, was
the fate of the *Verjudung* thesis in the socialist movement?

By and large, socialists retained their support for Jewish emancipation and
their disdain for traditional Judaism. As late as 1921 Karl Kautsky could not
have put it more bluntly: 'The Jews have become an eminently revolutionary factor, while Judaism has become a reactionary factor.'[26] But the theme
of 'Judaization' as such appeared only sporadically and then usually in somewhat defensive form. Given the orthodox materialist emphasis, it is not surprising that Marx's 'idealist' essay on the Jewish Question was virtually
forgotten until it was reprinted in the *Neuer Sozial-Demokrat* in 1872.[27] When
Eduard Bernstein reprinted extracts from these essays in *Der Sozialdemokrat*
in 1881, however, a certain ambiguity remained apparent. Bernstein accepted the notion of the 'Jewish spirit' but, especially in the light of the climate
created by Adolf Stoecker's antisemitic Berlin movement, tried to 'contex-
tualize' the problem. Somewhat disingenuously he warned of the danger of
'assuming precisely the opposite of what Marx excellently expounds, namely that the so-called Jewish spirit is a result of bourgeois society based on
the capitalist mode of production which, when there are no Eastern Jews produces Christian Jews, like the Christian-Germanic Jews in America.'[28] This
attack upon antisemitism *in terms* of the 'Judaization' thesis, the attribution
of 'Jewish' characteristics to non-Jews as a form of Jewish defence, was a
somewhat dubious tactic, a double-edged sword at best.

In an article entitled 'The Judaization of the Third Reich' (1881), Bernstein
maintained this ambiguity: 'Jewry' still symbolized huckstering. He deplored
the fact that popular revulsion was directed only at 'the circumcised Jews,
while uncircumcised Jewry at the helm (of State) was paid homage to and glo-
rified.' What had happened was that 'Huckstering had become the fundamental principle of the German Reich ... thanks to the Judaized outlook of the
Imperial Chancellor, the monarchical principle and the German monarchy itself
is completely judaized.'[29] Otto Bauer, the Austro-Marxist theoretician, could
approvingly quote the antisemite Baron Karl von Vogelsang's remark: 'If by
some miracle all our 1,400,000 Jews were to be taken from us, it would help
us very little, for we ourselves have been infected with the Jewish spirit.'[30]

Thus Marxist socialists, while at times inclined to equate the vulgar com-
mercialism of the *Gruenderjahre* with things Jewish, did not use the *Verjudung*

theme regularly and, when they did, it was usually in a deflective, albeit ambivalent, way. Their materialist class analysis and internationalist commitment prevented them from going much further than this. Such inhibitions did not pertain to those who were gradually building an ideology of socialism that was neither materialist nor cosmopolitan but rather idealist and nationalist. The rise of a national socialist ideology was, in many respects, a *voelkisch, fin-de-siècle* reaction to both bourgeois liberalism and Marxist socialism. These were propitious circumstances in which the *Verjudung* thesis could flourish. The role of the famous economist Werner Sombart in this development was both central and exemplary.

Sombart, significantly, began as a radical sympathetic to Marxism but ended up by including it in his pantheon of 'Jewish products'.[31] He was also, of course, instrumental in lending academic legitimacy to the identification of the 'Jewish spirit' with that of modern capitalism. His famous *Die Juden und das Wirtschaftsleben* (1911), while written in the idiom of social science, in reality simply systematized older, popular perceptions of the Jews and their facility for moneymaking and materialist gain.[32] The *Verjudung* of Germany could be counteracted only by the creation of a *German* socialism opposed to both the Jewish merchant and Marxist spirit.[33] In the best traditions of the 'Judaization' myth, Sombart, who had done so much to diffuse the image of the materialist Jew, argued that the 'Jewish spirit' was both an integral part of the Jewish group and was yet detachable and transmittable to non-Jews. Writing in 1934 in a Germany that had indeed attained National Socialism, Sombart stated: 'Here it is a question of overcoming and removing, in a feasible way, what is called the "Jewish spirit" ... This spirit first struck root among the Jewish people, and we must assume that it extended itself among them, because it corresponded with a frequently recurring racial trait in the Jewish people.' This was a kind of 'spiritual' rather than 'biological' racism, for Sombart argued that not all Jews were necessarily afflicted by the 'Jewish spirit': some could even be animated by its German antithesis. More to the point, however, was Sombart's insistence that the 'Jewish spirit' had radically spread: this did not attenuate the antisemitic animus; it meant simply that the range of attack had to be correspondingly widened, for Germany itself had become 'Jewish':

> Under the influence of the Jewish spirit the entire external structure of our existence has been formed and, as a matter of fact, *exists*, whether Jews are present or not. In other words, the Jewish spirit has become a part of us, it 'objectivates' in a thousand regulations and practices: in our law, our constitution, our style of life, our economics, etc. Our economy, above all ... In order to free ourselves from the Jewish spirit – said to be the chief

task of the German people and, above all, of Socialism – it is not enough to exclude all Jews, not even enough to cultivate an anti-Jewish temper. It will be far better to so transform the institutional culture that it will no longer serve as a bulwark for the Jewish spirit.[34]

We should keep in mind that in Wilhelmine Germany the perception of 'Judaization' was not limited to outright antisemites, conservative critics, or such circles as I have discussed above. The deep ambivalence attached to the transformation of Germany into a modern capitalist culture did not apply only to traditional classes or the new proletariat.[35] The very liberals and bourgeoisie who were bringing this metamorphosis about were also plagued by such doubts as older values came into conflict with newer economic practices. Given the obvious fact of Jewish participation in this process, liberal bourgeois non-Jews also voiced the sentiment – sometimes publicly, sometimes privately – that Germany was becoming *verjudet* without, for one moment, reneging on liberal support for Jewish emancipation. *Verjudung* was so useful precisely because it could function as a sublimative and deflective and 'symbolic' tool.

As one liberal put it in an address to the *Freies deutsches Hochstift* in Frankfurt in 1880, the new antisemitism, though attacking 'the Jews', was not really aimed at the Israelite population: 'Far from it, that movement represents an inarticulate manifestation of the feeling which has seized hold of our whole people. They feel that the insensate dance round the golden calf, the purblind pursuit of the pleasures of the flesh threaten to lead us, too, astray and onto paths of evil from which the lofty instinct of our people shrinks in horror.' Jews, the speaker went on, had of course contributed considerably to these materialistic developments, but 'Jewish' activities were not necessarily Israelite ones.

Indeed it is no secret that this circumstance led a long time ago to the adoption of a common useage [sic] of a new terminology which – let it be said, quite unjustly - designates all ruthless money-grabbers as 'Jews', even though they may be of German stock, no matter whether they are high or low born. It is these so-called Jews and their society, and not the Israelites, who are the targets of the movement of outraged indignation that is spreading wider in Germany every day. The German people are beginning to realize that they are in danger of losing their holiest and most cherished treasure, the heritage of our fathers, that noble contempt for worldly things, that humble reverence for the holy, that sublime striving for inner worth and the transfiguration of the soul, all those traits which have so far been shared by all Germans irrespective of differences of religious denomination.[36]

Liberals did not consistently distinguish between 'Jews' and 'Israelites'. The attack on Jewish civil rights was one thing, condemning the Jew as the embodiment of the 'Jewish spirit' quite another. Thus even self-consciously liberal periodicals, journals that advocated Jewish emancipation and opposed political antisemitism, reinforced this link. As Henry Wassermann has decisively shown, popular liberal publications such as the *Fliegende Blaetter* consistently connected Jews to the mammonization of German society:[37] Jews were granted a virtual monopoly in caricatures concerned with moneymaking and commerce in its dishonest and vulgar forms. This stereotype was reinforced by the popular middle-class German novels of Gustav Freytag and Wilhelm Raabe in which the distinction between honourable Christian and dishonest Jewish dealings was of central importance.[38] Liberal German *Buergertum*, embracing capitalism but locked into an older, competing system of values, found it easy to project the distasteful activity of making money and the commercialization of society onto the Jew.

There were, then, differing intentions behind, and divergent versions of, the 'Judaization' myth. But it was, nevertheless, fairly generally disseminated. All the circles described above – by employing its terminology and speaking its language – provided the idea with a certain legitimacy. Their role in the diffusion of this kind of thinking should not be underestimated. Still, here *Verjudung* was used mainly as a form of collective metaphor and in a deflective manner. This was not so for *voelkisch* ideologues, certain conservatives, and political antisemites. They constantly hammered the theme home: their attack was frontal, and the distinction between 'Jew' as symbol and as concrete embodiment was academic at best. While these groups must be differentiated, certain links and continuities need to be noted. The explicitly antisemitic versions of 'Jewification', at least in terms of their theoretical outlines, were also enunciated by self-defined 'progressive' radicals such as Richard Wagner and Wilhelm Marr. They, too, combined the traditional German 'noble contempt for worldly things' with the 'Judaization' myth: they also used the idealist tradition for their critique of Jewish materialism.

The translation of these themes into a self-proclaimed, revolutionary, redemptive antisemitism was effected by Richard Wagner. Although the idea and major themes of 'Judaization' had been circulating for a long time, it was a concept that awaited its name. No specific term had been coined. It was in Wagner's essay 'Judaism in Music' (1850) that the German neologism first appeared.[39] There the term connoted the transposition of the material on to the ideal, the corruption of the cultural by the philistine, the demeaning of the spiritual by the commercial. This concern – that the insides of Geman culture were being polluted and its basic values levelled by the 'Jewish spirit' – did not arise in a vacuum: it reflected the anxieties generated by the remarkable and rapid emergence of a new kind of Jew, the secular intellectual and artist destined to play a major role in the shaping of nineteenth-century German culture (Wagner focused his attack on Heinrich Heine, Felix Mendelssohn, and, of course, Giacomo Meyerbeer). Despite the conversion to Christianity of most of these intellectuals, many critics dismissed their work as 'arid' and 'soulless'. Juxtaposed to the noble, organic qualities of German culture, the 'Jewish spirit' was stigmatized as as an agent of decomposition. Jews, it was held, thrived in 'mechanical' rather than 'organic' situations. They thus flocked to Berlin – the very embodiment of 'Judaized' society – for there, as Heinrich Laube put it, even spiritual exercise was the product of mechanical forces.[40]

Wagner systematized these sentiments in sophisticated and radical terms, combining anti-Jewish rhetoric with sharp social observation. In what, he asked, did the *'Verjudung der modernen Kunst'* ('Judaization of modern art') consist?

According to the present constitution of the world, the Jew in truth is already more than emancipated: he rules, and will rule, so long as Money remains the power before which all our doings and dealings lose their Force. ... That the impossibility of carrying farther any natural, any beauteous thing, upon the basis of that stage whereat the evolution of our arts has now arrived, and without a total alteration of that basis – that this has also brought the public Art-taste of our time between the busy fingers of the Jew, however, is the matter whose grounds we here have to consider somewhat closer. ... What the heroes of the arts, with untold strain consuming lief and life, have wrested from the art-fiend of two millennia of misery, today the Jew converts into an art bazaar [*Kunstwaarenwechsel*]: who sees it in the mannered bric-a-brac, that is glued together by the hallowed brow-sweat of the Genius of two thousand years?[41]

For Wagner, the 'Judaization' process was partly the product of Jewish power over money; but it was also the beneficiary of a wider trend toward the 'commoditization' of culture. German culture was in a state of degeneration, and the decline of standards was clearly in the interest of the modern Jew who, given his 'rootlessness' and inalienable status as an outsider, was devoid of all authentic creative capacities. Cut off from its own tradition and the host society, the destructive 'Jewish spirit' merely reflected the Jewish condition. Genuine artistic creativity was a function of deep, unconscious, historical belonging.[42]

Wagner illustrates particularly well the fact that all theories of *Verjudung* functioned – in a more or less sophisticated way – as a means of self-appraisal, as foils for cultural criticism. Both the preconditions for, and ultimate success of, 'Jewification' were located in flaws and weaknesses in the German self and society.[43] The specter of *Verjudung* was thus clearly linked to the insecure sense of German national identity: the 'Judaized' society provided a countermodel against which the desired national state of affairs could be posited. In his essay 'Was ist Deutsch?' (1878) Wagner drew a picture of Jewish power and German failure where cultural pessimism and utopian vision functioned as necessary correlates. He stressed a theme later anti-semites were constantly to reiterate. *Juedischer Geist*, he argued, had pene-trated so deeply, had so undermined the people, that, under the spell of liberal Jewish organs, they would no longer be able to utter a sensible word. *Verjudung* was a kind of opiate. In terms of its purported capacity for spiritual conta-gion, as an agent of ideological contamination, Wagner could seriously fore-see a situation, close at hand, in which although the German *Volk* would persist in external form, its *Geist* would completely disappear.[44]

Wagner was even able to take the *Verjudung* critique beyond the hope for German national regeneration. Here the Jew and his negative 'spirit' became the negative symbol, the antitype, not only of the German nation but the counterconception to Wagner's idea of humanity itself. A redeemed, revo-lutionized world was a de-Judaized humanity.[45]

Like Marx's apologists, defenders of Wagner contend that Wagner did not attack 'ethnic' Jews but Judaism as a moral symbol.[46] Was not Wagner friend-ly with Jews like Hermann Levi, Karl Tausig, and Jacob Rubinstein?[47] The symbolic, plastic nature of the *Verjudung* argument made this distinction a popular one; many antisemites claimed that they had nothing against indi-vidual, particular Jews.[48] Judaism was here presented as a state of mind, a psycho-spiritual condition. Houston Stewart Chamberlain, an enthusiastic initiate of the Wagner entourage, put it thus:

> One does not need to have the authentic Hittite nose to be a Jew; the word indicates rather a special kind of feeling and thinking; a person may very rapidly become a Jew without becoming an Israelite; some need only to associate actively with Jews, read Jewish newspapers and become accus-tomed to the Jewish conception of life, literature and art. ... We must agree with Paul, the apostle, when he says: 'For he is not a Jew who is one out-wardly in the flesh, but he who is a Jew inwardly.'

This kind of 'spiritual anti-Judaism' allowed for the 'humanization of the Jew'. As Chamberlain archly put it, 'A wholly humanized Jew is no longer a Jew.' Of course, he stressed, it was easier to 'become a Jew' than the almost impossible task of 'becoming a German'.[49] But, at least in theory, the excep-tional Jew could overcome the 'Jewish spirit' within him.

The overwhelming majority of German Jews, while accepting the need for Jewish 'modernization', tried to balance their 'Germanism' and Judaism within some kind of honorable synthesis. A few extreme cases, however, not only accepted the antisemitic onslaught on Judaism in its entirety but made its purported 'spiritual' basis the means for 'overcoming' their own Jewishness. The Jewish writer Conrad Alberti (b. Konrad Sittenfeld), for example, totally accepted the anti-Judaic critique. He opposed active antisemitism on the grounds that it merely strengthened Jewishness! 'Judaism', he wrote, 'can be successfully combated only by Jews – the experience of Christ and Paul should have taught us that ... Only inner, spiritual self-disintegration (*Selbstzersetzung*) can liquidate and destroy Judaism.'[50] The self-proclaimed Wagnerian Otto Weininger made this spiritual anti-Judaism the cornerstone of a systematic and ultimately tragic attempt to transcend his Jewishness. Judaism was, for him, not a historical tradition or an ethnic or racial category. It was rather a Platonic idea, a psychic negative potential of all human beings. There are 'Aryans who are more Jewish than many Jews, and actual Jews who are more Aryan than certain Aryans', he wrote in his famous *Sex and Character* (1903).[51] Weininger was well aware of the projective nature of this phenomenon. Whoever hated Jews, he commented, hated the Jewish part within himself. But because it was an idea, a spiritual predisposition, he argued that Jewishness could be overcome. This could never be done on a collective basis. The only satisfactory solution to the Jewish Question would take place on the individual level, where after a profound, inner struggle Jewishness could be transcended.

Like the antisemites, Weininger claimed that he was not attacking 'individual Jews, to so many of whom I would have incurred highly unwillingly harm, to whom a great and bitter injustice would occur, if what I have said were to be turned against them.' Yet whenever this kind of distinction was drawn – and this was very often the case – there was an inevitable and alarming correspondence between the 'Jewish spirit' and real, everyday Jews. As Weininger put it, although Judaism was a universal human *possibility*, its 'overwhelming *realization* had occurred within historical Jewry.'[52] Weininger's attempt to 'spiritualize' the Jewish Problem relied upon the early Wagner and left out the more explicitly racist writings of the 1880s. But even in the early Wagner the ethnic ingredient was present no matter how elevated the metaphysical discourse appeared. The distinction between person and principle, 'spirit' and ethnicity, was an overwhelmingly fine one.[54] And although in his 'Judaism in Music', Wagner allowed for Jewish redemption in principle, in practice this was an almost impossible task. For the German, redemption entailed regeneration through self-destruction; in the case of the ethnic Jew a double self-destruction was required, an almost superhuman act of will.

After Wagner introduced the neologism in 1850, *Verjudung* rapidly became an indispensable part of the linguistic currency of anti-Jewish discourse. The term summed up a fear that went beyond explicitly antisemitic circles. The perception of disproportionate Jewish power was certainly not limited to radical and fringe groups. The concern that public opinion was being controlled by the 'Jewish press' was especially prevalent. For those who elaborated on the 'Jewification' of Germany, this was particularly important, for in an age of increasingly impersonal mass communications the press was regarded as the major agent of ideological infiltration, the vehicle through which the 'Jewish spirit' entered the German psyche. The Jewish press, one critic commented in 1865, had become so powerful 'that it does not need to be directed by Jews anymore; the Christian has become so Judaized that no significant differences can any longer be recognized.'[55]

Anti-Jewish circles concurred that the infection had spread; what differed were the diagnoses of, and proposed cures for, the disease. Clericals and conservatives agreed with radical antisemites that the 'Jewish spirit' was based on the principle of Mammon (a conviction with which, as we have seen, both socialists and Liberals did not really take issue). Such worldliness, conservatives argued, threatened to destroy the organic basis of society, to trample on traditional values of honest labor and authentic community. For such circles the process of 'Judaization' was the consequence of the decline of religion. The triumph of the Enlightenment, of the French Revolution and liberalism, had destroyed the Christian state and the old social order and prepared the way for the rule of Judaism. This age of Jewish materialism and liberal permissiveness had tempted and overcome the believing Christian. Only with the financial crash of the 1870s, Christian polemicists proclaimed, did they begin to regret their actions: 'You have made into your own God the calf that the Jew worship. You have helped the Jews', Paul Koehler wrote in his pamphlet, *The Judaization of Germany: The Path to Deliverance*, 'to destroy in the people the ideals of our Christian faith. Now do you wonder if Christian morality has disappeared? that Judaization has penetrated? that Germanism, which only flourished under the domination of Christian thought, was now declining? You are yourselves Judaized!'[56]

If *Verjudung* followed the breakdown of the Christian *Weltanschauung*, the ideological antidote was obvious: 'Whoever keeps his Christian faith high does not sink into Judaization. .... .Become Christian again and you will be freed of your *Verjudung*. .... .As long as the evangelical faith lives in the German people, to that degree it will not be Judaized. No real Protestant becomes a *Judengenosse*.'[57] This was a fairly wide sentiment. Still, most clericals and conservatives combined this hostility with a solution that was becoming increasingly antithetical to the radicals: total assimilation of the Jews through conversion to Christianity. De-Judaization of the Christian and Christianization of the Jew were their solution to the problem of *Verjudung*.

The emerging radical antisemites took a quite different, explicitly opposed view. They self-consciously based themselves on what they designated a 'nonconfessional' standpoint, thus denying to the religious factor a determinative role as either an explanatory or a therapeutic factor. More important, the new antisemites often combined their hostility against Jews with an attack upon Christianity itself. This was equally true for the *voelkisch* prophet of a regenerated Germanic religion, Paul de Lagarde, the professional anti-semite Wilhelm Marr, and the racist theoretician Eugen Duehring. Here was an antisemitism avowedly radical, secular and political in nature (although, when convenient, it too incorporated traditional Christian elements into its view). As such, their solution to 'Jewification' could obviously not be found in Christianization, for their attack upon Christianity was partly prompted by the argument that Christianity itself was the chief source, the major agent of *Verjudung* in Western culture. 'Judaization' was *not* the product of Christian weakness but rather the result of its *success*. Houston Stewart Chamberlain was already heir to an established tradition when he wrote in his *Foundations of the Nineteenth Century* (1899) that it was through Christianity that Judaism had become internalized and part of the non-Jewish soul. Were this not the case, he argued, the danger of 'flesh-and-blood Jews for our culture would be far smaller.'[58]

From Lagarde through Alfred Rosenberg, it became commonplace to argue that Christians had become weakened and corrupted through Judaization of the Church.[59] This kind of argument was considerably strengthened by someone who could hardly be accused of supporting political antisemitism, Friedrich Nietzsche. Yet his *On the Genealogy of Morals* (1887) and *The Anti-Christ* (1888) were clearly written in this idiom. A substantial part of his savage attack on Christianity was based upon the assertion of Christianity's thorough Judaization. The Jews, inventors of the slave revolt in morality, the revaluators of values, Nietzsche proclaimed, had been totally victorious. They had radically falsified 'all nature, all naturalness, all reality, of the whole inner world as well as the outer ... by their after effect they have made mankind so thoroughly false that even today the Christian can feel anti-Jewish without realizing that he himself is the *ultimate Jewish consequence*.'[60] Of course this was meant as an attack on Christianity, but the language was quite consistent with that of the antisemites:

This Jesus of Nazareth. ... was he not this seduction in its most uncanny and irresistible form, a seduction and bypath to precisely those Jewish values and ideals? Did Israel not attain the ultimate goal of its sublime vengefulness precisely through the bypath of this 'Redeemer', this ostensible opponent and disintegrator of Israel?. ... What is certain, at least, is that *sub hoc signo*, Israel, with its vengefulness and revaluation of all values, has hitherto triumphed again and again over all other ideals, over all *nobler* ideals.[61]

With all the important necessary qualifications, it is not surprising that, given the correct selective reading, certain anti-semites could turn to Nietzsche for inspiration (see Chapter 4). The Jews, more than any other people, Nietzsche wrote, had

> a world-historic mission. The 'masters' have been disposed of; the moral-
> ity of the common man has won. One may conceive of this victory as at
> the same time a blood poisoning (it has mixed the races together) – I shan't
> contradict; but this intoxication has undoubtedly been successful. The
> 'redemption' of the human race (from the 'masters', that is) is going for-
> ward; everything is visibly becoming Judaized, Christianized, mob-ized
> (what do the words matter!).[62]

In all probability Hitler did not read Nietzsche, but it does seem that at least a crude version of such thinking had filtered down to him. His remarks in conversation were virtually a direct paraphrase of Nietzsche's notions about the Jews and their overall 'democratizing', weakening effect in which the people, the mob, had been victorious as was his disdain for the 'Jewish Christ-creed with its effeminate pity-ethics'.[63]

There was an irony in Conrad Alberti's choice of Paul as the model of Jewish self-overcoming, for it was precisely this Pharisee Paul who was regarded by many antisemites as the instrumental agent of 'Judaization'. It was he who had brought his weakening doctrines to the West and with it broken the great power of the Roman Empire. His debilitating influence was a commonplace of these circles. Paul's role was central in the pamphlet by Hitler's mentor Dietrich Eckart, which had the significant title *Das Judentum in und ausser uns (The Judaism Within Us and Without)*. As a result of Paul's materialism and his literalism, the inability to understand that immortality was a spiritual not a corporeal matter, worldly Judaism had become an inte-gral part of the non-Jewish psyche. 'There is a large portion', Eckart wrote, 'unbelievably much Judaism that since Paul has become more and more and more part of our Christian being. ... Many Germans are not true Jews only because they are not circumcised'.[64] The Jew was now within.

For *voelkisch* critics like Lagarde, whose life and writings span the sec-ond half of the nineteenth century, the Paulinian influence on Christianity had been so disastrous that only the creation of a regenerative *Germanic* religion would be able to stem the tide of German decline and 'Judaization'.[65] In Wagnerian language, Lagarde wrote, 'The unregenerated German, like the unregenerated Jew, is only a different species of the same genus.'[66] For the Jew the choice was total assimilation or explusion. But the German task seemed even more essential, for Lagarde explained 'Judaization' in terms of German national inauthenticity. Lagarde addressed 'those who were not so *verjudet* that they could still recognize the illness which beset them'. These people could wage the battle: 'The sharper we express our character as a nation, the less place there will be in Germany for the Jews. ... Germany must become full of German people and German ways ... then there will be no room for Palestine in it. ... To the degree that we become ourselves, the Jews will cease being Jews.'[67]

The return to authentic essence was the key to redemption; *Verjudung* mirrored deviation from such authenticity. Not all those concerned with the dangers of 'Judaization' necessarily preached Jewish self-overcoming. On the contrary, for some it was assimilation itself that was the core of the problem. As the publicist Rudolf Pannwitz, an associate of the Stefan George circle put it, it was not the Jews but *Verjudung* that was so disturbing. 'You', he wrote to the Jews, 'have not preserved yourselves, and we have not preserved ourselves and this mutual neglect has led to demoralization.'[68] Whether German authenticity could be achieved through total Jewish assimilation or its opposite, traditional Jewish self-affirmation, was thus a matter of dispute. The fact of *Verjudung* itself was not.

Wilhelm Marr, who coined the term *Antisemitismus*, also found that 'Jewification' was ubiquitous and that Christianity was an integral part of the problem, not the solution. He regarded Christianity as a wild union of Jewish religion and Platonism. Its dominion had led to nothing short of the 'Judaization of mankind' (*Verjudung der Menschheit*). Through a process of religious superstition and mass mental indolence, Western humanity had become totally 'Judaized.'[69]

Unlike Lagarde and Wagner, Marr portrayed a Germany so completely *verjudet* that no hope for redemption existed. But, as Jacob Katz has pointed-ed out, this pessimism was a pose, a tactic.[70] Indeed Marr believed that the Jewish Question was powerful enough to stand on its own as an indpendent and unifying issue.[71] He was among the pioneers of a self-consciously political antisemitism, convinced that this was not a peripheral matter but rather the key question of German – if not world – society. In order to make this into an issue of overriding importance, one from which all other political issues derived, it was necessary to portray the all-encompassing nature of 'Judaization'. This was the basic message of Marr's unambiguously entitled

The Victory of Judaism over Germanism: Considered from a Nonconfessional Standpoint (1879). *Verjudung*, he stressed, was not merely a matter of individual Jewish influence but 'the Jewish spirit that has conquered the world.' It had penetrated the entire cultural and conceptual German domain: its ruling concept *Freiheit* ('freedom') was in reality *Frechheit* ('impudence'). The very innards, the thoughts of Germans were no longer their own.[72] Germany was enslaved.

Wagner, Lagarde, and Marr enunciated their antisemitism in clearly radical, nonconfessional ways. But if there was incipient racism – at least in principle if not in practice – they left room for the possibility of Jewish self-transcendence. With the emergence of full-blown racism, this was no longer an option. The spiritual and the biological became indissolubly fused. The possibility that the doctrine of 'Judaization' had always allowed – that of somehow distinguishing between the process and its agents – was now to all intents and purposes removed. Symbol and embodiment were one.

Eugen Duehring was one of the first theoreticians to attempt to articulate this notion systematically. As with most radical (and certainly all racist) antisemites, the *Judenfrage* was cast into world-historical terms, into a confrontation between the forces of good and evil. Unlike Marr, Duehring's work radiated an activist, dynamic energy. Both the problem and solution were posed in simple terms: 'Judaization of all relations and peoples is a fact', he wrote, 'de-Judaization the challenge.'[73]

Apart from the vital racist framework there was only one other ingredient Duehring added to the catalog of 'Jewification'. This, however, was an important one, destined to be crucial in the National Socialist brand of antisemitism. Previous formulations of the myth had equated *Verjudung* with liberalism, capitalism, materialism, and godless secularism. With Duehring, himself a socialist respected by leading figures of the German labor movement, Marxism (in at least one version the theory that had prophetically outlined the 'Judaization' of bourgeois society) was itself transformed into a 'Jewish' symptom, ironically labelled as the embodiment of precisely that *Verjudung* which it had lamented. Marx's Jewish origins, materialism, and cosmopolitanism were turned against Marxism itself and easily categorized as 'Jewish' principles. Hitler's later obsession with Marxism as a Jewish conspiracy is to be found already apparent in Duehring. Marxist socialism, wrote Duehring was really a *Judenallianz*, a scheme by which all nations of the world would be controlled and absorbed by a new *Judenreich*. This so-called communist Reich would, in reality, be the means by which the Chosen People dispense with the common treasure of the nations.[74]

It was, of course, during the Weimar Republic that the radical, and especially the racist, Right came into its own. Liberal Weimar with its sceptical, experimental culture, that system which, in Peter Gay's memorable phrase, had promoted the traditional outsider into insider,[74] was an easy target, one that was consistently, and apparently plausibly, cast as thoroughly *verjudet*. There were few additions to the anti-Jewish canon during this period. The notion of *Verjudung* simply became cruder and more extreme, able to reach a wider audience than ever before. Weimar was surely a 'Jew Republic'. With Walther Rathenau as foreign minister, on the one hand, and Marxist Jewish revolutionary leaders, on the other, who could have doubted this?

If there were no significant additions to the idea of *Verjudung* during the Weimar period, there was a kind of updating, fitting it into the *Zeitgeist* of an unprecedented permissiveness and placing it within the new era of technology and consumerism. This, at least, was the emphasis of racist ideologues and self-proclaimed 'culture critics' like Alfred Rosenberg and others. 'Judaization' now became the metaphor for the critique of mass society. The Jews, Rosenberg wrote, were undermining the nations by 'spinning our thoughts and trying with the goods of this world, with economics, trade, industry, and technology to draw us all away from our proper spiritual direction'. It was the Jews who relentlessly tried to remove individual pesonality and 'replace it with the chaos of those cosmetic levelling phrases of Humanity, Fraternity, and Equality'.[76] The modern city was the creation of, and dominated by, the 'Jewish spirit'; its result was mass, atomized man. The metropolis, Rosenberg stressed, constantly engaged in 'race annihilating work'. The major instrument of 'Judaization' was mass culture. It was Jewish management that, after all, had done away with creative acting and in its stead produced 'stars'; art and theater had been converted into a form of mass hypnosis and sensual excitement; the film was now the 'movie industry' and 'a means of infecting the *Volk*.'[77] But, Rosenberg stressed, if *Verjudung* was the leveling process – the creation of an utterly atomized society – the Jews exempted themselves from such a process. They would retain their international cohesiveness, blood ties, and spiritual unity.[78] (This perception, that Jews maintained their cohesiveness and sense of identity under all conceivable circumstances, was a source of both fear and envy. Indeed, for many antisemites this racial perserverance and historical continuity provided a kind of mirror-image model worthy of emulation.) The process of mass-levelling and Jewish dominance had gone so far, one commentator put it, that in all the newspapers, magazines, fashion pages, cinemas and revues, the very model of 'homogenization' was being fashioned in terms of Jewish expressions and body images.[79]

The early days of Nazism produced all kinds of crackpot versions of the 'Judaization' idea, schemes that tried to combine the spiritual with the biological, the religious with the racist. It was only in the confused post-World War I era that grotesque works like Arthur Dinter's novel *Die Suende wider das Blut* (*The Sin against the Blood*), (1918) could achieve great popularity and reach a mass audience. Dinter, the leader of early Thuringian Nazism, produced an entire philosophy of 'spiritual racism' in his novels and pamphlets. Spirit, he argued, was not the product of race but the reverse. Race was merely the earthly incarnation of *Geist*. Jews were the physical embodiments of deeply fallen spirits who in the *Ur*-time of creation had chosen egoism and materialism as their spiritual direction. Race was the vehicle through which such a spirit was transmitted. Even if Jews perceived this 'racial–spiritual' truth, and tried to change their ways, they had to be condemned to a tragic life, for they could not be permitted to join and thereby endanger the Aryan *Blutgemeinschaft*. The Aryan racial spirit was, of course, an idealistic one, but, given the fact that race was only a vehicle for basic spiritual orientations, one could also find egoistic-materialistic Aryan 'Jews'. In fact, this had occurred through the total 'Judaization' of both the Catholic and the Protestant churches: 'It is this Jewish-Christianity that has made us so receptive to the Jewish infection.'[80] The only way to save the Aryan race was to 'complete' the sadly Judaized original German Protestant Reformation.[81] 'The real challenge of a true Christianity', Dinter wrote, 'is overcoming 'the Jew' in ourselves and around us.'[82]

But Dinter's attempts to found a counter-Christian community threatened to drive potential Church-affiliated voters away and interfered with Hitler's tactical desire for co-operation with the established Churches. By 1929 he had been expelled from the party.[83] There were other attempts to permeate Nazism with non-Christian forms of 'spiritual' racism. In certain ways such ideas were crucial to the movement's self-definition. Works like L.F. Clauss's *Die nordische Seele* (*The Nordic Soul*) (1930), for example, argued that external appearance was not the essential hallmark of Aryanism but rather the race-soul, fount of all creativity, which Nordic blood had produced. The anti-semitic Kantian philosopher and outspoken Nazi Max Wundt viewed races as 'spiritual forces that have created bodies for themselves.'[84] The popular and ostensibly 'scientific' racist Hans F.K. Guenther, in effect, regarded racial types as physical representations of inner nature.[85] Anthropology and metaphysical categories of beauty and soul conveniently merged. As George L. Mosse has shown, the Nazi 'science' of race was integrated with a mystical, mythological version.[86] The book burnings of May 1933 gave graphic physical expression to this spiritual dimension. *Juedischer Geist* was to be exorcised and, as Goebbels put it, the hegemonic age of 'sophistic Jewish intellectualism' brought to an end.[87] 'You are leaving now to burn books', Alfred Baeumler told his students, 'in which an alien spirit uses the German word to fight us.'[88]

It was left to Hitler, of course, to give the notion of *Verjudung* its toughest and most racist expression. All previous distinctions between Jews and the 'Jewish idea' were utterly dismissed, race and spirit completely fused. As Hitler told Dietrich Eckart in the early 1920s: 'This is the point: even if not one synagogue, not one Jewish school, the Old Testament and the Bible had not existed, the Jewish spirit would still be there and have its effect. From the beginning it has been there and there is no Jew, not one, that does not embody it.'[89] The Jew was the physical incarnation of the very principle of evil.[90]

For all that, it is important to note that the metaphorical elements of the *Verjudung* myth were not dropped. They were simply fused with the racial. The traditional function of the overall critique of society and culture was maintained. The attack on the physical Jew was obvious and essential, but the all-encompassing process of 'Judaization' was also a rationale for broader political activity, a sanction for radical measures within society itself. For *Verjudung* had so sapped the vital energies of the people, so degenerated their basic values and instincts, that only a thorough purging, a radical reconstruction, would be able to regenerate Germany. *Mein Kampf* (1925) can, indeed, be read as a treatise on both the moral and physical 'Jewification' of the world and as a ruthless dynamic program for radically solving the problem. 'Judaization' had transformed the German respect for labor into a contempt for all productive physical work. It had penetrated everywhere, combining biological and mental corruption in the most intimate and primal areas,

> running parallel to the political, ethical and moral contamination of the people, there had been for many years a no less terrible poisoning of the health of the national body. Especially in the big cities, syphilis was beginning to spread more and more. ... The cause lies primarily in our prostitution of love. Even if its result were not this frightful plague, it would nevertheless be profoundly injurious to man, since the moral devastations which accompany this degeneracy suffice to destroy a people slowly but surely. This Jewification of our spiritual life and mammonization of our mating instincts will sooner or later destroy our entire offspring.[91]

This 'inner Judaization of our people', as Hitler put it,[92] was as dangerous as the tangible Jewish presence. The Jewish influence was the triumph of antinature over nature, of disease over health; *Verjudung* was the weakening of instinct and the loss of ability to resist infection.[93]

This unremitting vocabulary in the mystic–naturalistic–biological mode not only sanctioned ruthless and final measures against all Jews;[94] it also provided a convenient rationale for the 'positive' dynamic of the racial revolution, the 'natural' regeneration of the German *Volksgemeinschaft*, and a sanction for such totalitarian renovation. The idea of 'Judaization' could be pushed no further in thought – or in action.

4 Nietzsche, Anti-Semitism and Mass Murder

Each generation constructs its own, most appropriate Nietzsche – or Nietzsches. During the years of the Third Reich (and immediately after) Nietzsche appeared to be paradigmatically Nazi (while National Socialism seemed best understood as a kind of Nietzschean project).[1] Both National Socialists and their opponents tended to agree that Nietzsche was the movement's *most* formative and influential thinker, visionary of a biologized *Lebensphilosophie* society, fuelled by regenerationist, post-democratic, post-Christian impulses in which the weak, decrepit and useless were to be legislated out of existence. For those interested in making the case any number of prophetic themes and uncannily appropriate quotes were available. 'From now on', Nietzsche wrote in *The Will to Power*, 'there will be more favorable preconditions for more comprehensive forms of dominion, whose like has never yet existed. And even this is not the most important thing; the possibility has been established for the production of international racial unions whose task it will be to rear a master-race, the future "masters of the earth." The time is coming when politics will have a different meaning.'[2]

The paradigmatic Nietzsche of the 1930s, 1940s and early 1950s was then the Nietzsche who was regarded as the thinker most crucially and intimately definitive of the Nazi order. To be sure there were always dissenting voices (both within and without the Nazi camp) but the prevailing wisdom held that Nietzsche was proto-Nazi, that he uncannily prefigured and, indeed, in some way even 'caused' National Socialism and that in fundamental ways the movement itself had to be regarded as 'Nietzschean'.[3] This perception began to shift in about the mid-1950s and, although there have always been counter-challenges, it has so proceeded apace that, for many younger people educated from about the 1970s on, the identification seems virtually incomprehensible. Nietzsche's de-Nazification – and the de-Nietzscheanism of Nazism – I would argue, has become close to a *fait accompli* within Western culture (at least in English-speaking countries and France). This, in the main, has been the product of two, quite different, intellectual forces that – in consonance with wider political changes – has rendered the only other early major competitor and counter-interpretation, Georg Lukács' *Destruction of Reason,* with its guiding thesis that 'Hitler ... was the executor of Nietzsche's spiritual testament and of the philosophical development coming after Nietzsche and from him',[4] if not downright quaint then certainly a little anachronistic.

69

I am not sure if it is an exaggeration to claim that the basic aim of Nietzsche's most insistent and influential post-war expositor, translator and populariser, Walter Kaufmann, was to casuistically rid Nietzsche of these sullied associations and to provide him with the kind of liberal-humanist face consistent with American academic values of the time. His 1950 masterwork portrayed the Nazified Nietzsche as a pure, virtually inexplicable distortion. Essentially a good European, he was a thinker who had to be grasped in terms of his emphases on creativity, culture and critical individualism and whose dismissal of nationalism, racism and anti-Semitism could not have been more apparent.[5]

Kaufmann was, of course, a more or less systematic philosopher who insisted upon pressing Nietzsche's thought into a comprehensible and comprehensive system. Such systematisation is, of course, quite anathema to those who since, in a different, less liberally certain and determinate age, have most dominantly colonised Nietzsche (and at the same time been crucially shaped by him!) – those various exponents of what, for lack of a better name, we call post-modernism and deconstructionism (Foucault, Deleuze, de Man and so on). For them – as distinct from Kaufmann – the issue by and large goes quite unmentioned, unnoticed; the very need to refute the putative Nietzsche-Nazi link has been obliterated! Theirs is a Nietzsche that is quite dissimilar to Kaufmann's. Here he is the radically sceptical perspectivist, the anti-totalizing prophet of heterogeneity, *differance*, fragmentation and discontinuity.[6] But, like Kaufmann, they have also fashioned a rather sterilised Nietzsche[7] whose project appears as the diametrical opposite, even therapeutic answer to, National Socialism. With the important exception of Jacques Derrida (quoted at length a little later) they usually elide the more compromising aspects of his thought, those that sit less comfortably with their hero of ironic indeterminacy.

It may not be at all surprising that the post-war de-Nazification of Nietzsche occurred above all in France and the USA, where, given not only the brilliance but the remarkable elasticity of Nietzsche's oeuvre, he could be harnessed to new cultural and political agendas. In Germany, of course, loosening him from these moorings was a different matter. In the land where Nazism had arisen and flourished and where Nietzsche had become so identified with the regime, it should perhaps not surprise us that, for upholders of the new liberal-democratic regime, resistance to his renewed influence was perhaps the greatest. It is no coincidence therefore that the most vociferous contemporary critic of Nietzsche – as well as post-modernism and what he considers to be its parallel irrationalist, anti-Enlightenment thrust – is Juergen Habermas.[8] There are signs, I believe, that – perhaps with the slow demise of deconstructionist thinking – not only in Germany but elsewhere there has begun to occur another shift, or a rethinking, that, on a more sophisticated, qualified basis, will be able to seriously grapple with this question. The present chapter is an attempt to contribute to this renewed conversation.

Of course, particular readings and judgements of Nietzsche will determine whether we believe him to be implicated in Nazism. And, on the other hand, particular interpretations of National Socialism will influence our readiness to include him within its contours. But the very range and complexity of opinion is also related to the exceedingly charged nature of the issue. After all, both Nietzsche and National Socialism remain central to the twentieth century experience and our own defining cultural and ideological landscape and sense of self.[9] And this chapter, of course, deals with the entwinement in its most explosive dimension: not the general question of the interrelationship of Nietzsche and the Third Reich (this I have done in detail elsewhere[10]) but the connections between the philosopher and radical Jew-hatred as well as the possible connections between his thought and the genocidal project (and the other major mass murders) that stood at the dark heart of the Third Reich.

How may the historian deal with such vexed questions and what are the assumptions and materials that must be brought to bear? Anyone even vaguely acquainted with the history of Nietzsche's political and cultural influence and reception will know how manifold, pervasive and contradictory it has been. It is clear that no 'unmediated', causally direct relationship can be inferred or demonstrated. It would be an error to reduce Nietzsche's – exceedingly ambiguous, protean, elastic – work to an essence possessed of a single, clear and authoritative meaning and operating in a linearly determined historical direction. There should be no set portrait of the 'authentic' Nietzsche, nor dogmatic certainty as to his original intent. Clearly the essentialist representations of both Kaufmann and Lukacs – Nietzsche's thought as either *inherently antithetical to or the prototypical reflection, the ideational incarnation of the Nazi project* – prejudge precisely the question at hand. What needs to be sifted out, and analysed as precisely as possible, are the concrete mediating links, the transmission belts that demonstrate conscious appropriation, explicit acknowledgments of affiliation and influence, the recognised thematic parallels and (more speculatively) the preconditions, the creations of states of mind and sensibilities that fed into the horrors of the Third Reich and rendered them conceivable in the first place.

Let us first turn to the question of Nietzsche and anti-semitism and, most importantly, his annexation – or, perhaps, rejection – by German anti-semites from the Second Reich on. As always, Nietzsche's texts themselves provide a positive goldmine of varied possibilities, filled with ambiguities that his followers – and critics – could scavenge and turn in numerous, often quite

contradictory, directions (this was typical of Nietzsche's reception in virtually every area). However one interprets it one must stress the fact that Jews
and Judaism are intrinsically implicated in, if not crucially central to,
Nietzsche's work; in both his hostile and friendly deliberations he insisted
upon their absolutely fateful historical role within European civilisation.
(Who else could have written in such a simultaneously affirmative and omi-
nous tone: 'Among the spectacles to which the coming century invites us is
the decision as to the destiny of the Jews of Europe. That their die is cast,
that they have crossed their Rubicon, is now palpably obvious: all that is left
for them is either to become the masters of Europe or to lose Europe.'[11])

From our point of view it does not really matter whether Nietzsche's views
on Jews and Judaism are to be regarded as a unified and coherent element of
a larger systematic outlook or as disparate and self-contradictory.[12] For the
historian of culture what is important are the interpretive spaces open to those
who selectively read and received the texts. There were clearly sufficient
allusions, hints and themes to satisfy virtually all comers. Jew and anti-semites
alike were aware that both could find Nietzsche's work useful (and spent
much of their time in casuistically explaining away those passages that were
not compatible with their own particular outlook). *Voelkisch* anti-semites
interested in annexing Nietzsche had to contend with the knowledge that he
was no nationalist, indeed was perhaps the most pronounced critic of his contemporary Germans, and above all the most outspoken opponent of the anti-
Semitic 'swindle'. Turning around the very basis of his notion of *ressentiment*
Nietzsche even branded the herd, mass movement of anti-Semitism as itself
a kind of slave revolt.[13] To make matters worse for the anti-Semites, more
than any other European thinker he lavished extravagant praise on 'The *Old*
Testament ... all honour to [it]! I find in it great human beings, a heroic landscape, and something of the very rarest quality in the world, the incomparable naivete of the *strong heart*; what is more I find a people. In the New one,
on the other hand, I find nothing but petty sectarianism, mere rococo of the
soul, mere involutions, nooks, queer things'[14] – and the comparative virtues
of the European Jews of his own time: 'Jews among Germans are always the
higher race', he wrote, 'more refined, spiritual, kind. *L'adorable* Heine, they
say in Paris.'[15]

Those inclined to pick up and disseminate these positive Nietzschean
Jewish messages could easily do so (this is precisely what many in the Jewish
community consistently did[16]) and this, indeed, was the reason that many
anti-Semites from the time of the Second Reich and continuing through the
Nazi period either rejected Nietzsche entirely (Theodor Fritsch, Dietrich
Eckart and Ernst Krieck are only the best-known of many examples) or,
where they did appropriate his ideas, did so in a qualified, selectively har-

nessed fashion (for instance Adolf Bartels, Wilhelm Schallmeyer, Heinrich Haertle).[17] Even those many anti-Semites and Nazis who were wholeheartedly Nietzschean (Franz Haiser, Ernst Wachler, Alfred Schuler, Ludwig Klages and Alfred Baeumler among others) were aware that casuistic explanation of Nietzsche's pro-Jewish comments and his biting contempt for political anti-Semitism was needed. Variations on this theme were offered in abundance: The true 'Germanic', indeed, racist, Nietzsche had been consistently hidden by his Jewish mediators who had maliciously transformed him into a libertarian, nihilist internationalist.[18] Anyone familiar with Nietzsche, wrote Alfred Bauemler, knew how opposed to the Jews he actually was. His philo-Semitic comments were simply an attention-getting device – playing the Jews against the Germans was part of his strategy to get the Germans to listen to him![19] But the most important claim argued that in recasting the terms of the debate, by infinitely radicalizing the question and going beyond all its conventional forms, Nietzsche was in fact 'the most acute anti-Semite that ever was'.[20] He had, so the argument went, only opposed its traditional nineteeth-century varieties and its Christian versions because he stood for a newer and more radical form, one whose anti-Christian and biological sources pushed it far beyond the limited confessional, economic and social domains.[21]

No matter how selective an exercise this was, these anti-Semites were basing themselves upon, and finding inspiration in, particular readings of some of Nietzsche's most powerful – and extreme – texts. (Their reading, incidentally, was shared by Nietzsche's close friend and confidant, Franz Overbeck who remarked that although 'Nietzsche has been a convinced enemy of anti-Semitism as he had experienced it ... That does not exclude that his opinions about the Jews, when he spoke frankly, had a sharpness which surpassed by far every anti-Semitism. His position against Christianity is primarily founded in anti-Semitism.'[22]) The philosopher had, after all, endowed the Jews with a world-historical stain, the stain that his entire philosophy sought to uncover, diagnose and overcome. It was *On the Genealogy of Morals* that held the 'priestly people' responsible for nothing less than beginning 'the slave revolt in morality: that revolt which has a history of two thousand years behind it and which we no longer see because it – has been victorious.'[23] And as Nietzsche put it in *The Antichrist*, the Jews, with their desire to survive at any price, were nothing less than 'the *most catastrophic* people of world history.' Their sin was inconceivably heinous for they had radically falsified

all nature, all naturalness, all reality, of the whole inner-world as well as the outer ... out of themselves they created a counterconcept to *natural* conditions: they turned religion, cult, morality, history, psychology, one after the other, into an *incurable contradiction to their natural values* ...

by their aftereffect that they have made mankind so thoroughly false that even today the Christian can feel anti-Jewish without realizing that he himself *is the ultimate Jewish consequence.*[24]

It is true that Nietzsche was in the main referring to the priestly period but the force of the texts themselves submerged this somewhat and interested appropriators were certainly not going to bother themselves with such scholastic qualifications! (It may also be that Nietzsche's distinction between the Hebrews and – priestly – Judaism matched the same opposition between vitality and decadence that he posited between pre- and post-Socratic Greece. That may or may not have been the case but, in terms of reception history and political consequences, Greeks in late nineteenth century Europe did not constitute a politically vulnerable and threatened minority nor did Athens possess the same negative emotional valence that surrounded the question of Jews and Judaism in the Germany of that time. No comparable Nietzschean ethnic anti-Alexandrian movement can be identified.)

It was these radical themes that were picked up by extreme anti-Semites and certain Nazi supporters and that informed their everyday rhetoric. Nazism, wrote Heinrich Roemer in 1940, was indebted to Nietzsche's pivotal insight that Israel had denaturalized natural values. The clear implication was that National Socialism had to be regarded as the countermovement leading to renaturalization.[25] For such commentators the significance of Nietzsche's anti-Christian posture consisted in its anti-Jewish basis. His demonstration that Christianity was the ultimate Jewish consequence and that it engendered the spread of Jewish 'blood-poisoning' (Nietzsche's words)[26] made the Jews the most fateful people of world history. As one acolyte, Hans Eggert Schroeder, put it, Judaized Christianity, represented racial decline and decadence, 'the antiracial principle applied against the racial.'[27] It was in this way, according to these Nietzschean Nazis, that Nietzsche found his way to the race problem and then toward the solution of racial hygiene in an attempt 'to break the degeneration of a thousand years.'[28]

This kind of rhetoric was awash at every level of Nazi discourse, and if it was not the only source, it certainly served to canalize, reinforce and significantly radicalize already pre-existent anti-Semitic impulses. To be sure, it is almost certain that Hitler either never read Nietzsche directly or read very little.[29] Nevertheless his thoughts, sayings and speeches clearly espoused a popularized Nietzscheanism as it had percolated down to him during and after World War I – after all, a certain brutalized Nietzschean coin had become the basic currency of the radical right during that period. It was this that he selectively applied and melded into the *melange* that constituted his own peculiar mode of thinking.[30]

Historical transmission belts – the ways in which thought, ideas, moods and sensibility become translated into policy – are complex indeed and all this is not meant to draw a causally straight line between Nietzsche, his epigones and the destruction of European Jewry. As we have already pointed out, Nietzsche's influence was like his writings, always multivalent and never simplistically reducible to any single political or cultural current or direction.[31] Nevertheless, I would argue that these texts and the mediated sensibility they could embody possess a relevance to the problem at hand. They formed an explicit ingredient of – and a particularly radical way of canalizing – this kind of anti-Semitic consciousness, an influence that (for many, though obviously not for all) was openly acknowledged, and which constituted a crucial element of a radicalized mind-set that was a kind of precondition for what was to come.

This, at any rate, is how some recent historians have viewed the matter. Thus, as Conor Cruise O'Brien has argued, it was Nietzsche who was the decisive force in the fateful switch from a 'limited' Christian theological Jew-hatred to an unlimited, secular brand and who thus concretely paved the way to the Holocaust. Hitler, he writes, learned from Nietzsche 'that the traditional Christian *limit* on anti-Semitism was itself part of a Jewish trick. When the values that the Jews had reversed were restored, there would be no limits and no Jews.'[32] (We do not know if Hitler knew of the following Nietzschean passage but his utterances certainly echoed such sentiments: 'Decadence is only a *means* for the type of man who demands power in Judaism and Christianity, the *priestly* type: this type of man has a life interest in making mankind *sick* and in so twisting the concepts of good and evil, true and false, as to imperil life and slander the world.'[33]) And, as George Lichtheim would have it, only when Nietzschean ideas antithetical to the Judeo–Christian inheritance and its humanist offshoots had slowly percolated through and successfully gripped certain German minds did Auschwitz become possible: 'It is not too much to say that but for Nietzsche the SS – Hitler's shock troops and the core of the whole movement – would have lacked the inspiration which enabled them to carry out their programme of mass murder in Eastern Europe.'[34]

Before going on with the argument and trying to clarify some particular historical distinctions a few general remarks would be in order. While here, and elsewhere, I insist that for the cultural historian interested in grasping the role, dynamics and effects of ideas within a political culture, the question of 'valid' or 'invalid' interpretations and appplications must be set aside, this does not, of course, render irrelevant the role of the text – and here the Nietzschean text – within this process. Even if, for a moment, we retain the language of 'distortion' or 'misinterpretation', approaches such as Kaufmann's leave us oblivious to the possibility that, as Martin Jay has put it, 'the potential for the specific distortions that do occur can be understood as latent in the original text. Thus, while it may be questionable to saddle Marx with responsibility for the Gulag Archipelago or blame Nietzsche for Auschwitz, it is nevertheless true that their writings could be misread as justifications for these horrors in a way that, say, those of John Stuart Mill or Alexis de Tocqueville could not.'[35] Jacques Derrida, so much a part of the 'new' Nietzsche that we discussed at the beginning of the paper, has nevertheless similarly argued for a certain complicated complicity – 'one can't falsify just anything ...' – and notes the need

> to account for the possibility of this mimetic inversion and perversion. If one refuses the distinction between unconscious and deliberate programs as an absolute criterion, if one no longer considers only intent – whether conscious or not – when reading a text, then the law that makes the perverting simplification possible must lie in the structure of the text 'remaining'. ... There is nothing absolutely contingent about the fact that the only political regimen to have *effectively* brandished his name as a major and official banner was Nazi.

> I do not say this in order to suggest that this kind of 'Nietzschean' politics is the only one conceivable for all eternity, nor that it corresponds to the best reading of the legacy, nor even that those who have not picked up this reference have produced a better reading of it. no. The future of the Nietzsche text is not closed. But if, within the still-open contours of an era, the only politics calling itself – proclaiming itself – Nietzschean will have been a Nazi one, then is necessarily significant and must be questioned in all of its consequences.

> I am also not suggesting that we ought to reread 'Nietzsche' and his great politics on the basis of what we know or think we know Nazism to be. I do not believe that we as yet know how to think what Nazism is. The task remains before us, and the political reading of the Nietzschean body or corpus is part of it.[36]

To be sure, other historians and thinkers, of whom Berel Lang is the most recent example, have claimed the very opposite arguing that while ideas *are* central in grasping the genocidal impulse of Nazism,

> for Nietzsche's historical aftermath, what is at issue is an instance of misappropriation, not of deduction and not even ... of affiliation. Far from being entailed by the premises underlying Nietzsche's position, the conclusions drawn are inconsistent with them. To reconstruct in the imagination the events leading up to the Nazi genocide against the Jews without the name or presence of Nietzsche is to be compelled to change almost nothing in that pattern.[37]

This, it seems to me, is entirely unpersuasive. Of course, Nietzsche's influence permeated many – contradictory – political and cultural tendencies but an exceptionally wide range of historical actors themselves (many Nazis and their adversaries) as well as any number of later critics have, at different levels of complexity, identified a profound affinity and a thematic complicity of Nietzschean impulses in Nazism's definitive taboo-defying, transgressive core and its programmatic, murderous drives. To be sure, distinctions and not just commonalities need to be noted. It is remarkable that numerous victims of National Socialism have similarly intuited such a relationship and that a survivor of Auschwitz, Primo Levi, sought (whether successfully or not) to identify both the commonalities as well as the defining differences. It is worth quoting him in full.

'Neither Nietzsche nor Hitler nor Rosenberg', he wrote as if the connections between them were entirely obvious,

> were mad when they intoxicated themselves and their followers by preaching the myth of the Superman, to whom everything is permitted in recognition of his dogmatic and congenital superiority; but worthy of meditation is the fact that all of them, teacher and pupils, became progressively removed from reality as little by little their morality came unglued from the morality common to all times and civilisations, which is an integral part of our human heritage and which in the end must be acknowledged.
>
> Rationality ceases, and the disciples have amply surpassed (and betrayed) the teacher, precisely in the practice of useless cruelty. Nietzsche's message is profoundly repugnant to me; I find it difficult to discover an affirmation in it which is not contrary to what I like to think; his oracular tone irritates me; yet it seems that a desire for the sufferings of others cannot be found in it. Indifference, yes, almost on every page, but never *Schadenfreude*, the joy in your neighbour's misfortune and even less the joy of deliberately inflicting suffering. The pain of *hoi polloi*, of the *Ungestalten*, the shapeless, the not-born-noble, is a price that must be paid for the advent of the reign of the elect; it is a minor evil, but still an evil; it is not in itself desirable. Hitlerian doctrine and practice were much different.[38]

(Other intellectual survivors did not necessarily agree with this view. Thus another Auschwitz inmate, Jean Amery, viewed the philosopher quite differently to Levi. Nietzsche, he wrote, was 'the man who dreamed of the synthesis of the brute with the superman. He must be answered by those who witnessed the union of the brute with the subhuman; they were present as victims when a certain humankind joyously celebrated a festival of cruelty, as Nietzsche himself expressed it ...'[39])

At any rate, what I am proposing here is that both in its overall bio-eugenic political and medical vision, its programmatic obsession with degeneration and regeneration, whether in parodistic form or not, there are clear informing parallels with key Nietzschean categories and goals. From one perspective, as Robert Jay Lifton has recently persuasively argued, Nazism is about the 'medicalisation of killing'. Its genocidal impulses were implicit within a bio-medical vision and its vast, self-proclaimed programmatic task of racial and eugenic hygiene. On an unprecedented scale it would assume control of the human biological future, assuring health to positive racial stock and purging humanity of its sick, degenerative elements. Its vision of 'violent cure', of murder and genocide as a 'therapeutic imperative', Lifton argues, resonates, with such Nietzschean themes.[40]

While every generation may emphasise their particular Nietzsche, there can be little doubt that in the first half of this century various European political circles came to regard him as *the* deepest diagnostician of sickness and degeneration and its most thoroughgoing regenerative therapist. 'The sick', he wrote, 'are man's greatest danger; not the evil, not the "beasts of prey".'[41] To be sure, as was his wont, he employed these notions in multiple, shifting ways, as metaphor and irony (he even has a section on 'ennoblement through degeneration'[42]) but most often, and most crucially, it was represented (and understood) as a substantial literal danger whose overcoming through drastic measures was the precondition for the urgent recreation of a 'naturalized', non-decadent humankind. Although he was not alone in the wider nineteenth-century quasi-bio-medical, moral, discourse of 'degeneration'[43] – that highly flexible, politically adjustable tool that cut across the ideological spectrum, able simultaneously to locate, diagnose and resolve a prevalent, though inchoate, sense of social and cultural crisis through an exercise of eugenic labelling and a language of bio-social pathology and potential renewal[44] – he formed an integral part in defining and radicalizing it. He certainly constituted its most important conduit into the emerging radical right. What else was Nietzsche's *Lebensphilosophie*, his reassertion of instinct and his proposed transvaluation whereby the healthy naturalistic ethic replaced the sickly moral one (a central theme conveniently ignored or elided by the current post-structuralist champions of Nietzsche). 'Tell me, my brothers', Zarathustra asks, 'what do we consider bad and worst of all? Is it not *degeneration*?'[45] In this world, the reassertion of all that is natural and healthy is dependent upon the ruthless extirpation of those anti-natural *ressentiment* sources of degeneration who have thoroughly weakened and falsified the natural and aristocratic bases of life. Over and over again, and in different ways, Nietzsche declared that 'The species requires that the ill-constituted, weak, degenerate, perish.'[46]

The Nazi bio-political understanding of, and solution to 'degeneration', as I have tried to show here and elsewhere, was in multi-layered ways explicitly Nietzsche-inspired. From World War I through its Nazi implementation, Nietzschean exhortations to prevent procreation of 'anti-life' elements and his advocacy of euthanasia, of what he called 'holy cruelty' ('The Bibical prohibition "thou shalt not kill"', he noted in *The Will to Power*, 'is a piece of *naivëté* compared with the seriousness of the prohibition of life to decadents: "thou shalt not procreate!" ... Sympathy for decadents, equal rights for the ill-constituted – that would be the profoundest immorality, that would be antinature itself as morality!'[47]) both inspired and provided a 'higher' rationale for theorists and practitioners of such measures.[48]

The translation of traditional anti-Jewish impulses into genocide and the murderous policies adopted in different degrees to other labelled outsiders (Gypsies, physically and mentally handicapped, homosexuals, criminals, inferior Eastern peoples and Communist political enemies) occurred within the distinct context of this medico-bio-eugenic vision. There were, to be sure, many building-blocks that went into conceiving and implementing genocide and mass murder, but I would argue that this Nietzschean framework of thinking provided one kind of radical sensibility that helped to act as a trigger for its implementation.

Related to, but also going beyond, these programmatic parallels and links we must raise another highly speculative, though necessary, issue: the vexed question of enabling preconditions and psychological motivations. Clearly, for events as thick and complex as these no single theoretical or methodological approach or methodology will suffice. Yet, given the extraordinary nature of the events, more conventional modes of historical analysis soon reach their limits and demand novel answers (the study of Nazism has provided them in abundance, some more, some less convincing).[49] I am not thus claiming exclusiveness for the Nietzschean element at this level of explanation, but rather arguing for his continued and important relevance. To be sure, of late, many accounts of the ideas behind, and the psychological wellsprings enabling, mass murder have been, if anything, anti-Nietzschean in content. For Christopher Browning it was hardly Nietzschean intoxication, the nihilistic belief that 'all is permitted', that motivated the 'ordinary killers' but rather prosaic inuring psychological mechanisms such as group conformity, deference to authority, the dulling powers of alcohol and the simple (but powerful) processes of routinization.[50] For George L. Mosse, far from indicating a dynamic anti-bourgeois Nietzschean revolt, the mass murders represented a *defence* of bourgeois morality, the attempt to preserve a clean, orderly middle-class world against all those outsider and deviant groups that seemed to threaten it.[51]

These contain important insights but, in my view, leave out crucial experiential ingredients, closely related to the Nietzschean dimension, which must form at least part of the picture. At some point or another, the realization must have dawned on the conceivers and perpetrators of this event that something quite extraordinary, unprecedented, was occurring and that ordinary and middle-class men were committing radically transgressive, taboo-breaking, quite 'unbourgeois' acts.[52] Even if we grant the problematic proposition that such acts were done in order to defend bourgeois interests and values, we would want to know about the galvanizing, radicalizing trigger that allowed decision-makers and perpetrators alike to set out in this direction and do the deed. To argue that it was 'racism' merely pushes the argument a step backward for 'racism' on its own – while always pernicious – *has to be made genocidal* (in principle it may be compatible with policies of emigration, separation, enslavement and domination or even paternalism).

We are left with the issue of the radicalizing, triggering force. These may be many in number but it seems to me that Nietzsche's determined antihumanism (an atheism that, as George Lichtheim has noted, differs from the Feuerbachian attempt to replace theism with humanism[53]) and his apocalyptic imaginings and exhortatory visions, helped to render such a *possibility, such an act, conceivable in the first place* (or, at the very least – given the relevant selective readings – able to provide the appropriate ideological cover for it). This Nietzschean kind of thought, vocabulary and sensibility constitutes an important (if not the only) long-term enabling precondition of such radical elements in Nazism.

With all its affinities to an older conservatism, it was the radically experimental, morality-challenging, tradition-shattering Nietzschean sensibility that made the vast transformative scale of the Nazi project thinkable. Nietzsche, as one contemporary commentator has pointed out, 'prepared a consciousness that excluded nothing that anyone might think, feel, or do, including unimaginable atrocities carried out on a gigantic order.'[54] Those who looked to him to inspire – or rationalize – their imaginings could easily find what they sought and apply it to their own situation. For instance the passage where Nietzsche insists that 'master races' with their 'terrible claws' organized for war and that great leaders like Napoleon represented a 'synthesis of the *inhuman* and *superhuman*': 'He who can command, he who is by nature "master", he who is violent in act and bearing – what has he to do with contracts! One does not reckon with such natures; they come like fate, without reason, consideration, or pretext; they appear as lightning appear, too terrible, too sudden, too convincing, too "different" even to be hated. Their work is an instinctive creation and imposition of forms ... They do not know what guilt, responsibility, or consideration are, these born organizers.'[55]

Of course, Nazism was a manifold historical phenomenon and its revolutionary thrust sat side by side with petit-bourgeois, provincial, traditional and conservative impulses.[56] But surely, beyond its doctrinal emphases on destruction and violent regeneration, health and disease, the moral and historical significance of Nazism lies precisely in its unprecedented transvaluations and boundary-breaking extremities, its transgressive acts and shattering of previously intact taboos. It is here – however parodistic, selectively mediated or debased – that the sense of Nazism, its informing project and experiential dynamic, as a kind of Nietzschean Great Politics continues to haunt us.

AFTERWORD

I have purposely thus far omitted Ernst Nolte's very important, and often extremely insightful, analysis of the Nietzsche–Holocaust link (and the genocidal impulse in general) because, I believe it constitutes a kind of case study in itself and illustrates at the same time the way in which our perceptions of Nietzsche are usually tied into, and can be neatly subordinated by, wider political issues and agendas. In his rendering, beginning with the by-now classic of 1963, *Three Faces of Fascism*,[57] Nietzsche is portrayed as the most crucial figure of an ongoing impulse against bourgeois and Marxist 'realization'. It is he who, above all, incarnates the impetus to the sensuous 'renaturalization' of the world and points to the creation of a new, wholly nondecadent man. The Nietzschean and Nazi projects thus become virtually identical. Hitler, wrote Nolte, 'was possessed by "something" which was not trivial.' As 'terminal figure of an age', he was, in effect, the most radical manifestation of an impulse best articulated by Nietzsche.[58]

In this view, the notion of destruction or extermination – *Vernichtungsgedanke* as Nolte puts it – was bound to become central to Nietzsche's late philosophy.[59] It is worth quoting him at at length in this connection:

> Nietzsche's real enemy is obviously the concept of realization; it is at this that he aims such terms as *ressentiment, decadence*, and *'total degeneration'*. From a philosophical standpoint there is only one unassailable counterconcept: that of the wholly non-decadent man, the 'beast of prey, the magnificent, roaming blond beast lusting for booty and victory', the magnificent animality of 'the pack of blond beasts of prey'. ...
>
> It cannot be doubted that Nietzsche's whole thought represents a more radical ... more persistent countermovement to the Marxist conception and

that the idea of extermination *(Vernichtungsgedanke)* represents the negative aspect of its innermost core. For if history is not an *Attentat* thousands of years old, then only the extermination of the perpetrator of this crime can restore things to their true balance. Nietzsche is not in a banal sense the spiritual father of fascism; but he was the first to give voice to that spiritual focal point towards which all fascism must gravitate; the assault on practical *and* theoretical transcendence, for the sake of a 'more beautiful' form of 'life'.[60]

The Nazi exterminations were thus best understood as the most desparate (and essentially Nietzschean) 'assault ever made upon the human being and the transcendence within him.'[61] Although Nolte himself did not demonstrate the connections, as we have already seen, this indeed closely resembled the way in which various Nietzschean Nazi sources defined their own project – as the creation of an immanent, re-naturalized and anti-transcendental society.

In a much later work, Nolte spelled out the specifically Jewish turn Nazism gave to this Nietzschean framework. What Hitler meant by the word 'Jew', Nolte wrote in his controversial *The European Civil War 1917–1945* (1988) was that complex of phenomena related to 'progress', to industrialisation, the control of – and estrangement from – nature, emancipation and individualism

> that first Nietzsche and after him other Life-philosophers like Ludwig
> Klages and Theodor Lessing declared as a threat to *Life*. Hitler therefore
> had the same world-historical process in mind that for Marx was simul-
> taneously progress and decline, a process that one can call the intellectu-
> alisation of the world. But ... Marx and Nietzsche, Lessing and also Klages
> were always far from maintaining that this process was attributable to a
> concrete, human cause. Hitler then made the step, which was a radical
> overturning of all previous ideologies ... whereby he attributed to a human
> group the power to bring about a transcendental process.[62]

In Nolte's new book *Nietzsche and Nietzscheanism* (1990), Nietzsche remains the inspirational centre of the Nazi exterminatory drive.[63] There he focusses upon the nature of 'exterminatory' thought and language within the Nietzschean corpus. Once again, Nietzsche's positive quest for 'life-affirmation' is linked to his call for the brutal destruction of those life-denying, 'emancipatory' forms responsible for the prevailing decadence, degeneration and overall decline of vitality.[64] Nolte emphasises a (somewhat neglected) passage in *Ecce Homo* ('The Birth of Tragedy', 4) as a salient example of such intentions:

Let us look ahead a century and assume the case that my attempt to assassinate two millenia of anti-nature and human disfiguration has succeeded. That new party of life which would take the greatest of all tasks into its hands, the higher breeding (*Hoeherzuchtung*) of humanity, including the merciless extermination (*schonungslose Vernichtung*) of everything degenerating and parasitical, would make possible again that excess of life on earth from which the Dionysian state will also grow again.[65]

The list of Nietzsche's anti-life opponents – Christian priests, vulgar Enlighteners, democrats, socialists, the degenerate masses – is so great, Nolte now argues, that in a sense it *dwarfs* the Nazi 'implementation':[66] 'If [Nietzsche's] "extermination" is understood literally the result must be a mass murder, in comparison with which the later real "Final Solution" of the National Socialists assumes almost microscopic proportions. The "purity" of the conception was far more gigantic than the "impurity" *("Unreine")* of the reality.'[67]

Both the tone and grammar of this passage indicate that Nolte's Nietzsche has now become neatly embedded within his post-*Historikerstreit* ideological framework. In Nolte's view the same logic applies to both the Bolshevik and National Socialist implementations. In characteristically evasive – even convoluted – language (what constitutes 'pure' and 'impure' extermination?) Nolte explains these (unmediated) processes thus: Marx's revolution assumed an 'impure' character when the bourgeoisie refused to conform to their historically determined role and when the Bolsheviks were confronted with an obdurate, majority peasantry. What history could not 'naturally' finish would have to be done through a human exterminatory agency. He describes the Nietzsche case in the following (very unclear) terms: Nietzsche's conception had to take on 'impure' form when it became clear that it would not be a matter of the strong few destroying the many weak but rather a case where the anxiety and perception of threat 'set a biological, indeed, a metabiological, extermination into motion, in which humanity and, above all, the Master and Super-Race would be secured against the most dangerous of all assassinations ...'[68]

The philosopher here appears as a central protagonist, prophet of Nolte's all-embracing vision of the twentieth century world-historical *Buergerkrieg*, the war between the dialectically linked forces of Bolshevism and National Socialism. Here, Nolte's Nietzsche functions as the 'presager *(Vorhersage)* of the great civil war and the concept of the indispensable extermination.' Significantly, he weaves this extermination concept into his chronological and substantive account of the relationship between these two historic forces and their destructive drives. In this view, the cultured Nietzsche, almost despite himself, is driven to 'foresee the great world civil-war and create the extermination concept *(Vernichtungskonzept)* which was the counterconcept to another and more original (urspruenglicheren) exterminatory conception.'[70] Nietzsche is now ensconced within Nolte's dubious reduction of Nazism and its atrocities as a reaction to an earlier Marxist version of the same thinking[71] and in which the Holocaust is portrayed as a kind of anticipatory act of German self-defence, a preventive measure against the perception of Jewish (Bolshevik) genocidal intentions.[72]

The uses of Nietzsche, it appears, are still unpredictable and inexhaustible.

5 The German–Jewish Dialogue at its Limits: The Case of Hermann Broch and Volkmar von Zuehlsdorff

'Did I express myself so clumsily or is there simply no understanding between man and man, and thus not even between us two?'

Hermann Broch to Volkmar von Zuehlsdorff

The 1945–1949 correspondence between the great Austrian novelist Hermann Broch (1886–1951) and his much younger friend Volkmar von Zuehlsdorff (born 1912) provides us with a revealing 'moving picture' of the burning moral, political and existential issues that confronted thinking people in the wake of the collapse of National Socialism and the attempt to create a new post-war democratic German order. Broch and Zuehlsdorff variously debated the question of German guilt and responsibility; the extent of internal opposition to Hitler; the uniqueness (or otherwise) of Nazi crimes; the prospects for German democratization and the dangers of Nazi recrudescence; the nature of Allied behaviour and retribution; the conduct and disposition of Jewish Displaced Persons (DPs); the dilemma of returning to Germany – both spent the war years in the USA – and the meaning and implications of exile. Beyond these particular questions, the correspondence wrestled with the complexities of 'coming to terms' with a compromised national past (and outlined some of the early available strategies for alternatively confronting or evading it). Above all it is permeated by a tension over the possibilities and limits of mutual empathy in the face of atrocity and a tussle over Jewish and German claims to victimization. For the historian, the Broch–Zuehlsdorff exchange constitutes a compelling, almost prescient, study in the embryonic construction of divergent, and always passionately charged, post-Nazi 'German' and 'Jewish' stances, perceptions and memories.[1]

Little in the biography of either man made it likely that they would so sharply intuit and articulate 'German' or 'Jewish' gut feelings and 'collective representations'. Volkmar von Zuehlsdorff was a prominent activist in the exiled anti-Hitler German resistance, an intimate member of Hubertus Prinz zu Loewenstein's circle and a representative of those who self-con-

85

sciously designated themselves as belonging to a different and 'better' Germany. (Not all German exiles accepted the validity of this designation. To the chagrin of many of his fellow expatriates Thomas Mann argued that the very notion of a 'better' Germany too easily let one off the hook. There were not two Germanies, the good and the bad, he insisted, but only one: 'anyone who was born a German *does* have something in common with German destiny and German guilt.'[2])

The tensions and contradictions in Broch's complex case were legion. Although he later 'returned' to Judaism, Broch was an early (1909) convert to Catholicism (a sensibility that permeated his creative literary work to the end.[3]) He certainly was not specifically identified with Jewish causes or the organised Jewish community. Indeed, his 1932 masterpiece, *The Sleepwalkers*, indicted Judaism – 'this radical religiosity, dumb and stripped of ornament, this conception of an infinity conditioned by severity and severity alone' – as centrally complicit in what (the rather 'Catholically' conservative) Broch took to be the progressive collapse of Western civilization and the undoing of its integrated unity of values, style and sensuality. The Jew was the most advanced embodiment of this fragmented modernity: in his absolute abstractness and the 'immolation of all sensory content' he was 'to be regarded as the prevailing cause of the prevailing disintegration of values.'[4]

Both men, nevertheless, fashioned their responses in terms of recognizably 'German' and 'Jewish' lines of demarcation. Despite their common, impeccably anti-Nazi credentials, the incommensurability of perceptions, priorities and interpretations became apparent as soon as the correspondence began. In many ways they anticipated – indeed, gave shape to – a tendency that Saul Friedlander discerned for a later time: 'On a symbolic level ... one may speak of a Jewish memory of Auschwitz and of a German one. Although the incompatibility between these two memories may be growing, they are helplessly interwoven in what has been called a "negative symbiosis". ... Any re-elaboration of one memory directly impinges on the other; any neutralization casts an overall shadow of oblivion. Neither Jews nor Germans can relate to their own memory without relating to the other's as well.'[5]

To be sure, as Friedlander himself has pointed out, the model is too simplistic. No monolithic 'German' or 'Jewish' collective memory can be unequivocally located; differentiations and nuances are to be found on both sides. (And, as we have pointed out in Chapter 1, on the official level Germany did indeed accept responsibility for crimes committed in the past.) This was as true in the immediate post-war years as it is today. The New York exile journal *Aufbau*, for instance, often debated the same issues that preoccupied Broch and Zuehlsdorff and not infrequently that liberal Jewish organ supported the kinds of positions adopted by Zuehlsdorff.[6]

Still, the Broch–Zuehlsdorff correspondence self-consciously enunciated what amounted to (albeit enlightened) distinctly 'German' and 'Jewish' positions. Perhaps the theoretical ruminations of their dialogue did not approach the intellectual standard that characterised the Hannah Arendt–Karl Jaspers exchange (see Chapter 6); it is also obvious that Broch's letters to Zuehlsdorff seldom reflected the sophisticated – and tortuously complex – philosophical positions he adumbrated elsewhere.[7] But precisely because this is a record that is characterised by a rare candidness and captures gut reactions to current events and issues, it is peculiarly revelatory of the immediate emotions and responses of the time.

As early as July 1945, in his very first letter to Zuehlsdorff, Broch intuited the essence of this 'negative symbiosis'. He did this in the context of a discussion concerning the possible return of Jews to Germany. He was, he told Zuehlsdorff, against the idea for in the presence of victims 'no guilty conscience can grow'.[8] In later letters he expanded upon this negative interdependence: the sight of the victim would merely harden and render impenitent the perpetrator, especially as the victim would now be seen – and conduct himself – as the 'victor'. Broch perceptively recognised this psychological dialectic even before the negative impact of the DPs in Germany became palpable. A precondition for German regeneration was the absence of Jewish returnees, for even the best-intentioned amongst the Germans, he wrote, would 'seek the "guilt" of the victims, not only because this "excuses" his own guilt (that is, his indifference), but rather because it is part of the general nature of people to regard the suffering as guilty, a fact that perpetuates the Hitler-seed.'[9]

The difference between the two was immediately evident in their respective attitudes towards post-war Germany. While Broch's view was instinctively critical Zuehlsdorff exuded a patriotic identification. 'In you', wrote Broch, 'the *Heimatsgefuehl* is much stronger than in me.'[10] Zuehlsdorff's rhapsodic description of his return in November 1946 – 'Now we are back in Germany and I can hardly describe to you how happy I am. The fourteen years of exile, the hopeless assault against evil and stupidity lie behind one, and it is as if one has escaped a serious illness' – and his ecstatic celebration of the German character was testament either to a magnificent indifference to the ethnic divide between the two friends or, given recent events, astonishingly obtuse in its disregard for Broch's fragile Jewish sensitivities: 'The most shattering and at the same time most uplifting, that one is filled with joy, courage and hope and with such a great love for this people; the contradiction between the harshest poverty, suffering and bodily want, and against this a purity and clarity of the spiritual realm, a flowering of Christian virtues, brotherly love, cheerful tolerance and a depreciation of all earthly possessions.'[11]

Broch disregarded these rhetorical flourishes and concentrated on a more general point. To a certain degree, he was prepared to concede, suffering and catastrophe did ennoble. But, unlike Zuehlsdorff, he was not prepared to attribute such ennoblement to peculiarly German national characteristics. 'Every Volk has until now behaved well under catastrophic conditions, the English like the Serbs, and the Russian like the French. The Germans are average people like all others.'[12] To be sure, he was genuinely shocked by the descriptions of German suffering and repeatedly told his younger friend so. But, unlike Zuehlsdorff (and this was an ongoing matter of contention), he sought to place this contemporary distress into a larger historical – and somewhat different empathic – perspective. German misery was genuine enough, but what he found most disturbing, he wrote, was the unrepentant and self-pitying tone of the hundreds of letters he had received (mainly from Austrians). In the face of the great inhumanities that had taken place, he complained, the Germans and Austrians seemed to demonstrate no remorse at all – the humiliation of others remained a matter of indifference and the only shock they had genuinely experienced was their own immediate want.[13]

Broch was, in effect, groping towards a conception of what amounted to a *Vergangenheitsbewaeltigung*, suggesting to Zuehlsdorff some of the minimum prerequisites for an authentic working through of the past. He was aware that this could not realistically be expected until the country's material condition had somewhat improved. Nevertheless, as he repeatedly maintained, contemporary German regeneration would only occur through an honest confrontation with, and open acknowledgment of, its own recently committed crimes.

Of course Zuehlsdorff in no way denied the occurrence of these catastrophic events but he did refuse to endow them with the same weight that Broch desired nor was he willing to provide the kind of priority to the past that Broch regarded as essential. It was not only the contemporary economic situation that was in need of amelioration. What was also required, he wrote, was a transformation in political conditions. Only then could the *Schuldfrage*, the question of coming to terms with German guilt, be properly confronted. In the absence of sovereign institutions that could provide the nation with a modicum of legitimacy and self-respect the task of coming to terms with the past was well-nigh impossible. 'As long as Germany remains a Stateless vacuum in which the self-consciousness of the nation has no means to express itself', he wrote in 1947, 'it will necesarily be silent.'[14] By the 1990s the problem of German Statehood had been resolved in a maximalist way probably inconceivable to Zuehlsdorff at the time. Yet, while the political vacuum has been filled, his comments still maintain their relevance. The continuing debates about the German past still resonate with the demand that a proper recognition of past horrors can only take place within the framework of a more balanced and 'legitimate' national historical narrative. (To what degree such narratives erase rather than facilitate recognition of the dark underside of that history remains a matter of much current contention.)

The tension between these two men was most palpable in their – obsessively recurring and often mutually uncomprehending – discussions of the Jewish Question. The correspondence is littered with Broch's (usually rather exaggerated) fears of an immediate Nazi revival and repeated allegations as to the continuation of anti-Semitism in Germany[15] and Zuehlsdorff's rebuttals. Upon his return to Germany Zuehlsdorff wrote, 'I have sensed little anti-semitism ... I am told that after the capitulation there has been absolutely none [*sic*] (it was never a "popular feeling" [*Volksgefuehl*]) and it is for their passivity that one must reproach the Germans – by the way, also the Jews, not after 1933, but before, when the majority did not lift a finger against Hitler and very many greeted him in the hope that it would only go against the *"Ostjuden"* ...'[16]

But Zuehlsdorff went further than reminding Broch of this complex historical Jewish divide between 'Eastern' and 'Western' European Jews (a sensitive gulf that anti-Semites had often exploited[17]). He also noted that the occupying Americans were more anti-semitic than the Germans – a familiar claim at the time.[18] But most ominously he warned that any perspective that focused on the events and miseries of the present through the partial prism of the Jewish Question – as did Broch – was 'not only incorrect but also dangerous – especially for the Jews themselves.' Singling out Jews as victims (and concentrating so heavily on exclusive Jewish matters) merely replicated the 'race thinking' they had both struggled to defeat. 'You do not draw the dividing line between the Nazis and their victims (under which the Jews constituted only a fraction in numerical terms) but between "Jews" and "Germans".' Much as Hitler had done, he reprimanded Broch, 'you shut Jews out of the German *Volksgemeinschaft* (to which one could add a row of casuistic questions: What about half and quarter Jews? Or are the Nuremberg Laws still simply valid?).'[19]

These arguments apart, Zuehlsdorff recognised that the issue had to be addressed head-on, especially as it touched upon Broch's major concern and repeated indictment: the charge of indifference. Even before the rise of Nazism to power, Broch's work minutely anatomised the nature and evil of human indifference. (Indeed, this was a crucial ingredient of his *The Sleepwalkers* which he regarded as '*the* prophetic novel, demonstrating the predestination of the German people to Hitlerism.'[20]) The Jewish Problem, Broch declared, demonstrated the 'guilt' of the German people. For a full twenty years the Germans had regarded the most idiotic Jew-baiting with 'bestial indifference'[21] that itself became an accomplice to a 'bestial-systematic mass mur-

der': 'Every German who was not in the concentration camps is at least suspected of this contribution to murder by dint of such indifference.' Even earlier, in a radio talk addressed to the German People (although apparently
never broadcast) Broch adverted to the language of his famous novel and
argued that because of 'their voluntary blindness' the German Volk was complicit in bringing about world war and in monstrosities committed in the
'murder factories of Maidanek, Oswiecim, Buchenwald, Nordhausen,
Ravensbrueck. The German *Volk* was blind like a sleepwalker. In blind, sleepwalking manner the German people delivered its destiny into the hands of
liars and criminals, blindly sleepwalking it took part in their crimes and apa-
thetic in the face of foreign suffering took upon itself responsibility for the
crimes of the war and the worst atrocities in all of human history.'[22]

Zuehlsdorff sought to directly counter Broch's admonitions. Nothing, he
claimed, drew resistance to National Socialism more than the Jewish question: the broad masses were in no way anti-Semitic. Certainly there was
knowledge of concentration camps for these were the explicit means of political terror but as far as the exterminations were concerned the population
neither knew about it – nor would they have believed it. In any case, 'if SS
man X in Warsaw was killing Jews, what could Herr Schulze in Augsburg
do?'[23] It is by no means clear how, retrospectively, the historian should assess
the nature of these debates and the validity of these remarks. Subsequent
scholarship tends to agree that, by and large, the Herr Schulze's did indeed,
not 'know' about the mass murders – but that, by and large, the lack of knowledge was a result of a choice not to know.[24] (There was, in any case, something of the logic of the Freudian Jewish joke here. They didn't know, but if
they did they wouldn't have believed it and anyway they couldn't do anything about it![25]) To some extent, Zuehlsdorff's comments were beside the
point for, as his letters to Zuehlsdorff attest, Broch made it quite clear that
he did not equate indifference with anti-Semitism but rather regarded it as
the crucial factor enabling increasingly brutal anti-Jewish measures to proceed unimpeded. The relationship between popular anti-Semitism, indifference and genocide is a complex one as the final chapter of this book attests.
At any rate, it was precisely to these psychologically convoluted mechanisms
and rationalizations that Broch, for many years, had called attention.

The deepest gulf between these friends lay in Broch's – sometimes explicit, most often implicit – belief that the mass murder of European Jewry was,
in some critical way, a novum of human cruelty and Zuehlsdorff's unwill-
ingness to grasp (or at least acknowledge) the enormity and special character of Nazi crimes against the Jews. This was blatantly evident in his consistent
attempts to undercut Broch's assertions by means of arguments of comparative equivalence. Short memories are prone to assume that the strategy of

historical relativisation was somehow a product of the *Historikerstreit* of the 1980s. In fact it began almost concurrently with the events themselves and – whatever its intrinsic merits – was from very early on integrated into justificatory constructions of a more acceptable national self-image. How, Zuehlsdorff wondered, could one begin to judge Herr Schulze – living under a controlled press, a terrorist regime and the threat of concentration camps – in the light of the recent killing of 200,000 men, women and children of an already defeated enemy?[26] (He was, of course, referring to the American bombing of Hiroshima on August 6 1945.)

But Zuehlsdorff's outraged comparative comments were, above all, animated by various Allied actions aimed at Germany itself (especially the Potsdam plan and the mass expulsions from the East[27]) and what he saw as the vindictive spirit of revenge exemplified in the various plans of the occupying powers for Germany's future. As he wrote – rather bitterly and shockingly – to Broch: 'And he who is bent on revenge can now be satisfied, for the ovens of Auschwitz have become the glowing fires of Hamburg and Dresden, of Berlin, Munich, Leipzig, Cologne, Essen, Dortmund ... and so the millions of beaten and dispossessed, the terrors of Koenigsberg, Breslau and the Sudetenland and the anaemic hunger whose victims are now falling in flocks (here in Amorbach alone there were six deaths in the last four days), dissipation, destruction, defeat through the merciless victor that has destroyed National Socialism and placed itself in that same spiritual image.'[28]

The extremity of these Allied actions and conditions did indeed occasion genuine anger and fear and certainly lessened any impulse to confront the lessons of one's own recent past. Total war did produce actions and behaviour that was more than reprehensible and not only on the German side. But Zuehlsdorff attributed much of this to a peculiarly 'Jewish' impulse. He was incensed by Henry Morgenthau's – and Bernard Baruch's – advisory role in the Allied councels of power. Zuehlsdorff wrote that it is 'tragic that such people have so much power to bring entire nations into misfortune and that the American Jews can go with him, like the Catholics with Franco. ... or the Germans with Hitler.'[29] Time and time again he obsessed about Morgenthau. Morgenthau's plan for the re-agrarianisation of Germany was a blueprint for murder and, as Zuehlsdorff wrote later, had it succeeded would have resulted in the destruction of millions.[30] But of Morgenthau and Jewish support for him there was in point of fact a lively debate within the Jewish community where his proposals evoked much opposition, especially among the exiles.[31] As Hannah Arendt noted in 1945: 'The rejection is so general that it becomes superfluous to quote special sources. The reasons are obvious: there is an overwhelming and altogether justified fear that half of Europe would starve if German industry ceased to function.'[32]

Still, Zuehlsdorff insisted, it was clear that Germans were not the only guilty ones and that 'Roosevelt–Morgenthau Nazism had to be denounced just as National Socialism in its time. ...'[33] To be sure, by thus labelling American policy Zuehlsdorff rendered 'Nazism' as the code-word for ultimate evil – but in applying it to other policies already relativised its impact and historical specificity. Indeed, as he wrote elsewhere, the crimes of the Allies may have been even more blameworthy for they were committed 'in the name of democracy! It is *this* that today one must damn, against which one must be indignant and fight – as we then did National Socialism ... it is the same destructive, infernal force that drove Versailles, Hitler and Potsdam.'[34] For Zuehlsdorff the continuum was clear – these were all indistinguishable forces 'directed at the same goal, the destruction of Europe, indeed, at humanity and the end of the Christian mission on earth.'[35]

Broch, of course, regarded matters somewhat differently. Zuehlsdorff's unceasing attacks on Morgenthau, he wrote at the beginning of 1949, were misplaced. If he had pursued a politics of hate, it may not have been statesmanlike but it certainly was humanly understandable. By now that hate would likely have dissipated as it had for the majority of Jews. In any case, he wrote (and here the gulf made itself most apparent), Zuehlsdorff's comments were misdirected; they should have been aimed not at Morgenthau but at the German petit-bourgeoisie. These 'philistines *(Spiessbuerger)* deserved such hate and perhaps still do. I was in Austria until '38 and what I experienced of the meanness and vileness of the *Spiessbuerger* is positively indescribable. Despite this I can no longer muster any more hate.'[36]

These cognitive and emotional dissonances were most clearly highlighted in concrete issues of the time. A case in point concerned the campaigns to aid hungry Germans caught in the chaos and dislocation of the immediate post-war years. For survivors, like Jean Amery, who, as he put it, had experienced German atrocities as 'collective ones', the Germans were 'laden with collective guilt, and it was rather indifferently that I helped some Quakerly-inspired persons to load a truck that was bringing used children's clothes to impoverished Germany.'[37] Zuehlsdorff too sought to put Broch to such a Jewish test. Wouldn't it be advisable, he asked, 'to organise a Jewish *Hilfsaktion* for the hungry and famished German children just as the Quakers and Protestants have done – first, for the sake of the children and secondly, to make it clear that Morgenthau does not speak for "the Jews"'[38]?

Broch's reply was characteristic. The Jewish *Hilfsaktion*, he wrote, would perhaps accomplish a reduction in anti-semitism and he would indeed support it – were it implementable. But 'the Jew is no *Uebermensch*, and the refugee, to whom the appeal is above all directed, least of all.' Were there energy enough for welfare activities it would have to be expended on Jewish rather than German goals for, it could well be argued, 'Jewish suffering in Europe is no smaller than the German which ultimately caused it.' In a pre-redeemed world each would have to take care of his own.[39] The conditions prevailing in Germany, he wrote in another letter, were indeed very harsh but things were even worse elsewhere (especially in south-east Europe). Germans were still better dressed and fed than people in other lands. One should not allow this to turn into an emotional appeal – a *Traenenkampagne* – which the Nazis could turn to their advantage.[40] (Erich Kahler – at whose Princeton home Broch resided – put the dilemma posed by the appeal suc-cintly enough: 'I have the fiercest discussions with one side and with the other – with Einstein, say, whose hostility toward eveything German is bound-less, and along with him a large number of well-intentioned and intelligent persons who simply react to this problem with instant blind fury; and on the other side, *with the Germans who once more, in their bitterness over the obvious sins of the Allies, have forgotten what endless harm has emanated from their own people.*'[41])

An even more emotive contemporary issue concerned policy towards and the behaviour of DPs. In 1945 there were approximately 300,000 displaced persons within the territory of the former German *Reich* and of these some forty thousand were Jews (almost exclusively from Eastern Europe). In 1946 Jewish and other DPs poured in to the US zones and by December the num-ber amounted to no less than 1.2 million.[42] Recent scholarship has confirmed that after the initial shock had worn off not only large segments of the German population but the Allies too tended to treat Jewish DPs as quite distasteful creatures (thereby confirming Broch's early intuitions). General George Patton may have been the most extreme when he (privately) exclaimed that DPs were not human beings 'and this applies particularly to the Jews, who are lower than animals.'[43] But it is clear that in the context of the chaos and economically desparate conditions there was increasingly less sympathy or understanding for the plight of the DP Jews, and little inclination to 'under-stand' their unsavoury black market activities.[44]

Zuehlsdorff's perceptions on this matter were strikingly similar to broader attitudes of the German population as described by Frank Stern: 'The revela-tions about the German crimes, the reasons for the situation the survivors found themselves in, the question of guilt and responsibility were not at all central in German discussions. Rather, during a period of severe food shortages, what caught the eye of the German population was, for example, the food truck con-voy passing on through town to be unloaded at the DP camp. What the popu-lation was preoccupied with was the problem of food supply and housing.'[45]

The antipathy to the DPs, Zuehlsdorff noted, was not motivated by racial concerns but there 'was much evil riff-raff who in the beginning robbed, plundered and murdered and then became the main centre of the black market, many the victims of circumstances, but many just so. Naturally there are many Jews amongst them, but when nationality is mentioned it is less Jewish than Polish.'[46] It was difficult, he argued elsewhere, 'to speak of anti-semitism in a people where there were virtually no Jews [*sic!*], whereas the black market is in the hands of Jewish DPs who have all the privileges and against whom a tank corps had to be brought in in order to evacuate them from their entrenched blackmarket headquarters in Zeilsheim.'[47]

Earlier on he put this in less virulent form but in a frame that again sought to equate what many would have argued were essentially incomparable phenomena: 'I am against the higher rations for Displaced Persons, just as earlier I opposed less rations for the Jews. And I am equally against nutritional distinctions between democrats and Nazis, for one cannot make food a political tool.'[48] Any such distinctions merely replicated Nazi logic. What was needed now was to punish the criminals and then get on with the business of recovery, human brotherliness and forgiveness.

The Broch–Zuehlsdorff exchange was one of the earliest post-war exchanges that explored and debated the ethical implications of war atrocities and mass murder and the responsibilities entailed in the reconstruction of a sullied national identity. Ultimately both men recognized that the possibilities for recovery and the reassertion of human solidarity were umbilically tied to a struggle over the weight and meaning of the past (and, consequently, of the present). Throughout this issue was expressed in a dispute over who currently most authentically constituted 'the victim.' Already in February 1946 Zuehlsdorff wrote: 'For fourteen years we denounced the National Socialists, who now lie destroyed as no other regime before. And today the wheel has turned. Today the Jews and Poles are not the victims, but Germans irrespective of their political persuasions. When that injustice occurred to Jews and Poles (and Germans!), we lifted our voices; and today, when it is happening to Germans, should we keep silent?'[49] All the world was outraged by what had happened in the past, he wrote later, yet there was silence over the injustices of the present. Indeed, it took special courage to protest them. 'Today the oppressed, persecuted, sick and hungry, degraded and scorned are here, the Germans in Germany, and this has nothing to do with my patriotism: the Czechs and Negroes concern me just as much.'[50]

Broch, it should be clear, was fully cognizant of the dubious nature of Allied actions both outside and within Germany. But the historical perspective through which he viewed these matters and the yardstick by which he measured them differed from that of Zuehlsdorff. 'I see in the atom bomb', he wrote on 5 September 1945, 'and the use without warning of this weapon of atrocity as a very grave misfortune that will compromise the "white man" and his democracy for decades to come.' Yet he also parenthetically formulated the problem within the prism of his even greater fear of the Third Reich. Its invention, he wrote, was unstoppable and in Hitler's hands would have become the instrument of a far greater human extermination.[51] With regard to contemporary German suffering, Zuehlsdorff had rendered Roosevelt and Churchill responsible. But these leaders were not superhuman and their greatness had to be measured in terms of the successful accomplishment of what had been their most essential historical task – defeating Hitler (without them, he wrote, this primary goal may not have been possible).[52] For Broch, it was the concrete atrocities of Nazism that remained the ultimate evil – in the face of which other injustices (however real) paled.

It is not as if the structure of the divide between the two men was hidden. Both were very consciously and acutely able to identify it. 'Dearest Hermann', wrote Zuehlsdorff, 'in the last analysis we want the same thing. Only it seems more important to you for one above all to speak of the Fascism of the past, while it strikes me as important to at least speak of the persecuted and injustice of the present. ... Whoever today, at least in Germany, speaks of the past and is silent about the present is a hypocrite.'[53] Broch agreed that they held common views on many matters. But, he protested, it was quite wrong to say that he gave priority to past Fascism over the injustices of the present: 'The crimes of the past reach into the present and has become part of the presently perpetrated injustice; one can only struggle against both.'[54]

These positions and juxtapositions remain strikingly familiar through to our own times. The same tensions, still unresolved, continue to surface. What in the eyes of one side appears to be a certain moral obtuseness, a refusal or incapacity to indulge in genuine soul-searching over unprecedented German crimes,[55] in the eyes of the other appears as essentially a form of hypocrisy, the imposition by the victor of an impossibly self-insulating double standard. Though the correspondence is marked throughout by mutual protestations of friendship and a common anti-Nazi and pro-liberal agenda, its limits were defined from the outset by essentially different empathic frames and opposed conceptions as to the moral interrelationship between past and present and the imperatives of collective historical responsibility.

Any cursory examination of Broch's literary and theoretical writings from the 1930s to the 1950s will reveal the degree of his obsession with analysing and overcoming the Nazi experience. It may be that in his great experimental literary masterpiece, *The Death of Virgil* (1945) Broch divined and gave well-nigh classical expression to the breakdown of traditional conceptions of beauty and language and their inadequacy for coping with human suffering, brute power and the onset of barbarism.[56] But like most intellectuals whose lives were transformed by this *novum* he had tremendous difficulty in forging the *theoretical* and *cognitive* tools necessary for grasping this unprecedented reality. At any rate, the lack of relevant master-models, this *'Begriffslosigkeit'*,[57] meant that in coming to terms with Nazism he relied in the main on past experiences and older interpretational systems and, in the final analysis, rather tortuously transposed these onto the new reality.[58]

Broch's admiring friend, Hannah Arendt, twenty years his junior, did self-consciously set out to provide an essentially new 'master-model'. Indeed, it was through this prism that she couched her critique of Broch. Whether or not her remarks were valid she held that Broch's categories and values, and especially his emphasis on death, were characteristic of the generation of World War I. Broch 'remained limited to this ... horizon of experience; and it is decisive that this horizon was broken through by the generation for whom not war but totalitarian forms of rule were the basic, the crucial experience. For we know today that killing is far from the worst that man can inflict on man and that on the other hand death is by no means what man most fears.'[59]

Regardless of the success or failure of her project, Arendt was one of the very few who set out in radical fashion to think through the problem of Nazism and totalitarianism and to provide the missing cognitive and ethical equipment necessary for the task. It is to her controversial work and her friendship with Karl Jaspers – a friendship that demonstrated the possibilities rather than the limits of the German-Jewish dialogue – that we must now turn.

6 Hannah Arendt and Karl Jaspers: Friendship, Catastrophe and the Possibilities of German–Jewish Dialogue

The extraordinary friendship between Hannah Arendt (1906–1975) and Karl Jaspers (1883–1969), and the recent publication of their correspondence spanning the years 1926–1969, provides the historian with an intimate, highly sophisticated documentation of 'the German–Jewish dialogue' at its points of greatest crisis and radical reassessment.[1] From the formative years of their relationship (still very much in the professor–student mould) in the troubled late Weimar years to its post-1945 maturation as the proportions of the National Socialist catastrophe became apparent, this was essentially a 'dialogue amid the deluge',[2] a friendship forged in its shadow and shaped by the urge to grasp its nature and consequences. 'Their letters to each other', Gordon Craig writes, 'were the product of the dissolution of their normal world, and their substance was enriched, rather than impoverished, by that experience.'[3]

Although the correspondence ranges widely in its topics,[4] it is most revealing as a sequence of intellectual snapshots tracing Arendt's and Jaspers' passionate and open engagement (the kind that was quite unimaginable with Arendt's other teacher, Martin Heidegger[5]) with questions of Germanness and Jewishness, their evolving attempts to grasp, at ever-deeper levels, the nature and consequences of Nazism and the interrelated political metamorphoses of their thought.

To be sure, this sustained dialogue was in no way a 'representative' one. Neither Arendt nor Jaspers regarded themselves (or were regarded) as official spokespeople. On the contrary, this was a friendship nourished by a fierce assertion of intellectual independence and by the attempt (albeit not always successful[6]) to rise above accepted communal postures and conventional pieties. If anything, here was a 'German–Jewish dialogue' that explicitly challenged what was perceived to be the unreflexive, self-celebratory nature of group affiliations. This ultimately rendered Jaspers and Arendt as acute critics rather than mirrors of their respective communities, often implacably at odds with both the 'German' and 'Jewish' establishment.

The unorthodox proclivities of both thinkers – as well as their most intimate engagement with the German–Jewish 'symbiosis' – were reflected in their basic biographical choices. Thus, Arendt's second husband Heinrich Bluecher was not only not Jewish, he was, to boot, a proletarian and so nonconformist a German Marxist that as an adolescent he joined a section of the Zionist youth group, the *Blau Weiss!*[7] Arendt clearly took pride in the generally subversive nature of these intertwined committments. As she confided to Jaspers in January 1946: 'If I had wanted to become respectable I would either have had to give up my interest in Jewish affairs or not marry a non-Jewish man, either option equally inhuman and in a sense crazy.'[8]

While the Bluecher–Arendt alliance was a product of a Paris exile following the Nazi rise to power, Jasper's marriage – by all accounts an idyllic one – to Gertrud Meyer, the daughter of a devout Orthodox Jewish Prenzlau family, took place as early as 1911. During the dark years of National Socialism, the Jaspers' survived precariously as a 'privileged mixed marriage' – a category never enshrined in law and one that eroded ever more rapidly as the Third Reich faced defeat.[9] Jasper's loyalty to his wife never flinched. Early on they determined upon a mutual suicide pact by cyanide in the event of arrest. (The planned transport for the couple was to take place on April 14, 1945. On March 30, Heidelberg was liberated by the Americans.[10]) Jaspers never sought public credit for this. On the contrary, as he argued in his speech delivered at the opening of Heidelberg University: 'When our Jewish friends were led away, we did not go out into the streets, we did not shout until we too were liquidated. No, we preferred to stay alive, with the feeble though correct thought that our death would not have been of any use anyhow. It remains our guilt that we are still alive.'[11]

To some degree both Jaspers[12] and Arendt self-consciously regarded themselves as embodiments of the (Jewish) 'pariah' type that Arendt so extolled. It was these people, Arendt wrote in 1944, 'who really did most for the spiritual dignity of their people, who were great enough to transcend the bounds of nationality and to weave the strands of their Jewish genius into the general texture of European life.'[13] Of course, such positive self-assessments were not always shared by the publics these thinkers addressed. Jaspers, we should not forget, was heavily criticised for his 1946 *Die Schuldfrage* [*The Question of German Guilt*],[14] that pioneering, but to many contemporary Germans threatening, *Vergangenheitsbewaeltigung* document, and taken to task as a preachy moraliser who abandoned his country in 1948 for a professorial post in Basel.[15] Through her critical writings on Zionism and Zionist policy[16] and, later, through her explosively controversial reading of the

Eichmann trial, Arendt (whether fairly or not) came to be regarded by significant sections of established Jewish communities as a heretic, even a self-hating enemy.[17] In the wake of the Eichmann book she was consistently reproached for her cold, even malicious, tone, and the tendentious harshness by which she judged and criticised the behaviour of the Jewish people while bending over backwards to empathically understand its persecutors;[18] Arendt, one analyst wrote, was more sensitive to the wrong done *by* the Jews than to that perpetrated *upon* them.[19]

Her response to such accusations was best summed up in her answer to Gershom Scholem's admonitions – occasioned by the Eichmann book – that she lacked *Ahavath Israel* ('Love of the Jewish people'):[20] 'I have never in my life "loved" any people or collective – neither the German people, nor the French, nor the American, nor the working class or anything of that sort. I indeed love "only" my friends and the only kind of love I know of and believe in is the love of persons. Secondly this "love of the Jews" would appear to me, since I am myself Jewish, as something rather suspect.'[21]

That this had very little to do with the 'self-hatred' so often attributed to her became clear in that same letter to Scholem: 'I do not "love" the Jews, nor do I "believe" in them. I merely belong to them as a matter of course, beyond dispute or agreement.' Her biography amply demonstrated this. After all, beginning in the early 1930s and continuing over many years, Arendt intensively involved herself on the practical as well as intellectual level with Jewish and Zionist matters. This was an identification which she not only never hid but made programmatically central and explicit (especially to her non-Jewish friends): 'Politically', she wrote to Jaspers in 1946, 'I will always speak only in the name of the Jews ...'[22] As late as 1967 in the wake of the Six Day War (and despite all the strains induced by the Eichmann affair) she reaffirmed this existential centrality to Mary McCarthy. 'I know', she proclaimed, 'that any real catastrophe in Israel would affect me more deeply than almost anything else.'[23]

Certainly, then, neither Arendt nor Jaspers can be regarded as classic disaffected intellectuals, as universalist non-Jewish Jews. (Or, for that matter, non-German Germans![24]) If classifiable at all, they most closely approximated Michael Walzer's portrait of 'connected critics', intellectuals whose thought flowed not from detachment but rather from passionate, if rather ambiguous, engagement.[25] Indeed, it was precisely because she wrote as a kind of insider, as an identified and self-consciously Jewish intellectual, that Arendt so infuriated the Jewish establishment.

Whatever their critics may have thought, it was then on *the basis* of Arendt's and Jaspers' respective – admittedly idiosyncratically conceived – commitments to Germanness and Jewishness that the dialogue took on much of its resonance and assumed its underlying significance. Certainly what in 1964 Arendt noted about her relations with non-Jewish Germans in general must apply too to Jaspers: 'there should be a basis for communication precisely in the abyss of Auschwitz.'[26] In them the whole problem of the German–Jewish symbiosis, its tensions, breakdown (and their own personal reconstitution of it) constituted an integral part of the bond. What Arendt wrote about an earlier, admittedly different period of persecution, nevertheless surely also characterised the essence of her dialogue with Jaspers:

> I so explicitly stress my membership in the group of Jews expelled from Germany at a relatively early age because I wish to anticipate certain misunderstandings which can arise only too easily when one speaks of humanity ... I cannot gloss over the fact that for many years I considered the only adequate reply to the question, Who are you? to be: A Jew. . . ... In the case of a friendship between a German and a Jew under the conditions of the Third Reich it would scarcely have been a sign of humanness for the friends to have said: Are we not both human beings? ... In keeping with a humanness that had not lost the solid ground of reality, a humanness in the midst of the reality of persecution, they would have had to say to each other: A German and a Jew, and friends.[27]

The differences between being a 'German' and a 'Jew' underlie the tension reflected in the correspondence between Arendt's and Jaspers' interpretations of *Deutschtum* (interpretations challenged and transformed by the rise of extreme nationalism and the Nazi experience). Their dialogue about the nature of Germanness in January 1933 acutely mirrored the troubled times in which it was written and the different sensibilities that informed the thought of a young, brilliant Jewess and a more established, rather conservatively-oriented German professor. What becomes immediately apparent was Arendt's sensitivity to the rumblings of anti-semitism and the (decent) *naïveté* of Jaspers, quite unable to comprehend the brutal nature of the political developments surrounding him (and still prey to the apolitical, anti-Western tradition of thought typical of German critics of mass society).[28] Upon the Nazi seizure of power he told Arendt that it would soon pass and that her proposed emigration would be the greatest stupidity of her life.[29]

Jaspers' ideas and ideals of Germanness were expressed in his lifelong reverence[30] for Max Weber whom he portrayed (in his 1932 book on the sociologist) as *the* great German, embodying the 'German essence' conceived as 'rationality and humanity originating in passion.'[31] For her part, Arendt throughout opposed the notion of a German, indeed, any national, 'essence' (including a Jewish one). As she wrote to her mentor in 1933, both the question of essence and Weber's imposing power-patriotism gave her difficulties. 'What troubled me first of all of course', she wrote, 'is the term "German character." You say yourself how misused it is. For me it is almost identical with misuse. ... Perhaps I have not understood what you meant by an emerging historical totality. I took it to mean that this character manifests itself from time to time in history. It would remain, then, despite its basic indeterminateness, something absolute, something untouched by history and Germany's destiny. I cannot identify with that, because I do not have in myself, so to speak, an attestation of "German character".'[32]

Her disagreement with Jaspers on this question, however, went well beyond theoretical objections to the notion of 'essence'. The real sticking point revolved around Jewishness. Arendt at that time voiced her reservations in terms of a Weimar Zionist sensibility that she had appropriated (albeit idiosyncratically) from another close mentor, Kurt Blumenfeld: 'You will understand', she proclaimed to Jaspers, 'that I as a Jew can say neither yes nor no and that my agreement on this would be as inappropriate as an argument against it. ... For me, Germany means my mother tongue, philosophy and literature. I can and must stand by all that. But I am obliged to keep my distance, I can neither be for nor against when I read Max Weber's wonderful sentence where he says that to put Germany back on her feet he would form an alliance with the devil himself. And it is this sentence which seems to me to reveal the critical point here.'[33]

Unlike Jaspers, Arendt restricted her Germanness to matters of language and culture. 'I can't simply add a German historical and political destiny to that. I know only too well how late and how fragmentary the Jews' participation in that destiny has been, how much by chance they entered into what was then a foreign history.' It should be noted that however much Arendt's attitude was coloured by Zionist spectacles, she was already adamant in refusing the validity of pre-cooked ideological recipes for she hastened to add: 'What my Germany is can hardly be expressed in one phrase, for any oversimplification – whether it is that of the Zionists, the assimilationists or the anti-Semites – only serves to obscure the true problem of the situation.'

Precisely because he so deeply accepted the Enlightenment vision of a German–Jewish symbiosis (on this question, to his credit, he was in no need of a catastrophe to change the course of his thinking) Jaspers was baffled by this willful Jewish acceptance of a necessary distance: 'How tricky this business with the German character is!', he wrote. 'I find it odd that you as a Jew want to set yourself apart from what is German.' Still, though he did not concede the point, he was aware of the difficulties inherent in defining this German essence. 'I do not isolate the German character as a type ... When I say the German character is rationality, etc., I am not saying that rationality is exclusively German .../ The word "German" is so much misused that one can hardly use it all anymore. I made the attempt, hopeless perhaps, to give it ethical content through the figure of Max Weber. That attempt', Jaspers wrote, his words endowed with an aura of nobility (especially as they were written in January 1933), 'however, would have proved successful only if you, too, could say: That's the way it is. I want to be a German.'[35]

Jaspers maintained this position throughout. 'What it comes to in the end', he wrote in 1952, 'is that I will never cease claiming you as a 'German' (you know that, of course), although as Monsieur [Heinrich Bluecher] would say, I am, along with you and many other Germans, "not a German", namely not in the political sense (even though I am a German according to my passport, but that gives me no pleasure).'[36] Nevertheless, although Jaspers' sense of *Deutschtum* (especially after 1933) was always critical, he retained the belief in an elevated core.[37] Both the critique and the idealization were apparent in his comments to Arendt about the condition of 1949 Germany: 'There is no denying that I do not belong among *those* Germans. That makes me all the more eager to write my Germany book, for there is something in the German character that I love above all else ... In the Western world, there are three peoples from whom individuals have peered into the depths – Jews, Greeks, Germans. But to put it that way is surely arrogant – let's at least conceal that arrogance.'[38]

But the dialogue was not limited to questions of Germanness. The specifically Jewish ingredient of these discussions revolved in the main around Arendt's critical analysis of the flawed dynamics of the alleged German–Jewish symbiosis, especially as it appeared in her (by now classic) study of Rahel Varnhagen. Because she began writing the work in 1929, only more or less completed it when she left Germany in 1933, added the last two chapters in the mid-1930s and extensively revised it before publishing it for the first time in 1957 (in English)[39] the issues raised by the book formed a sustained and recurring focus around which both Arendt and Jaspers formulated and developed matters that remained passionately central to them. *Rahel Varnhagen*, we should remember, took shape against the Weimar backdrop of accelerating anti-Semitism and was animated by a peculiarly German brand of Zionist critique; it contained many of the seminal, sometimes dazzling, insights into the tortured duplicities and psychology of assimilation that were incorporated into her later work.[40]

Just prior to her undertaking this task Jaspers confided to Martin Heidegger that he was was convinced that both by education and inclination Arendt was 'predestined' to compose this work.[41] Jaspers' intuition was quite correct but precisely because – as its varying stages of composition unambiguously revealed – it threw a harshly critical light upon the very possibility of an authentic 'German–Jewish' dialogue, *Rahel* consistently evoked from him an uneasy, critical, even testy response. In what appeared to be an ironic reversal of expected roles Jaspers summed up the ongoing emotional and symbolic stakes of this Rahel debate: 'I wanted to defend. ... the many remarkable people who have lived as German Jews.'[43]

Already in 1930 Jaspers was troubled by the way in which Arendt proposed to treat Rahel. His critique was couched within the existential frame he had taught her. 'You objectify "Jewish existence" existentially', he wrote to his student, 'and in doing so perhaps cut existential thinking off at the roots. The concept of being-thrown-back-on-oneself can no longer be taken altogether seriously if it is *grounded* in terms of the fate of the Jews instead of being rooted in itself. Philosophically, the contrast between floating free and being rooted strikes me as very shaky indeed.'[44] In her reply Arendt argued that she was 'not trying to "ground" Rahel's existence in terms of Jewishness' but rather 'to show that on the foundation of being Jewish a certain possibility of existence *can* arise that I have tentatively and for the time being called fatefulness. This fatefulness arises from the very fact of "foundationalessness" and can occur *only* in a separation from Judaism.'[45]

But Jaspers' scepticism remained. After reading the full manuscript in 1952 he not only (correctly) discerned the autobiographical nature of the work but remained convinced, even after the full dimensions of the German–Jewish catastrophe were revealed, of the potentially humanizing capacities of post-Enlightenment German–Jewish co-existence. In perhaps the most incisive and revelatory letter of the correspondence (and thus worthy of quoting at considerable length) he wrote that the book:

> still seems to me to be your own working through of the basic questions of Jewish existence, and in it you use Rahel's reality as a guide to help you achieve clarity and liberation for yourself. Because that was so, it made possible these analyses that now have an objective existence of their own. But because that was so, it also made possible the peculiar mood of the whole work, as if Rahel seems to have wakened neither your interest nor your love, or as if the book takes Rahel as a point of departure to then deal with something altogether different. No *picture of Rahel* herself emerges but only, so to speak, a picture of the events that chose this individual as their vehicle. I think it likely that you could do Rahel greater justice today, mainly because you would see her not just in the context of the Jewish question but, rather, in keeping with Rahel's own intentions and reality, as a human being in whose life the Jewish problem played a very large role but by no means the only one.
>
> ... everything you cite from 'enlightened' thinking is illustrated with negative examples (Dohm, Friedlaender) and then leads to pejorative presentations. But it was the greatness of the Enlightenment – of what made

Lessing what he is and ultimately, Goethe, too – that carried Rahel. And it was part of Varnhagen too, though in an even more denatured form. I wonder if the way in which you present the 'Enlightenment' not only underplays it but also distorts it. Basing your view on 'Die Erziehung des Menschengesechlechts', you see Lessing's 'reason' as historically based and set it over against Mendelssohn. That seems wrong to me. Even in Lessing, the origin of reason itself is – thank God – above history, and his thinking with history goes beyond history. The bewitchment of historians by a deified history was still in the future. Mendelssohn is doubtless flatter, more complacent than Lessing, naïve and dogmatic. Even though he may not stand comparison with Lessing, the impulse that linked them as friends is common to them both and an undeniable truth.

Your view of Rahel is, I feel loveless. ... The great figure of this woman – who trembles and bleeds, without home and homeland, without a world and without being rooted in her one love – who is so honest, reflects ceaselessly, understands, misunderstands, and casts off that misunderstanding – who constantly loses her way, loses track of herself, and has to re-create herself and deceives neither herself nor others about that – who reaches that mysterious territory where lies can appear as truth – you let this figure speak, but not from her core, that is, not as this human being herself who is not in her nature a Jew but who passes through this world as a Jew and therefore experiences the most extreme things, things that happen not only to Jews. ... On the one hand, you let Rahel dissipate herself in disjointed experiences; on the other, you force everything under the rubric of being a Jew. You make the reader feel the emotional impact of all that, but you don't let Rahel's brilliance appear in all that confusion and achieve its full glow.

You have to permit Rahel her errors, just as you have to permit everyone, even Goethe, his errors; and you have to perceive those errors in the context of the individual's stature, as the darker side of truth. And in the case of an 'exception' like Rahel, justice and love demand this of us even more.

What starts to take shape in your work but is then lost in sociological and psychological considerations (which should not in any way be omitted but should be incorporated into a higher level) is the unconditional aspect of Rahel ... , the quality of her personal influence, the totality of her insight, her secret knowledge of things, the timeless in the temporal, all the things for which being a Jew is only the outward guise and only the point of departure.

Your book can make one feel that if a person is a Jew he cannot really live his life to the full. It is surely infinitely difficult as soon as the Jew is no longer firmly rooted in the faith of his ancestors. But it can be done ...

Jaspers was able to link his critique directly to the personal circumstances of Arendt's life. 'You wrote this book', he told Arendt, 'before Heinrich Bluecher came into your life. ... But now, I think, you could reduce Rahel's Jewishness to one element in your presentation and let the greatness of her soul stand in the foreground. What the Christian world imposed. ... should not be minimized. ... But that shouldn't be the primary focus. What is important is that Rahel was a human being, liberated by the Enlightenment, who traveled individual paths that didn't work out for her and ended in blind alleys, but she also remained on the one true way, and that persists despite her failure.'

'Finally, and most important of all, that true profound "Jewishness", which is so uniquely historical in its effects without being aware of its historical-ness, should be made clearer in Rahel, without its being called Jewish, for that always has an equivocal effect.'[46]

Revealingly, the mature Arendt retorted that her earlier observations about the nature of assimilation and the Jewish condition remained valid. The reality of social assimilation and political emancipation, she insisted twenty years after writing *Rahel*, in effect did not permit Jews to really 'live'. Her focus was on the Enlightenment 'as it was relevant to Rahel, and by that I mean as a Jewish girl who had to bring about her own assimilation (that is, had to do consciously what others at a later time would have simply handed to them). Under those special circumstances the Enlightenment played a highly questionable role.'[47]

But in other, more pressing, ways the passage of time *had* induced a significant change of perspective. The experience of Nazism and knowledge of the Final Solution had clearly transformed Arendt's analytic priorities and the weight of considerations she had previously regarded as primary. The *Rahel* project, she told Jaspers in 1952, 'has not been very important to me for a long time'. It had been 'written from the perspective of a Zionist critique of assimilation, which I had adopted as my own and which I still consider basically justified today. But that critique was as politically naïve as what it was criticizing.'[48]

It is instructive at this point to note the privotal way in which both Jaspers' and Arendt's thought was metamorphosised by the catastrophe: previously very much in the non- (or even anti-) political mould characteristic of pre-1933 German philosophical discourse, both now became determinedly 'political' (however idiosyncratic their respective conceptions of the political may have been). In Jaspers' case, Nazism (together with the invention of the atom bomb) rendered political nationalism both dangerous and an anachronism.[49] Whereas for previous generations mankind had been a concept, a distant ideal, in his view it had now become an urgent reality translatable through

Jaspers' (pre-Habermasian) insistence on the primacy of communication and his federative notions of world citizenship.[50]

This is not the place to analyse and locate the nature of Arendt's political thought but it is clear that here, as with everything else she wrote, her penchant for paradoxical originality was the source of much of the brilliance, the strangeness and conceptual and historical confusions.[51] Various commentators have remarked upon her apparently arbitrary distinctions between the political and the social, and her idealized – even bizarre – conception of politics as the sphere of necessarily *disinterested* action.[52] Others have emphasised her continued, even if contextually transformed, debt to the assumptions of a peculiarly German (especially Heideggerian) existentialism and a Weimarian 'decisionism' devoid of any guiding and substantial political norms.[53]

However that may be, what needs to be noted in our context is the fact that it was above all the traumas of historical experience that constituted the key to the politicization of her thought in the first place.[54] It informed both her 'negative' historical analyses of totalitarianism (man as infinitely degradable, the stamping ground upon which to prove that 'everything is possible') and her related 'positive' philosophy with its (patently existential) emphases on natality and radical new beginnings.[55] Jaspers perceived the link between these destructive and creative moments, the desire to grasp but not to succumb to catastrophe, in Arendt's project: 'What begins to take shape. ... is a sense that there is a mysterious history inherent in a totality of events that is calling completely new forces into existence. These forces are melting down everything that has preceded them and are themselves absolute in nature. Over against that you also see, of course, the one great opportunity, human existence itself, that is continually being reborn, and you suggest that briefly and movingly.'[56]

The most urgent and initially central aspect of Arendt's 'politicization' was grasping what she believed to be the absolute *novum* of 'totalitarianism' and its related devestating inhumanities. As she wrote in her reply to Jaspers' comments on *Rahel Varnhagen*, her earlier critical remarks on Jewish assimilation were now bound to create serious misunderstandings and were clearly no longer the relevant, central concern. She then went on to acutely identify a causal confusion that haunts discussions of German–Jewish behaviour and the history of 'assimilation' to this day. 'I am afraid that people of goodwill will see a connection', she wrote in 1952, 'which does not in fact exist, between these things and the eradication of the Jews. All this was capable of fostering social hatred of the Jews and did foster it, just as it fostered, on the other side, a specifically German breed of Zionism. The truly totalitarian phenomenon – and genuine political anti-Semitism before it – had hardly anything to do with all this. And precisely this is what I did not know when I wrote this book.'[57]

To be sure this radical disconnection between her analysis of Jewish assimilation and the Final Solution was far more starkly and simply stated in her letter to Jaspers than her published work in fact intimated. Certainly *The Origins Of Totalitarianism* never makes this distinction sufficiently clear. Indeed, the way in which the dynamics of Jewish assimilation do eventually get incorporated is at best inconsistent with, or even contradictory on, this point.[58] Her rendering – in Part I – of the absolute centrality of the role of the Jews in the creation of the modern state and economy, her insistence on the inner logic (rather than the accidental nature) of the Jews assuming a place at the very storm center of events,[59] was salutary in its unprecedented moral and conceptual earnestness, its desire to grasp anti-Semitism at its most deadly and serious level and it was this that so many secular Jewish intellectuals found so beguiling and attractive. (After reading her penetrating analysis, Irving Howe reminisced, 'we could no longer escape the conviction that, blessing or curse, Jewishness was an integral part of our life.'[60]) But her analysis was informed by a problematic, and to many of her opponents almost sinister,[61] insistence that in crucial ways the Jews bore some responsibility for their predicament, that their actions and historical roles were not disconnected from the emergence of modern anti-Semitism. Arendt's view in *The Origins of Totalitarianism* was traceable to her belief that Jews, like all historical actors, exercised certain historical choices for which they were to be held responsible (a thesis she was to make much more explicit and radical in *Eichmann in Jerusalem*). Her critics argued that it was those who bore the hatred that needed to be analysed and that Arendt's work, by locating the sources of anti-semitism directly within Jewish history and functions rather than in external forces, was essentially an exercise in blaming the victim.[62]

Arendt's analyses may not have evoked unanimity but there is no denying the remarkably original and pioneeering nature of her major preoccupation of the 1940s and 1950s: coming to grips with what she regarded as the politically novel core of Nazism and Stalinist Bolshevism, the nature of their atrocities, and the genesis and dynamics of totalitarian dehumanization. Her later fame justly rested on these efforts to radically (and thus controversially) think through such matters, to provide what at that time was still a badly-needed conceptual framework in which to grasp these unprecedented phenomena. Her galvanising intellectual energy, her knack for perceiving unexpected relationships and making (almost recklessly) large generalizations in quite novel ways rendered her always an exciting, almost 'shocking', thinker, capable, on later reflection perhaps, of widely missing the mark but also of rare illumination.[63]

Totalitarianism, Nazism, the killing of the Jews and the nature of German guilt were, then, the major issues around which the Jaspers–Arendt correspondence revolved at that time. The ease with which they communicated, the self-questioning they encouraged – as well as the mutually supportive posture they assumed against outside criticism – contributed to the genesis and disposition of much of their post-1945 work.[64] To be sure, Jaspers' *Die Schuldfrage* consisted of lectures given in 1945 and early 1946 and was ready for publication by April of that year and many of Arendt's pioneering insights that were integrated into her *Origins of Totalitarianism* were already published in January 1945.[65] (Whereas their correspondence, which had been broken off for the last time in September 1938, was resumed only on October 28 1945.) Their resumed dialogue, set almost entirely under the shadow of the catastrophe, nevertheless now functioned as a mutually receptive sounding board for their respective ideas.

Jaspers' *Die Schuldfrage* has become a historical document as the first public attempt to come to terms with the questions of German guilt and responsibility. That notwithstanding, its deficiencies and weaknesses are, by now, reasonably well known.[66] Early on, Arendt, while admiring the work, was sceptical of the residues it contained of Jasper's pre-war nationalism and his rather Protestant emphasis on national German 'redemption'. But given her intuition concerning National Socialism's radically novel character, she most strongly disagreed with his attempt to think through the Nazi experience within familiar categories of guilt and responsibility. Her August 1946 response is worth quoting in full:

Your definition of Nazi policy as a crime ('criminal guilt') strikes me as questionable. The Nazi crimes, it seems to me, explode the limits of the law; and that is precisely what constitutes their monstrousness. For these crimes, no punishment is severe enough. It may well be essential to hang Goering, but it is totally inadequate. That is, this guilt, in contrast to all criminal guilt, oversteps and shatters any and all legal systems. ... And just as inhuman as their guilt is the innocence of the victims. Human beings simply can't be as innocent as they all were in the face of the gas chambers (the most repulsive usurer was as innocent as the newborn child because no crime deserves such a punishment.) We are simply not equipped to deal, on a human, political level, with a guilt that is beyond crime and an innocence that is beyond goodness or virtue. This is the abyss that opened up before us as early as 1933 (much earlier, actually, with the onset of imperialistic politics) and into which we have finally stumbled. I don't know how we will ever get out of it, for the Germans are burdened now with thousands or tens of thousands or hundreds of thousands of people who cannot be adequately punished within the legal system; and we Jews are burdened with millions of innocents by reason of which every Jew alive today can see himself as innocence personified.[67]

Jaspers did not comment on this early, almost wilfully perverse, symmetry Arendt constructed between Nazis and Jews and the new-found problem of the 'burden' of Jewish innocence. Instead, he incisively pointed to a problem that to this day bedevils (!) thinking and polemicising over the Nazi experience: the temptation to regard it within demonic – and thus absolutistic–moralistic – terms. His letter also prefigured – and may have planted the seed for – Arendt's later ruminations in *Eichmann in Jerusalem* on the 'banality of evil' (her *Origins of Totalitarianism* was still much taken with the Kantian notion of 'radical evil'):

You say that what the Nazis did cannot be comprehended as 'crime' – I'm not altogether comfortable with your view, because a guilt that goes beyond all criminal guilt inevitably takes on a streak of 'greatness' – of satanic greatness – which is, for me, as inappropriate for the Nazis as all the talk about the 'demonic' element in Hitler and so forth. It seems to me that we have to see these things in their total banality, in their prosaic triviality, because that's what truly characterizes them. Bacteria can cause epidemics that wipe out nations, but they remain merely bacteria. I regard any hint of myth and legend with horror, and everything unspecific is just such a hint. ... The way you do express it, you've almost taken the path of poetry. And a Shakespeare would never be able to give adequate form to this material – his instinctive aesthetic sense would lead to falsification of it – and that's why he couldn't attempt it. There is no idea and no essence here. Nazi crime is properly a subject for psychology and sociology, for psychopathology and jurisprudence only.[68]

Arendt's reply indicated her ability to absorb criticism from Jaspers as well as the still groping, tentative nature of her thinking:

I found what you say about my thoughts on 'beyond crime and innocence' in what the Nazis did half convincing; that is, I realize completely that in the way I've expressed this up to now I come dangerously close to that 'satanic greatness' that I, like you, totally reject. But still, there is a difference between a man who sets out murder his old aunt and people who without considering the economic usefulness of their actions at all (the deportations were very damaging to the war effort) built factories to produce corpses. One thing is certain: We have to combat all impulses to mythologize the horrible, and to the extent that I can't avoid such formulations, I haven't understood what actually went on. Perhaps what is behind it all is only that individual human beings did not kill other individual human beings for human reasons, but that an organized attempt was made to eradicate the concept of the human being.[69]

In her 1951 letters to Jaspers (as in her *The Origins of Totalitarianism* of the same year) 'radical evil' remained a key to comprehending the enormity wrought by Nazism, an enormity incomprehensible through traditional spectacles.

All traditional religion as such, whether Jewish or Christian, holds nothing whatsoever for me anymore. I don't think either, that it can anywhere or in any way provide a basis for something so clearly political as laws. Evil has proved to be more radical than expected. In objective terms, modern crimes are not provided for in the Ten Commandments. Or: the Western tradition is suffering from the preconception that the most evil things human things can do arise from the vice of selfishness. Yet we know that the greatest evils or radical evil has nothing to do anymore with such humanly understandable, sinful motives. What radical evil really is I don't know, but it seems to me it somehow has to do with the following phenomenon: making human beings as human beings superfluous (not using them as means to an end, which leaves their essence as human beings untouched and impinges only on their human dignity; rather, making them superfluous as human beings). This happens as soon as all unpredictability – which, in human beings, is the equivalent of spontaneity – is eliminated. And all this in turn arises from – or, better, goes along with – the delusion of the omnipotence (not simply with the lust for power) of an individual man. If an individual man *qua* man were omnipotent, then there is in fact no reason why men in the plural should exist at all – just as in monotheism it is only God's omnipotence that makes him ONE. So, in this same way, the omnipotence of an individual man would make men superfluous. (Nietzsche, it seems to me, has nothing to do with this, or Hobbes either. The will to power always wants simply to become more powerful and so remains within the comparative, which still respects the limits of human existence and does not push on to the madness of the superlative.)[70]

These thoughts not only informed her magnificent chapter on 'Total Domination' in which the concentration and extermination camps are viewed as 'the laboratories in which the fundamental belief of totalitarianism that everything is possible is being verified',[71] but alo provided the frame (still very relevant in our own time of 'ethnic cleansing') for her pioneering analysis of the general disenfranchisement of minorities and the profoundly dehumanizing implications attendant upon forced 'statelessness, the newest mass phenomenon in contemporary history.'[72] Regardless of the deficiencies and erosion of the analysis of 'mass society' as both the cause and effect of total-itarianism and, indeed, of the totalitarian model itself, the magnificence of these insights remain.[73]

If Arendt held the Western philosophical tradition not altogether innocent in this matter of superfluity – given what she now regarded as its unclear sense of the political, its emphasis on man as an individual and its incapac-ity to deal directly with the fact of plurality – this was less important than the fact that in her view the crucial culprits were those new forces that cre-ated and then constituted mass society. Arendt was not prepared to relin-quish the humanising capacities of culture nor to indict deep structures and tendencies of European civilization as implicated in the catastrophe. (Whether or not this was a blindspot, induced, as Ernst Gellner has recently argued, by her own committment to romantic and existentialist traditions that were themselves implicated in National Socialism – Jaspers, as we have just seen, similarly noted that her rhetoric uncomfortably resembled the 'demonic' idiom of romanticism – must remain unanswered here.[74]) The tradition, she emphasised, was in no way causally linked to the Nazi catastrophe. Although she did not mention Volume 1 of Karl Popper's *The Open Society and its Enemies*, first published in 1945,[75] she heatedly dismissed the contention that 'Hitler had anything to do with Plato.' Rather, she told Jaspers, 'One com-pelling reason why I took such trouble to isolate the elements of totalitarian governments was to show that the Western tradition from Plato up to and including Nietzsche is above any such suspicion.'[76] Arendt's 'respect for the mind', Jaspers proclaimed, 'kept her from making the great thinkers partially responsible for the horrors that occurred in the reality that her book ana-lyzes.'[77]

These observations were essentially correct. From the beginning Arendt's analyses flowed from her observations about the destructive aspects of rup-ture and the murderousness of new, modern phenomena. It was not the destruc-tive forces of past thought (or even their dialectically dangerous potential *à la* Horkheimer and Adorno (whom, incidentally, Arendt despised[78]), not tra-dition and continuity but breakdown and mass modernity that constituted the problem.

It was not only the discontinuities that counted for Arendt but also her adamant refusal to regard Nazism as the logical outcome of German histo-ry, its mind and polity. Arendt appears almost as a philosophical counterpart to the analyses of the more staid conservative German historians such as Gerhard Ritter[79] and Friedrich Meinecke[80] who argued that the rise of Nazism had less to do with internal, 'organic' German development than with the importation of essentially alien and corrupting modern mass practices and ideologies. Nothing more antithetical to the *Sonderweg* thesis is imaginable than her 'Approaches to the German Problem', published as early as 1945. 'Nazism', she wrote there, 'owes nothing to any part of the Western tradition, be it German or not, Catholic or Protestant, Christian, Greek or Roman. Whether we like Thomas Aquinas or Machiavelli or Luther or Kant or Hegel or Nietzsche – the list may be prolonged indefinitely as even a cursory glance at the literature of the "German problem" will reveal – they have not the least responsibility for what is happening in the extermination camps. Ideologically speaking, Nazism begins with no traditional basis at all, and it would be better to realize the danger of this radical negation of any tradition, which was the main feature of Nazism from the beginning (though not of Fascism in its first Italian stages).'[81] The Nazis did, to be sure, employ the traditional political rhetoric of Europe and all its ism's but 'only the experts with their fondness for the spoken or written word and incomprehension of political realities have taken these utterances of the Nazis at face and interpreted them as the consequence of certain German or European traditions. On the contrary, Nazism is actually the breakdown of all German and European traditions, the good as well as the bad.'[82]

Nazism was part of a wider catastrophe that had threatened European culture for more than a century; it was nihilism activated, 'basing itself on the intoxication of destruction as an actual experience, dreaming the stupid dream of producing the void.'[83] To be sure, the situation in Germany (its late development as a nation, lack of democratic experience, military defeat and postwar inflation and unemployment) rendered it peculiarly vulnerable to the breaking of all traditions but 'it is still true that these had to be broken, so that it was not any German tradition as such but the violation of all traditions which brought about Nazism ... This is the only tangible psychological meaning of the "German problem". The problem lies not in the German national character but rather in the disintegration of this character.'[84]

For Arendt, then, Nazism had to be understood as a consequence of the vacuum created by the almost simultaneous breakdown of Europe's social and political structures, the point when all safeguarding traditions had lost their force. New concepts and forms of understanding were required to grasp the novel nature of this polity – totalitarianism – that emerged to fill the vacuum. Jaspers was aware not only of the brilliance and the excitement this work generated but also of its loose inner structure and methodological peculiarities. To critics, he sought to sympathetically elucidate her approach. What she had set out to do, he wrote, was 'to reveal relationships among ideas. ... No one can ascertain how great a bearing they had on the actual course of events. Hannah never claimed that English imperialism produced Hitler and

Stalin, nor did she claim that there was any intellectual identity anywhere among them. But the analogies in the phenomena, which ultimately made the whole disaster possible, would still be there if there even if there were no causal relationships at all. What she has done is perceive those relationships and present them with remarkable vividness.'[85]

Because their trust was so great they were able to freely criticise each other in the intimacy of their correspondence although in public their stance was always mutually defensive and laudatory.[86] Jaspers, for instance, keenly understood his student's (almost perversely) combative instincts and tried as best he could to protect her from the inevitable onslaughts. As she prepared for the Eichmann trial he presciently stated: 'I'm afraid it cannot go well. I fear your criticism and think that you will keep as much of it as possible to yourself.'[87] Throughout that storm he provided Arendt with a critical ear strengthening even more a friendship that was tempered throughout by the self-conscious desire to forge an imagination of disaster that would also provide a space for humanity to remain alive.

For them, of course, a crucial part of that humanity lay in their own self-consciously German–Jewish friendship. What Arendt had written about Lessing and 'humanity in dark times' surely applied to her relationship with Jaspers: only where there was incessant and continual discourse about the affairs of men could there be friendship, and where friendship survived so too did humanness.[88] Theirs was a discourse that matched the passion of public affairs with the deepest of personal trust. Reading the correspondence one feels like an intruder, witness to the most touching (almost embarrassing) testaments that the Jewish 'student' and the German professor confidentially presented to each other as their friendship matured under the scar of historical trauma:

'I want to thank you', Arendt wrote to Jaspers on his birthday, 'for the seventy years of your life, for your existence, which would be cause enough for gratitude. I want to thank you for the early years in Heidelberg when you were my teacher, the only one I have ever been able to recognize as such; and for the happiness and relief I found that one can be educated in freedom. I have never forgotten since then that the world and Germany, whatever else they may be, are the world in which you live and the country that produced you.'

'I want to thank you for your friendship; you know what it means to me. It is such a great gift precisely because the mere fact of your existence would have been enough.'

'... And I hope, too, that the world will honor you as much as I would like to honor you, because it seems to me that everyone would do well to put ceremony aside and examine his life in the light of yours.'[89]

These were not only private convictions. As Arendt said of Jaspers in a 1964 interview: ' ... where Jaspers comes forward and speaks, all becomes luminous ... I don't want to make him responsible for me, for God's sake, but if anyone succeeded in instilling some sense in me, it was he. And this dialogue is, of course, quite different today. That was really my most powerful postwar experience. That there can be such conversations! That one can speak in such a way!'[90]

The mutuality was always evident. In 1946, before the rubble had cleared, Jaspers wrote to Arendt: 'In you I finally hear someone speaking whose seriousness is beyond any doubt, someone who, I feel, values the same things I do. The only difference is that you strike me as braver than I am.'[91]

And after years of separation through the catastrophe he reacted thus to seeing her reproduced face again:

'How happy we are to have your pictures. They are truly you, instantly recognizable. The same brilliant gleam of your eyes, but also etched in your face the sufferings of which your youth had no inkling. From your letters I have known for a long time now that you have come through undiminished. That was obviously not easy, and in these pictures I can see that it wasn't. You are a prodigal human being.'[92]

7 Small Forays, Grand Theories and Deep Origins: Current Trends in the Historiography of the Holocaust

This chapter does not purport to provide an overall history and evaluation of Holocaust historiography nor does it even pretend to comprehensively cover the state of present research. The beginning of this complex task has been competently undertaken by others.[1] Rather, I shall attempt to analyse certain key works and place into context some of the major interpretive issues that define the fluid – indeed, rather bewildering – condition of the field.[2]

All historiography – its agenda, emphases, systems of selection and intepretive perspectives – is bound to proceed, and reflect changes, within wider informing cultural and political contexts. The study of the *Shoah* is no exception to this rule. Despite an understandable (though, in my view, misguided) impulse to insulate the Holocaust from normal historiographical rules and practice, to regard it as somehow 'above history' and as humanly incomprehensible,[3] an event of this centrality and magnitude will inevitably undergo constant interpretive reshaping, benefited by (or prey to) shifting modes of cultural and political understanding.

The great historiographical debates of the 1980s that had a bearing upon the Holocaust were directly or indirectly related to the politics of the Federal Republic and the attempt to somehow rehabilitate German history and national identity. This gave resonance to the attack on the notion of a *Sonderweg*, an entrenched historiographical tradition that posited a distinct German mind and polity – integrally different from the liberal-bourgeois West – that was bound to culminate in Nazism.[4] The contemporary political dimension was even more obvious in what became known as the *Historikerstreit*, the debate over the alleged attempt by certain German historians to 'relativize' the Holocaust by placing it squarely within a causally connected continuum of ongoing twentieth century genocides.[5]

The challenges, however, were by no means confined to German questions. Saul Friedlander, always sensitive to changing cultural and political

115

currents and their moral and philosophical implications for the study of the *Shoah*,[6] has recently edited a volume drawing our attention to the role that a prevalent 'post-modernist' discourse has begun to play in problematizing and rendering more self-conscious the grounds of Holocaust historiography.

By asserting that historians in effect create their own object (which they then pretend to describe 'realistically' and analyse 'objectively') post-modernism poses a problem for historical discourse in general. But, as both advocates and opponents make clear in this volume, it raises in particularly acute form the problem of the 'limits of representation' of both Nazism and its crimes. Its rejection, as Friedlander puts it, 'of the possibility of identifying some stable reality or truth beyond the constant polysemy and self-referentiality of linguistic constructs challenges the need to establish the realities and truths of the Holocaust.'[7] Despite the plenitude of 'participant' documentation – of survivors, perpetrators and onlookers – the overall epistemological problem, many of the contributors argue, remains. As Martin Jay puts it, the Holocaust is 'itself ... a post-facto conceptual entity not in use at the time, which no one individual ever witnessed and whose truth or meaning, however we fashion the relation between these two very different concepts, cannot be proved by stitching together all of the individual testimonies.'[8] The volume spans positions ranging from Hayden White's argument – that historical narrative is essentially constituted by a limited number of rhetorical forms and choices that imply specific emplotments, explanatory models and ideological stances and that, therefore, neither 'the historical record' nor any 'objective' external criteria exist to provide access to the 'truth' or yardsticks for the preferability of one interpretation or another[9] – to the more traditionalist and fierce defence of a prior concrete historical reality (grounded in the testimonies of individual witnesses) by Carlo Ginzburg.[10]

The political and cultural debates of the 1980s and early 1990s thus made it increasingly clear that the impulse to conceive of both Nazism and the Holocaust in absolute, moralistic terms, cut off from broader epistemological questions (and crises) and the flow of wider historical processes would increasingly face serious challenge. This was symptomatized by the calls for the 'historicization' of National Socialism by Martin Broszat[11] (and Thomas Nipperdey who wrote that 'the moralized past ultimately destroys true history. We must "historize" National Socialism'.[12]) This was greeted with suspicion by Friedlander and other historians who argued that the insertion of Nazism into conventional historical narrative would inevitably shift the focus from what was central and unique to that regime – its criminal nature and the unprecedented atrocities it had committed.[13] 'Auschwitz', wrote Dan Diner, 'is a no-man's land of understanding, a black-box of explanation, a vacuum of extrahistorical significance, which sucks in attempts at historiographic interpretation. ... As the ultimate extreme case, and thus as an absolute standard of history, this event can hardly be historicized.'[14]

Yet to a large extent such proclamations begged the question at hand. Despite – perhaps because of – its attendant difficulties, the very magnitude of Auschwitz rendered inevitable a plethora of attempts at interpretive historical comprehension. 'After fifty years', Arno Mayer has written, 'the question is no longer whether or not to reappraise and historicize the Judeocide, but rather how to do so responsibly'.[15] (We shall shortly consider whether or not Mayer has successfully pursued his own challenge.)

If any unifying element linking these diverse (and often mutually incompatible) historiographical exercises can be identified it is, perhaps, the manifold attempt to integrate the Holocaust into wider historical and comparative processes and more complex explanatory structures and informing contexts. Their cumulative effect is to revise older explanations that privileged anti-Semitism as an autonomous factor, that viewed it as the singular key to the long-term roots and as the driving force in the detailed, immediate evolution of this event.[16] Such emphases are, of course, not entirely new. Many years ago, Hannah Arendt pointed out the deficiencies of historical doctrines positing 'an "eternal antisemitism" in which Jew-hatred is a normal and natural reaction to which history gives only more or less opportunity. Outbursts need no special explanation because they are natural consequences of an eternal problem.'[17] Contemporary examinations of the Holocaust increasingly revolve around such 'special explanations', seeking to identify the enabling circumstances and the broader context that allowed Jew-hatred to assume this particular, unprecedented genocidal form.

These treatments do not, of course, banish anti-Semitism so much as relocate – and recontextualize – it and in the process thereby shift its explanatory weight and determinative historical influence. This thrust has, in the first place, been apparent in a series of rather small-scale, empirical studies. These forays have typically problematised older assumptions concerning the unmediated continuity and universality of anti-Semitic attitudes as a linear, galvanising force leading almost inexorably to genocide. Research into pre–1933 Germany and indeed the Third Reich itself provides a complex, differentiated picture of the salience, functions and intensity of anti-Semitism within that society. As Michael Marrus has pointed out, no clear connection between intense *popular* anti-Semitism and the destruction process has been found.[19] Prior to 1914 anti-Semitism in Eastern Europe and even in a comparable society such as France was almost certainly greater than in Germany.[20] In the polarised post-war Weimar Republic there were, of course, very significant pockets of anti-Semitism – the entire political right contained anti-Jewish planks[21] – but it was very unevenly distributed and varied in style, intensity and nature (from more 'mild', 'conventional' forms to the far more extreme expressions of a – vocal – minority).[22] Indeed, numerous local studies suggest that anti-Semitism was often more a result of being won over to Nazism rather than the cause of the attraction.[23] Moreover, as Oded Heilbronner has recently shown, in the crucial years of their rise (1929–33) the Nazis quite consciously muted their anti-Jewish propaganda in order to broaden their popularity and establish their 'respectability'.[24]

A similar differentiated picture emerges from recent studies of German popular opinion and the 'Final Solution' itself. Although research continues, and no consensus may be said to exist, it is becoming increasingly clear that no clear link between a murderous, popularly generated anti-semitism and the Holocaust can be established. Genocide certainly did not entail mass-mobilization or represent the pent-up fury of an enraged citizenry: on the contrary, for the majority of the population *repression* of the event was the order of the day. As David Bankier puts it in his recent work *The Germans and the Final Solution*: 'Clearly there was no scarcity of information. There is no doubt that those who wished to know had the means at their disposal to acquire such knowledge. Those who did not nor could not believe reacted so because they did not want to believe. In one sentence: they knew enough to know that it was better not to know any more.'[25]

At issue, of course, remains the correct interpretive framework in which to view the attitudes underlying repression. Bankier (and Otto Dov Kulka and Aron Rodrigue[26]) stresses the explicit, determining role of anti-Semitism as a shaping factor: 'Since the Nazis were merely carrying out programmes of political anti-Semitism which had been in circulation for half a century, the exclusion of Jews from the German nation did not contradict the basic values of a society which was "traditionally" anti-semitic. Thus the bulk of Germans endorsed anti-Semitic policy fully aware that a pure racial community could not be achieved if one were unduly sensitive to morality.'[27] Ian Kershaw, on the other hand, argues for the relatively minor role played by the 'Jewish Question' in the overall formation of German opinion during the war. While acknowledging the role played by latent anti-Semitism, he places far more stress on indifference, passivity and apathy – characteristics typical of behaviour towards minority 'outsiders' in all authoritarian societies (and to some extent, even in liberal democracies) – that allowed the ruling ideological elite to propel and radicalise anti-Jewish policy into genocide.[28]

It should be clear, however, that while both indifference *and* 'conventional' anti-Semitism allowed the destruction process to proceed relatively unimpeded, neither of these factors set it in motion or were responsible for its implementation. What is perhaps most disturbing is the added possibility, increasingly stressed by numerous scholars, that at the heart of the killing itself, those who operated the 'machinery of destruction' (the middle-echelon 'desk' murderers and the 'little men' who did the dirty work at the bottom of the hierarchy) could carry out their duties impelled more by a series of bureaucratic incentives and socio-psychological imperatives than by anti-Semitic motives. Already in 1961, in his still-unequalled study of the bureaucratically organized destruction of European Jewry, Raul Hilberg demonstrated that anti-Jewish sentiments functioned as rationalizations, rather than causes, of atrocities that were perpetrated.[29] Hannah Arendt's portrait of Eichmann and the mental dynamics of the 'banality of evil'[30] and Stanley Milgram's perceptive analysis of the deep compulsion to obey authority within hierarchical structures[31] chillingly demonstrated the possibility of mass murder in which in which hatred of one's victim was rendered relatively unimportant, a result rather than a cause of the act committed.

Perhaps even more depressing was Christopher Browning's 1978 study of the anti-Jewish bureau of the Nazi Foreign Office. The mainsprings behind the actions of the bureaucrats he studied was neither anti-Semitism nor, even, fanatical obedience but rather old-fashioned careerism and the desire not to tarnish one's progress as a conforming civil servant.[32] In his illuminating 1992 study of Reserve Police Batallion 101 and the 'Final Solution', Browning demonstrates the incremental processes by which 'ordinary men' became mass murderers, rounding up and killing (with increasing ease and ferocity) Jewish men, women and children in 1942 Poland.[33] The 'Final Solution' was brought into being by the policies of the Nazi leadership, Browning reminds us, and the 'banal' bureaucrats implemented it, but the actual killing was the work of such 'ordinary men': 'Ultimately', he writes, 'the Holocaust took place because at the most basic level individual human beings killed other human beings.'[34]

Batallion 101, composed of middle-aged, mainly working class men from Hamburg (a city that particularly resisted the rise of National Socialism), was 'hardly a promising group', as Browning puts it, 'to recruit mass murderers on behalf of the Nazi vision of a racial utopia free of Jews.'(p. 48). Yet it was these men who, unlike the desk bureaucrats, had to view their victims face to face. Browning describes the inuring mechanisms by which the majority could kill with ever-decreasing compunction. (The word 'majority' is used advisedly. At the beginning of the killings there were various ways in which these men could opt out. 10–20 per cent availed themselves of the opportunity and, significantly, for the few who refused to participate, no punishment was meted out.) For those who remained, however, the killing was facilitated not so much by virtue of ideological conviction as by group conformity, deference to authority, the dulling powers of alcohol, processes of routinization (simply getting used to the killing) and a series of quite chilling rationalizations. As one killer later reported:

'I made the effort, and it was possible for me, to shoot only children. It so happened that the mothers led the children by the hand. My neighbor then shot the mother and I shot the child that belonged to her, because I reasoned with myself that after all without its mother the child could not live any longer. It was supposed to be, so to speak, soothing to my conscience to release children unable to live without their mothers.'[35]

As Browning portrays it brutalization was the effect rather than the cause of these men's behaviour (p. 161). With time the initially horrific business of mass killing became almost normal, a matter of routine. It is not as if anti-Jewish sentiment and stereotypes played no role – for these men the Jews 'stood outside their circle of human obligation and responsibility' (p. 73) – but rather that this factor became integrated into a complex cluster of general dehumanizing processes that ultimately facilitated such actions.[36] The Holocaust was an anti-Jewish project – but it could be carried out precisely because its murderous impulses operated within far more general shaping processes, structures and modes of behaviour that rendered it a 'human' possibility.[37] 'I must recognize', Browning writes, 'that in the same situation, I could have been either a killer or an evader – both were human – if I want to understand and explain the behavior of both as best as I can. ... Not trying to understand the perpetrators in human terms would make impossible ... any history of Holocaust perpetrators that sought to go beyond one-dimensional caricature' (p. xx).

But these studies refer to middle and lower level functionaries, implementers of the destruction process. *They do not address the underlying motivational factors, the level of ideology and policy-making at the very top, the driving force of a small elite that set all this machinery into motion.* This was the gravest shortcoming, the blind spot, of most 'functionalist' studies of the 1970s and 1980s. They did, to be sure, considerably enlarge our understanding of the processes of Nazi decision-making, stressing the polycratic, even chaotic nature of the regime and its contingent, largely non-ideological groping towards the 'Final Solution' (the extreme versions portraying it as an almost accidental occurrence.[38]) But, by and large, such accounts paid only lip service to the broader background, the larger contextual and mental structures that *shaped the choices made*, guided action and created the atmosphere in which decisions proceeded and the machine operated. This, surely, must be regarded as a decisive level of explanation.

How have scholars recently sought to address this question? What are some of the major frames in which they seek to locate the event? Perhaps because of its tragic recurrence in our own times, historians are beginning anew to pursue the general history of 'ethnic cleansing'. In effect, they follow – without necessarily acknowledging – Hannah Arendt's pioneering analysis of the general disenfranchisement of minorities and the profoundly dehumanizing and potentially genocidal implications attendant upon forced 'statelesness, the newest mass phenomenon in contemporary history'.[39] There is, too, an emerging consensus that the various manifestations of 'ethnic cleansing' – from expulsion and mass resettlement policies through atrocities to genocide – are contingently linked to the enabling and brutalizing circumstances of war (especially the two great World Wars).[40] The 'ethnic cleansing campaigns' undertaken during – and immediately after – World War II alone affected the lives of over 100 million people, including Poles, Slavs, Germans, Soviets, Serbs, Croats and Ukrainians (often in interchangeable roles as victims or perpetrators). In this view – as articulated both by the 'revisionist' German historian Andreas Hilgruber[41] and, more recently, by Istvan Deak[42] – the Holocaust must be regarded as a particularly odious phase in an (ongoing) European tendency of ethnic purification within the context of increasingly dehumanizing, total wars. The Jews were the most unfortunate group of victims, Deak argues, because they were 'both wholly defenceless and the object of an official Nazi policy obsessively bent on eliminating them.'

The general framework may be persuasive. But as shocking as the various expressions of 'ethnic cleansing' may be, mass resettlement did not always amount to genocide nor does this generalized category explain *why* it was the Jews that became the object of an official and obsessive Nazi genocidal thrust. This Arno Mayer has set out to do in his controversial, explicitly revisionist[43] 1988 work *Why did the Heavens not Darken?* As its sub-title, The *'Final Solution' in History*, suggests, Mayer seeks to locate and analyse what he calls the 'Judeocide' within the largest possible historical context and explanatory structures (the term 'Holocaust' is vehemently unacceptable to him, too tied to an ideological, ahistorical cult of Jewish memory[44]). The Judeocide, he argues, possesses homologous qualities characteristic of other major historical convulsions, namely the Thirty Years War (of the seventeenth century) and the First Christian Crusade of 1095–1099. The former, he argues, resembled its twentieth century counterpart in that for both 'the traditional foundations of Europe were shaken by a general crisis in civil and political society which was at once cause and effect of total and monstrous war' (p. 31). But the very generality of the comparison makes it of little value and Mayer does not overly press his case acknowledging the fundamental difference in the scale and systematic nature of the atrocities committed in what he terms the Twentieth Century Thirty Years War.

Mayer's second comparison, however, gets us closer to the central – and most dubious – thesis of this work. 'Just as the first mass murder of the Jews since antiquity had been closely tied to the First Crusade of the late eleventh century', Mayer argues, 'so the epochal Judeocide of the twentieth century was closely interwoven with the Nazi-led crusade against bolshevism from 1941–1945.'[45] The original target of the Crusade was the Muslim infidels, while for the Nazi crusaders the Bolsheviks and the Marxist Soviet Union were the *real* and ultimate foes. In both cases, according to this version, the mass murder of the Jews functioned as a *kind of explosive side-effect of a frustrated project*. Had the Wehrmacht been triumphant, Mayer argues, the unsystematic killing of Jews would have continued but ultimately they would have been deported to the far interior of Russia or to an overseas colony.[46] (A totally unsubstantiated assertion made, as many dismayed critics noted, in the absence of any footnotes or supporting documentation.[47]) It only became genocidal when the drive against Bolshevik forces began to fail, at the point when, according to Mayer, in the late fall of 1941 the Eastern campaign bogged down and the real enemy became less and less accessible.

There are significant empirical omissions and interpretive deficiencies in this version. Mayer provides no evidence about German despair in the summer which would substantiate the sudden genocidal drive and pays no attention to the fact that historians have variously dated the decision to systematize the murders from as early as March 1941.[48] Others argue that the decision was made during the summer not out of frustration or disappointment with impending defeat but rather in the *euphoria* of the early victories of the Barbarossa campaign.[49] The exact, immediate precipitating circumstances surrounding the decision will probably never ever be known. But, the apocalyptic atmosphere surrounding Barbarossa notwithstanding, both euphoria and disappointment seem to me to be peculiarly lame and inappopriate explanatory categories, bypassing the underlying factors that allowed for the possibility of genocide to arise as an option in the first place – whatever the 'propitious' circumstances may have been.

Mayer asks us to believe that between 1941–45 (as in 1095–99) the war on the Jews was essentially an act of *deflection*, a kind of *surrogate* mass murder in which the Jews, the most easily accessible victims, were singled out by frustrated perpetrators unable to reach – or defeat – their real enemy: 'Once Hitler and Himmler realized that the allegedly bestial soldiers and callous Bolshevik commissars of the Red Army were thwarting the peerless Wehrmacht, they increasingly vented their rage on the Jews.'[50] This version is saved from being a ludicrously simplistic scapegoat theory[51] only by Mayer's argument that Jews were attacked because they were considered 'the primary carriers of the Bolshevik system and ideology' (p. 270). But Nazi anti-

Semitism as a species of anti-bolshevism excludes many of its most obsessive and defining characteristics. It does not, for instance, account for the animus against non-communist Western, or indeed Polish Jews (the *prior* Nazi concentration of Polish Jewry in specially created ghettoes was surely centrally related to the ultimate genocidal decision); it is unable to reveal why so much energy was invested to extricate for extermination a few Jews from remote Greek islands nor, indeed, can it explain the special venom reserved for those traditional, 'caftan' Jews most removed from any Bolshevik associations.[52]

Against all his pronounced broadening intentions, the effect of Mayer's work is ultimately a narrowing, ideological one in which virtually every aspect of the Nazi experience is essentially reduced to a species of anti-Bolshevism.[53] But while Nazism was obviously anti-Bolshevist it was not merely that. It was equally contemptuous of the liberal democratic and, indeed, the wider Western Enlightenment tradition. Indeed, it is a continuing error to regard National Socialism merely in terms of its negations. For here was a movement that envisaged a new world order to be created through programmes of vast magnitude, holding out, as Eugen Weber has put it, 'the ultimate revolutionary promise: *changer la vie*, an absurb project unless associated with *changer l'homme*, Nietzsche's *noch nicht festgestellte Tier.*'[54] Nazism sought to implement a radically different (but still modern) alternative to both Marxist and liberal conceptions of modernity.[55] Its propelling dynamic flowed from its own sustaining vision of a 'positive' biological politics and a racial re-organization of the world, implemented through hitherto undreamt-of large-scale eugenic schemes of regeneration and destruction. This was to be conducted on peoples and minorities – including 'impure' elements among the Germans themselves – that had nothing to do with Bolshevism. It was *not*, Daniel Jonah Goldhagen points out,

> anti-Bolshevism that caused the Nazis to regard Jewish bodies as racially polluted ... to sterilize the physically debilitated Germans, to kill the German insane, to mass murder Gypsies, to decimate homosexuals, to seek the extermination of the Polish intelligentsia, to intend the destruction not only of the Bolshevik state but also of the Russian people, to envisage the climax of this apocalyptic enterprise as the eradication of the Christian churches.[56]

It was these integral, defining tendencies and aims, not their 'blighted dreams' as Mayer argues, that 'led the Nazi regime to violate most traditional political, moral, and religious norms and, more importantly, the notions of humanity defined by them, so that naked power now normalized brutality as its own response to its own irreversible loss of control.'[57]

Basic motivational clues are to be found where both Mayer (and, for that matter, the functionalists) demonstrate a peculiar insensitivity: in the shaping powers of racism as the overarching Nazi principle of policy emanating (no matter how vaguely) from the very top of the State and informing the choices made by bureaucracies at every level. The structure and dynamics of its defining logic have recently been ably analysed by Michael Burleigh and Wolfgang Wippermann. The Third Reich, they remind us, 'became the first state in world history whose dogma and practice was racism.'[58] Here was a State whose ruling elite was animated by the belief, as Walther Darre the Nazi agrarian ideologist put it, that a 'people can only reach spiritual and moral equilibrium if a well-conceived breeding plan stands at the very *centre* of its culture.'[59] Burleigh and Wipperman demonstrate in detail the programmatic implementation of this vision characterised by a variety of inter-linked measures of inclusion and exclusion, combining 'positive' philogenerative and social-welfare measures for the *Volksgemeinschaft*[60] with a series of increasingly radicalized measures purging 'abnormal' and 'unwanted' elements. The programme of total extermination was reserved only for the Jews – a fact which all revisionist accounts and relocations still need to explain – but it existed within a general eugenic framework defined both by its 'regenerative' and radically exclusionary and murderous impulses (between 1941 and 1944 the Nazis killed about 7 million civilians in Russia and in Poland – where the figures vacillate extremely – anywhere between 800,000 to 2,400,000 non-Jewish Poles). Indeed, in inextricable fashion, the murderous impulses of the death-camp Auschwitz can only be comprehended within the context of an overall plan to ethnically 'purify' and reconstruct and re-Germanise the surrounding upper Silesian areas. Himmler regarded such towns as Auschwitz, Blachstadt, and Saybusch as relics of medieval German colonisation and sought to convert these into model ecological, urban and architectural centers.[61]

Burleigh and Wippermann implicitly demonstrate that it was not so much the autonomous strength of Jew-hatred that impelled it to assume its entirely novel, systematically genocidal form but rather its integration within the implementation of a total, eugenic vision of racial community. In this view the Holocaust is comprehensible only as part of a continuum – of which it represented the extreme edge.

In line with such analyses, over the last few years there has been a marked trend to document these (previously relatively neglected) 'eugenic' and 'racial hygiene' programmes and demonstrate, either implicitly or explicitly, their possible relation to the Holocaust. It is only over the last few years that the nature and scale of the Nazi programme of compulsory sterilization has become apparent. Between 1934 and the outbreak of war, approximately 350,000 so-called 'hereditarily ill' Germans (or 0.5 of the population) underwent such procedures (the numbers incidentally, did not even approximate the optimal hopes of the 'racial hygienists' responsible for the programme).[62] The 'euthanasia' programme – and its key links in both method and personnel to the Holocaust – is better known although still not sufficiently integrated into the wider whole.[63] Like other major atrocities there was a clear awareness about the optimal conditions under which this should take place. As Hitler told the Reich Physicians Leader Dr. Wagner, 'such a problem would be more easily solved in war-time'.[64] The so-called 'destruction of worthless life' (including mass gassings of mental patients) 'officially' took place between October 1939 and August 1941 and took the lives of about 93,000 'handicapped' people. Contemporary research is establishing that, contrary to conventional wisdom, this programme was not after all stopped by popular pressure. Rather, while it came to an end within the T4 German killing centres, it was now redirected to the East where, under the conditions of total war, its horizons were made even broader. The *Einsatzgruppen*, one must remember, were instructed to kill all Jews and communists active as partisans but they 'also killed all the Gypsies and patients of mental asylums they could find.'[65] The methods, ideology and personnel of this programme were thus exported and adapted; the same people who had done the work in Germany now sought the 'sick' in concentration camps in the East and set up variations of the gas installations used on mental patients for use on Jews in the death camps.[66]

It is similarly only with reference to this informing framework of eugenic biopolitics that the persecution and murder of other so-called 'degenerative' elements – the 'asocials' (criminals, vagrants, etc.), the Gypsies,[67] homosexuals – becomes comprehensible. Outside of Germany these kinds of population programmes became even more grandiose in conception. Himmler's *Generalplan Ost* envisaged shifting 31 million non-Germans across Eastern Europe in order not only to get rid of 'inferior' people but also to facilitate the resettlement of *Volksdeutsche*.[68]

The role of 'experts', university-trained lawyers and public servants (excluding Heydrich, seven of the fourteen participants at the Wannsee Conference held doctoral degrees in law as did a disproportionately high amount of *Einsatzgruppen* officers),[69] academics and natural and social scientists in the inspiration, construction and implementation of these racial and eugenic programmes has been long recognised and has lately again been underlined.[70] Recently, however, the special centrality of doctors – and indeed of medicine itself – both in defining the vision and in putting it into practice has become increasingly the focus of attention.

Relative to other professional groups, from the begining doctors were heavily overrepresented in the Nazi party.[71] They were actively involved in mass murder at all levels – as batallion physicians in the East instructing soldiers and police on the most effective modes of face to face killings;[72] as architects and virtually the sole practitioners of the sterilization and euthanasia programmes; and, ultimately, as key figures at Auschwitz where, the infamous medical experimentations apart, they were the sole authorities to make the selections for the gas chambers.[73] Indeed, Robert Jay Lifton has argued that the 'medicalisation of killing' constituted the very essence of Nazism. Its genocidal impulses were implicit within what can only be described as a bio-medical vision and its vast, self-proclaimed, task of 'racial hygiene'. Assuming control of the human biological future, assuring health to positive racial stock and purging humanity of its sick, degenerative elements, entailed a mission of 'violent cure', of murder and genocide as a 'therapeutic imperative.'[74]

All these works illuminate the workings of the Nazi state and its murderous impulses in new and broadening ways. But they too mostly leave unanswered the even more complex and elusive (but nevertheless still extremely necessary) question of *long-term historical influences and dynamics*. More and more, cultural and intellectual historians are drawing our attention to the fact that the genocidal building blocks discussed here – racism, eugenics (or *'Rassehygiene'*), the notion of 'degeneration', the historical role of doctors in the diagnosis and stigmatisation of 'outsiders' (such as the insane, the homosexual, the Gypsy, the Jews) – had their roots not merely in the Nazi experience or even in German history[75] but constituted an integral part of nineteenth and early twentieth century modern *European* self-understanding.[76] These longer-term approaches argue that the *Shoah*, though certainly not inevitable,[77] cannot be regarded as an accident or a self-explanatory bureaucratic exercise or simply the outcome of a brutalising war-dynamic but sprang from far wider structures and inbuilt attitudes.

George Mosse's statement that 'nothing in European history is a stranger to the holocaust'[78] is no doubt somewhat hyperbolic but points to a variety of approaches, best described as the history of 'predisposing structures and mentalities', in explaining Nazism and its atrocities. All of these approaches, to be sure, have their difficulties. More often than not they do not sufficiently establish the transmission belts that concretely relate 'origins' to the act, the mediating links in the chain of historical causality. They tend too to 'indict' abstract categories – 'modernity', 'capitalism', 'medicine',[79] the 'bourgeoisie' – thereby often collapsing distinctive developments into ahistorical generalisations. Nevertheless, precisely because they deal head-on with underlying motivational questions, they at least confront a dimension that functionalists and others leave relatively untapped. In this respect the more conventional modes of historical analysis soon reach their limits and leave one with a sense of frustrating incompleteness.

Mosse's own intellectual career, his life-long search for those aspects of German and European history that relate to the Holocaust, illustrates some of the historiographical shifts explored in this paper.[80] His famous work on the intellectual roots of the Third Reich published in the mid–1960s[81] emphasised three inter-related aspects of the problem. In the first place, anti-Semitism was regarded as definitional of National Socialism: Nazism was, above all, 'the anti-Jewish revolution'. This anti-semitism, moreover, was analysed as a peculiarly German, *voelkisch*, phenomenon, integrally related to its nineteenth century *Sonderweg* history. Finally, both Nazism and the atrocities that accompanied it had to be seen as the radical, irrational *antithesis* of (what was taken to be) rational, liberal, bourgeois modernity.[82] Over the years Mosse has considerably revised these views. In the first place, the notion of a peculiarly illiberal German *Sonderweg* is now dismissed. World War I is now the crucial event, the galvanising turning point. Only that war, defeat and concomitant brutalization propelled *Voelkisch* ideology and racist nationalism – now represented as previously rather fringe phenomena – to the center of national life.[83] Prior to 1914, Mosse has often argued, it was not in Gemany but in France that the most pernicious proto-Fascist, anti-Semitic and racist tendencies were to be found.[84]

Most dramatically, Mosse now views Nazism not as the antithesis but as the essential expression of bourgeois predilections, the very source of its criminality. Mosse's Nazi implements – in radicalised form – that wider European alliance between nationalism and middle-class morality that, from the early nineteenth century on, together defined modern standards of 'respectability', creating ever-tightening distinctions between outsiders and insiders, ideal types and anti-types, 'normality' and 'abnormality'.[85] The new man of National Socialism, Mosse argues, was the (radicalised, corrupt) 'ideal bourgeois'[86] intent on cleansing his world and preserving it against what he regarded as the forces of degeneration. Nazism emerges here as the most radical actualization of a more general middle-class movement toward the classification and denigration of the Other. The euthanasia programme against the handicappped, insane and criminal; the persecution and murder of homosexuals, gypsies and communists and, of course, the 'Final Solution', Mosse insists, were not anti-bourgeois acts but the expressions of middle-class men attempting to maintain the values of manliness, order, cleanliness, hard work, honesty and family life against these outsider groups who, in their eyes, seemed to morally and aesthetically desecrate the basic tenets of bourgeois morality and respectability.

The Holocaust is now directly located within the larger context of the dynamics of European bourgeois society. To be sure, distinctions remain. The project was most fatal to Jews (and to some extent, Gypsies) because they were separate 'people-races' whereas (at least in Germany) other 'abnormals' were partial insiders (non-Jewish asocials, mentally and physically handicapped Germans) or deemed capable in principle of undoing their degeneration (homosexuals). The separateness and vulnerability of the Jew was reinforced, of course, by the long-standing tradition of anti-Semitism. But, again, in this conception it is not the autonomous force of anti-Semitism that is crucial, but rather its encasement within this middle-class hierarchy of values, its integration into a radicalising, systematic racism that created and actualized this genocidal potential.[87]

This is suggestive but is extremely incomplete. If National Socialism represents a 'corruption' and 'radicalization' of middle-class values we need to spell out these transformative processes in detail. Bourgeois morality may perhaps have been characteristically intolerant but it was never before genocidal: knowledge of the relevant radicalizing forces thus become crucial in the metamorphosis. Such forces were almost always – explicitly and implicitly – 'antibourgeois' in nature. Nazism was an uneasy combination of both bourgeois and antibourgeois elements. Embodying this dualism it managed to radically transcend middle-class morality at the same that it paradoxically embodied it. Inheriting older materials and attitudes it also forged them in ways that went beyond all previously established limits. Determining the nature and content of those factors that went into National Socialism's attraction to these outmost limits, its unprecedented transvaluations and boundary-breaking extremities remains a central task in the study of Nazism and the 'Final Solution'.[88]

This is not only a long-term historical issue but also, of course, a phenomenological question: penetrating the inner consciousness and experiences of these elite murderers. This is notoriously difficult. Nevertheless, precisely because of its transgressive extremities unless such explanations are at least attempted a crucial dimension of what is understood by Nazism may be left untapped. There have been various attempts to penetrate this level. Most invoke explicitly non or anti-bourgeois factors. For Hannah Arendt the camps provided the site where the nuclear troops of the totalitarian state and its most radical possibilities could be fully tested. Without its momentum, 'the dominating and the dominated world would only too quickly sink back into the "old bourgeois routine"; after early "excesses", they would succumb to everyday life with its human laws.'[89] As one who experienced such atrocities on his own person, Primo Levi argued that the very essence of Hitlerism was constituted 'by widespread useless violence, as an end in itself, with the sole purpose of creating pain, occasionally having a purpose, yet always redundant, always disproportionate to the purpose itself.'[90]

In 1965, Raul Hilberg, discussing the definitive evolution of anti-Jewish policy into the ultimate 'Final Solution', sought to delineate the taboo-breaking, philosopho-experiential dimensions of this momentous decision:

> Blood was to be shed. This act – this work – was never to be undone. A landmark in history, it was cast in "monumental" proportions ... This was no episode. It was a deed.
>
> In the middle of the end, a final cognition was felt. The perpetrator was gazing upon a forbidden vista. Under the murky huts of Auschwitz, Germans stood alone as they lined up their victims, herding them into gas chambers. These guards were living through something ultimate. Experience *Erlebnis* was reaching its outer limits. The act had become knowledge, and that knowledge was unique, for the sensation of a first discovery is not repeatable.[91]

More recently Saul Friedlander has alluded to the necessity for this level of explanation and, for his part, invoked what he terms *Rausch* (a state of intoxication) that accompanied (and perhaps produced) the staggering dimensions of the event. The perpetrators, he argues, were 'beings seized by a compelling lust for killing on an immense scale, driven by some kind of extraordinary elation in repeating the killing of ever-huger masses of people.'[92] To be sure, as Friedlander himself has pointed out, these kinds of speculations are fraught with intrinsic difficulties;[93] they also stand in contradiction to the aforementioned (including Hilberg's – see note 29) far more prosaic psychological accounts that privilege numbing, rationalization and sheer routinisation in explaining the killings.

As with the question of killer's motivations so too will certain explanations concerning 'deep origins' be more plausible than others. Thus in his recent (and otherwise excellent) ruminations on the moral and philosophical ramifications of the *Shoah*, Berel Lang dubiously indicts the Enlightenment itself. In its totalizing and universalizing rationalism, its principled intolerance of particularities (such as Judaism), he proclaims, it 'establishes a ground of possibility or causal evocation of the Nazi genocide'. Lang does not argue for a relation that is one of direct cause and effect but rather 'that the ideational framework in which the act of the Nazi genocide was set involved – *required* – a number of concepts that had been central in Enlightenment thought.'[94] If the Enlightenment (and especially Immanuel Kant) proposed a universal and rationalist notion of humanity, he argues, those not deemed to possess the appropriate characteristics would be excluded from such a definition of humanity and the way opened to genocide. The Enlightenment concept of humanity 'is inapplicable without a criterion of exclusion (without such a criterion there would be nothing that was not a self).'[95]

But Lang nowhere elicits the connecting links in an argument that presents Nazism as the most radical embodiment and implementer of a world view it utterly despised and against which it set itself in contemptuous opposition. (With Lang there is not even, *à la* Adorno and Horkheimer, a *dialectic* of enlightenment!) He can adopt the position he does in part because he simply dismisses the relevance of an ongoing, ever more radical 'Counter-Enlightement', the intellectual tradition with which Nazism overtly identified itself.[96] But, equally importantly, his argument is based upon a very questionable interpretation of Enlightenment and especially Kantian thought.[97] Leszek Kolakowski has pointed out that it is precisely the particularist jargon of the 'concrete', empirical human being – as a race, class or nation – that permits some sections of humanity to deem others as natural objects while Kant's 'abstract' – i.e. universal and moral – conception of humanity stands as the most potent conceptual safeguard against legitimizing genocide.[98] Moreover, as Emil Fackenheim has written:

> That human personality is an end in itself is the heart and soul of Kant's categorical imperative. As for the Third Reich, *its* heart and soul was the aim to destroy just this principle – by no means only in the case of Jews, 'inferior races', and enemies of the Reich, but also, and perhaps above all, in the case of the 'master race' itself. From the start the great dream was to stamp out personality as the Volk marched in unison at the Fueher's behest ...[99]

Whatever its shortcomings, Lang's emphasis on the Kantian Enlightenment as creating the 'ground of possiblity or causal evocation of the Nazi genocide' stands in line with a larger tradition that asserts – in widely varying, and often quite contradictory, ways – the paradigmatic *modernity* of Nazism and the Holocaust, as an event comprehensible only within its informing technological, bureaucratic and mental structures.[100] This was always in tension with another view of National Socialism as an essentially 'anti-modern' movement.[101] The latter notion fostered a conception of the Holocaust as either ideologically and psychologically *regressive* – 'The holocaust', George Steiner wrote in 1971, 'is a reflex, the more complete for being long inhibited, of natural sensory consciousness, of instinctual and polytheistic and animist needs' [102] – or, at best, as embodying a self-destroying contradiction: 'Industrialization', Wolfgang Sauer wrote, 'was sought in order to destroy industrial society, but since there was no alternative to industrial society, the regime must eventually destroy itself. This was the situation of Nazism. The Nazis built an industrial machinery to murder the Jews, but once in operation the machine would have had to continue and would have ruined, indirectly at least, first the regime of civilized society and then the fascist regime. Industrialization of mass murder was, thus, the only logical answer Nazism had to the problems of industrial society.'[103]

In his recent work the sociologist Zygmunt Bauman has sought to systematise the view in which the Holocaust is regarded neither as regressive nor even as dialectically in contradiction with modernity but rather as one of its inherent, quintessential possibilities. It flowed, he writes, from 'everything we know about our civilization, its priorities, its immanent vision of the world' (p. 8). The Nazi murder of the Jews must not be considered to be a 'matter of pathology' but rather viewed from within 'the context of cultural tendencies and technical achievements of modernity.'[104] Nor, he argues, must the *Shoah* be regarded either as simply a Jewish tragedy, the culmination of European Christian anti-Semitism, or as a purely *German* crime for such analyses would make it 'comfortably uncharacteristic and sociologically inconsequential.' (p. 1) It must, rather, be comprehended as the result of a dialectical combination between uniqueness and normality: *'the Holocaust was an outcome of a unique encounter between factors by themselves quite ordinary and common.'*[105]

Such analyses provide valuable antidotes to excessive *Sonderweg* interpretations, reminding us that it was not only the 'abnormal' course of German history or peculiarly German national characteristics, but also 'universal', generalised aspects of human behaviour that under certain conditions allowed the event to occur, and rendered it a deeply 'human' possibility. (An even older scholarly theory, that of mass society, similarly exculpated the German historical experience. 'It was not any German tradition as such', Hannah Arendt wrote in 1945, 'but the violation of all traditions which brought about Nazism.)[106]

Studies that emphasise (the variously understood) long-term factors and the more generalised 'universal' or 'human' structures seem to me to be an indispensable ingredient in grasping the deeper motivational dimensions underlying Nazism and its atrocities. Yet if such generalised explanations – 'Enlightenment', 'the bourgeoisie' – are to be in any way satisfactory they must demonstrate the mediated connections, the transmission belts and concrete ties linking such general structures with the actual event or the particular context in which it unfolded. Failure to do so means, as Burgleigh and Wipperman argue in terms of Bauman's work, that 'the unique horrors of the Third Reich disappear within a fog of relativising, sociological rhetoric. The fact of Nazi Germany's murder of millions of Jews, Sinti and Roma, and others at a specific point in time is obscured by talk of general genocidal impulses allegedly latent beneath the thin civilised crust of all "modern" societies.'[107]

This is not the place the place to discuss the manifold pitfalls that characterize those analyses of Nazism that mechanically emphasize its relationship to the problematics of 'modernity'[108] or 'capitalism' – too often they carry blatant ideological baggage and advocate simplistic contemporary political messages in which the actual historical atrocities of National Socialism seem to meld indiscriminately with present problems, practices and the allegedly murderous nature of our own civilization.[109]

Nevertheless, it is essential to mention the most controversial current project (undertaken by a number of younger German historians[110]) that regards the 'Final Solution' (and related National Socialist crimes) as an eminently 'rational' expression of the logic of capitalism, a 'normal' variation in its – always potentially murderous – process of modernisation. For Goetz Aly and Susanne Heim, the genocide of the Jews is to be located not within the realms of pathology and political irrationality but rather as a 'sensible' means of structural and developmental planning. The 'Final Solution', they hold, was grounded upon rational utilitarian-economic and power-political considerations and should be regarded as the outcome of specialised thinking on economics, population policy and *Ostraum* planning.[111] In this view it was the (relatively lowly placed) 'experts' – demographic scientists, economists, geographers and so on – who were the practical initiators of the Final Solution. They were not primarily ideologically inspired but motivated by considerations of 'pragmatic rationality ... They did not revel in myths of blood and race, but thought in categories of large-scale economic spaces, structural renewal, and overpopulation with its attendant food problems; and they were resolved to effectuate more rational methods of production, standardize products, and improve social structures.'

Between 1939 and 1941, Aly and Heim argue, the experts devised the genocide of the Jews 'for logical reasons and implemented it in conjunction with the war against Russia. The "final solution" evolved from studies and proposals of subordinate planning officials, gradually moving from the lower to the higher bureaucratic echelons. ... these planners ... did not themselves make the decisions but suggested them to superiors.'[112] Only by radically dealing with Poland's endemic overpopulation problem, they believed, could the massive 'Germanic development program' be undertaken. Such a goal could be achieved 'if they found a way to eliminate the sizeable Jewish minority from the population.' Polish Jews were unredeemably poor and 'the ghetto economy was anachronistic. It tied down resources. ... without even remotely attaining the desired modern level of production. The deportation and the killing of unemployed Jews meant a massive saving ... Overpopulation theories and ruthless economic rationalization provided an immanently rational reason for the destruction of the Jews. This was true in the summer of 1941 when the Nazi regime pushed its utopian social redevelopment schemes at the height of its power; and this remained true even when its military successes took a turn for the worse.'[113]

This thesis, of course, turns on its head the traditional view that the essence of the Final Solution was to be found in its determinedly *anti-economic* character. Though Aly and Heim have been taken to task for this (and many other aspects of their thesis),[114] their delineation of the role of social and economic planners, their argument that the *Endloesung* took place against the backdrop of a wider Nazi *Ostpolitik*, and the suggestion that there is an economic dimension to the atrocities may well merit further consideration. To be sure, such reconsideration will have to take into account the fact that the 'Final Solution' was not limited to poor Polish Jews and explain why Jews were obsessively rounded up from all over Europe (and beyond). The economic profiles of these Jews were as a rule quite different from Polish Jewry and, more often than not, they played essentially productive roles in far more developed economies. What is most problematic about the Aly–Heim analysis, however, is the dubious explanatory framework in which they cast their work. Precisely because they analyse the problem in terms of the dynamics of capitalist modernisation, they tend to regard its 'imperatives' as somehow autonomous, as a primary force, rather than as an economic system interacting with, and responsive to, the policies of political elites. Particularly within the Nazi state, such political and ideological guidelines were crucial. The actions of those lower-level functionaries and experts operated within a specific ideological and political setting. Their perceptions and, indeed, the very possibility of selecting victims and making particular policy choices (such as genocide) cannot plausibly be seen outside of the official racial–biological policies prescribed by the State. It was not, as their account implies, capitalism that *necessitated* the transition to extermination but rather the overarching ideological framework that, in the context of an ever more brutalising war, allowed genocide to become an option, a possibility, in the first place.

In effect the work of Aly and Heim work exemplifies a problem that characterizes many of the tendencies that we have studied in this essay. The attempt to re-place the Holocaust within broader, informing structures and relate it to more universal structures, salutary as many of these efforts may be, often does not sufficiently explain why, to begin with, the Nazi elite, the critical makers and movers of policy, were so fixated on the 'Jewish Question'. On that level, this galvanising anti-Jewish obsession still requires special attention and explanation. The road that led to the death camps – those utterly unique institutions – was certainly twisted, cobbled with contingencies and part of a general structure but, nevertheless, inconceivable without this factor.

To be sure, the nature, continuity, distribution and historical origins of this anti-semitic obsession continues to be variously interpreted and a matter of much debate. Thus, in a provocative recent work Paul Lawrence Rose has attempted to identify the specifically 'German' and radical nature of this obsession. He portrays a peculiar non-liberal, revolutionary vision that transcended all conventional 'left–right' distinctions and that fused 'revolutionary' and 'reactionary' categories. This was a broadly enunicated 'German' ideology that consistently regarded the Jews as the crucial separatist force, the central impediment, frustrating the attainment of both national and, indeed, 'human' redemption. It was not, Rose argues, the application of biological theories but the advent of these new visions of revolution and redemption that modernized the old Jew-hatred. For the realisation of these redemptive ideals, the possibility of self-fulfillment itself, became inextricably dependent upon the extirpation (variously and ambiguously conceived) of Jewish being.[115] In rather controversial fashion, Rose stresses the long-term nature of this *Sonderweg* political tradition, linking not only Kant to Wagner but, indeed, Luther and Hitler.[116] Shulamit Volkov, on the other hand, has emphasised the discontinuities between what she takes to be an essentially old-order, 'written' anti-Semitism of the *Kaiserreich* and the emergent, post-War radicalised Nazi version rooted in a 'spoken' demagogic mass-culture of 'action'.[117] However one views the roots of this hatred, there is no doubt about the fact that Hitler and the top leadership directed their most vicious animus against the Jews. In their eyes, they represented the very negation of the governing racial scheme, the embodiments, as it were, of an insidious unnatural principle, of 'anti-race.'[118]

Future historiography will have to better comprehend and integrate into the wider frame the particular nature of Nazi anti-Jewish fixations. Nevertheless the current emphasis on informing context, the activating mechanisms that translated such impulses into organized mass murder, still seems to me to be of considerable importance. For it suggests that only because Jew-hatred operated within a particular, official matrix, part of the continuum of racism (bereft of any idea of overall 'human' redemption, Paul Rose's thesis notwithstanding) that it could assume its unprecedented genocidal form. The overall dynamic of this state-sanctioned ideology provided the essential frame whereby the 'Final Solution' became conceivable in the first place and thereafter – however fitful and contingent the process may have been – translated into a horrible reality. The interlaced connection, the interdependence, between these two factors was made crystal clear by Hitler (without whom this event still remains virtually inconceivable) at the end of his *Political Testament* written at the moment that his Reich was being utterly demolished. 'Above all', he wrote, 'I charge the leadership of the nation, as well as its followers, to a rigorous adherence to our racial laws and to a merciless resistance against the poisoner of all peoples – international Jewry.'[119]

We need, however, to place these historiographical developments, including our own speculations and preferences, into perspective. Jacques Derrida has written that we do not 'as yet know how to think what Nazism is. The task remains before us ...'[120] It would be foolhardy to speculate on the future directions historiography may take. Nevertheless, it is dubious in the extreme that we will somehow ever achieve a definitive grasp of 'what Nazism is' and that historiographies of the future will yield 'ultimate' interpretive conclusions. I say this not because I regard Nazism and its atrocities as in some deep way 'incomprehensible' or because I adhere to some post-modernist notion of historical indeterminacy but because there can be no such thing as 'closure' within the ongoing historical enterprise. This certainly will apply to such a mulifarious phenomenon as Nazism and so complex and dense an event as the *Shoah* where no theoretical or methodological monopoly can possibly be expected to pertain. Rather, we can be sure that the field will continue to be fluid, marked by an ongoing plurality of approaches and perspectives that reflect not only the complexity of the event itself but also the multiple ways in which contemporary experience inevitably reshapes our questions about, and understandings of, the historical past. Surely the task now must be to keep an open scholarly, and always vigilantly critical, eye on such proceedings.

Notes and References

1 Culture and Catastrophe

1 For an anthology – and analysis – of the culture National Socialism sought to propagate (in both the 'high' and everyday sense) see George L. Mosse, *Nazi Culture: Intellectual, Cultural and Social Life in the Third Reich* (New York, 1966).

2 These themes are developed in more detail in Chapters 3 and 7.

3 On this problematic, see Israel Bartal, '"The Heavenly City of Germany" and Absolutism à la Mode d'Autriche: The Rise of the Haskalah in Galicia', in Jacob Katz (ed.), *Toward Modernity: The European Jewish Model* (New Brunswick and Oxford, 1987), pp. 33–42.

4 On the self-creation of German Jewry within the German high cultural image, see David Sorkin, *The Transformation of German Jewry 1780–1840* (New York and Oxford, 1987) and George L. Mosse, *German Jews Beyond Judaism* (Bloomington, 1985). On anti-Semitic perceptions of Jewish cultural dominance within Germany, see Chapter 3.

5 See *At the Mind's Limits: Contemplations by a Survivor on Auschwitz and its Realities*, translated by Sidney Rosenfeld and Stella P. Rosenfeld (Bloomington, 1980), p. 8. Amery emigrated to Belgium in 1938 whereupon he adopted his new name, an anagram of the original Mayer. Hans became Jean. He joined the Resistance Movement and was caught in 1943, tortured by the SS and survived the following years in the camps.

6 *Ibid.* The quotes appear on pp. 10, 12 and 19 respectively.

7 See Nico Rost, *Goethe in Dachau*, with a foreword by Anna Seghers (Frankfurt am Main, 1983). This was published originally in 1948.

8 *Ibid.* For instance the entry of 6 February, 1945, p. 179: 'Sometimes I have the feeling as if Goethe has not been through the hell of human thought as have the likes of Hoelderlin, and van Gogh, Poe and Dostojevski, and that he is lacking something that characterises the really great!' Such criticism of course had nothing to do with either an indictment of thought and culture in general or German culture in particular.

9 The more complete comparison reads thus: 'Dachau was one of the first National-Socialist concentration camps and thus had, if you will, a tradition; Auschwitz had been created only in 1940 and to the end was subject to improvisations from day to day. In Dachau the *politi-*

cal element predominated among the inmates; in Auschwitz, however, by far the great majority of prisoners consisted of totally unpolitical Jews and politically very inconstant Poles. The internal administration of Dachau lay for the most part in the hands of political prisoners; in Auschwitz German professional criminals set the tone. In Dachau there was a camp library; for the ordinary inmate of Auschwitz a book was something hardly still imaginable. In Dachau ... the prisoners had in principle the possibility to oppose the SS state, the SS structure, with an intellectual structure. That gave the intellect there a *social function*, even if this maintained itself essentially in political, religious, or ideological ways and only in rare cases, as that of Nico Rost, at the same time philosophically and esthetically. In Auschwitz, however, the intellectual person was isolated, thrown back entirely upon himself. Thus the problem of the confrontation of intellect and horror appeared in a more radical form ... in a *purer* form. In Auschwitz the intellect was nothing more than itself and there was no chance to apply it to a social structure, no matter how insufficient, no matter how concealed it may have been.' See *At the Mind's Limits*, p. 6.

10 Primo Levi, *Survival in Auschwitz: The Nazi Assault on Humanity*, translated by Stuart Woolf (New York and London, 1976), Chapter 11. The quote appears on p. 102. The work was originally published in Italian in 1947.

11 Zvi Jagendorf, 'Primo Levi Goes for Soup and Remembers Dante', *Raritan*, 12 (no. 4, Spring 1933) pp. 31–51. In a sensitively crafted exposition Jagendorf demonstrates the layered complexities, the numerous relevancies and analogies, contained in this act of Dante remembrance.

12 *Ibid.*, p. 49.

13 For Levi's disagreement with Amery – 'To argue with a dead man is embarrassing and not very loyal. It is all the more so when the absent one is a potential friend and a most valuable interlocutor' – see Chapter 6, 'The Intellectual in Auschwitz', in *The Drowned and the Saved*, translated by Raymond Rosenthal (London, 1988), pp. 102–20. The quotes appear on p. 102 and p. 111.

14 Michael Andre Bernstein reports an incident in which a colleague of his gave a talk on Levi to a local Jewish community several members of whom bitterly attacked the Dante chapter for this reason. See his *Foregone Conclusions: Against Apocalyptic History* (Berkeley, 1994), pp. 49–50.

15 Hannah Arendt, *The Origins of Totalitarianism* (Cleveland, 1963), p. 447.

16   See the chapter 'A Season in Hell' in Steiner's *In Bluebeard's Castle: Some Notes Towards the Re-definition of Culture* (London, 1971), especially pp. 47–8.

17   Levi, 'The Intellectual in Auschwitz', p. 112.

18   Much of the following analysis is culled from Mann's talk 'Germany and the Germans' (May 29, 1945), *Thomas Mann's addresses delivered at the Library of Congress, 1942–1949* (Washington, 1963), pp. 51, 65.

19   See the translation by Walter D. Morris, *Reflections of a Nonpolitical Man* (New York, 1983). In this wartime tract Mann glorifies many of the same traits he later associated with Geman demonism and their degeneration into atrocities committed by National Socialism. For an analysis of this work in its original context, see my *The Nietzsche Legacy in Germany, 1890–1990* (Berkeley and London, 1992), pp. 148–53.

20   Critics, especially Marxists, often took Mann to task for maintaining these discredited categories, employing suspect epiphenomenal notions and bourgeois mystifications such as the 'daemonic.' The East German Marxist critic, Stanislaw Lem, wrote of Dr. Faustus that fascism was an impersonal mechanism not a mythical devil, and its meaning could not be dislosed by reference to some traditional higher cultural order. Western critics, like T.J. Reed, respond that the devil–Faust myth is animated by the Nietzschean Dionysian one, transformed into a psychological irrational force that provides greater plausibility and that Mann employs mythological themes in dynamic rather than static fashion and as a critical tool to analyze forces observable in man and society. See his *Thomas Mann: The Uses of Tradition* (Oxford, 1974), pp. 393ff.

21   Mann, 'Germany and the Germans', p. 64.

22   *Ibid.* The respective quotes may be found on pp. 51, 64, 61.

23   *Ibid.*, p. 51. There, already in 1945, Mann outlined in theoretical terms what his Dr. Faustus was to achieve in more strictly literary fashion. 'And the Devil, Luther's Devil, Faust's Devil, strikes me as a very Germanic figure, and the pact with him, the Satanic covenant, to win all treasures and power on earth for a time at the cost of the soul's salvation, strikes me as something exceedingly typical of German nature ... .isn't this the right moment to see Germany ... .is literally being carried off by the Devil? ... .[Faust] should have been musical. ... Music is a demonic realm.'

24   For Lukács's appreciation of Mann as the great realist of the bourgeois world especially its German incarnation see his *Essays on Thomas*

Mann, translated by Stanley Mitchell (London, 1964). Lukács, as we know, was exceedingly Orthodox – in many ways he even defined the Orthodoxy – but he differed from many other Marxists in his positive reading of the critical nature of Dr. Faustus: 'Mann's devil is ... a historical critic of the entire bourgeois culture of imperialism' (p. 76).

25 Lukács sought to trace the forms of bourgeois reactionary irrationalism, especially its German centre and to document 'Germany's path to Hitler in the sphere of philosophy ... how this concrete path is reflected in philosophy, and how philosophical formulations, as an intellectual mirroring of Germany's concrete development towards Hitler helped to speed up the process.' See *The Destruction of Reason*, translated by Peter Palmer (Atlantic Highlands, NJ,1981), p. 4.

26 Lukács consistently repeated this line, lumping radically disparate figures into an essentially undifferentiated irrationalist-reactionary pattern. As he wrote elsewhere, 'Schopenhauer and Wagner, Nietzsche and Freud, Heidegger and Klages are without exceptions Germans, international leaders in a much larger sense than the reactionary ideologists of other nations. The political and social reaction of the world acquires its highest (so far), its "classical" form in Hitler's Germany.' See 'The Tragedy of Modern Art' in Lukács, *Essays on Thomas Mann*, p. 95.

27 Lukács, *The Destruction of Reason*, p. 753.

28 See the translation by John Cumming, *Dialectic of Enlightenment* (New York, 1972).

29 For a still reliable and interesting exposition of this work see Ch. VIII of Martin Jay, *The Dialectical Imagination: A History of the Frankfurt School and the Institute of Social Research, 1923–1950* (New York, 1973).

30 *Dialectic of Enlightenment*, p. 44.

31 See the critical remarks by J.G. Merquior, *Western Marxism* (London, 1986), Chapter III, especially p. 115.

32 The lack of clarity concerning such definitions (and links) stems from the masterwork itself. As Leszek Kolakowski has noted, Adorno and Horkheimer's 'concept of "enlightenment" is a fanciful, unhistorical hybrid composed of everything they dislike: positivism, logic, deductive and empirical science, capitalism, the money power, mass culture, liberalism, and Fascism.' See his *Main Currents of Marxism*, Vol.3., translated by P.S. Falla (Oxford, 1978), p. 376.

33 See Chapter 7, 'Genocide and Kant's Enlightenment' in Berel Lang, *Act and Idea in the Nazi Genocide* (Chicago, 1990), especially pp. 169, 190.

34   This question is more fully and critically discussed in Chapter 7.

35   See Kolakowski, *Main Currents of Marxism,* Vol. 3, p. 372.

36   See his 'After Auschwitz' in the 'Meditation on Metaphysics', Part III
     of *Negative Dialectics*, translated by E.B. Ashton (New York, 1973).
     The German original was published in 1966.

37   This famous phrase is to be found in his essay 'Cultural Criticism and
     Society' in *Prisms*, translated by Samuel and Sherry Weber (Cambridge,
     Mass., 1983), p. 34.

38   See 'Herbert Marcuse and Martin Heidegger: An Exchange of Letters',
     New German Critique (no. 53, Spring/Summer 1991), pp. 28–32.

39   See Richard Rorty's fascinating essay, 'Heidegger, Kundera, and
     Dickens', in his *Essays on Heidegger and Others* (Cambridge, 1991).
     As Rorty reminds us (p. 72), Heidegger remarked that the 'forgetful-
     ness of Being' may 'easily go hand in hand with a guaranteed living
     standard for all men, and with a uniform state of happiness for all men.'

40   As Friedrich George Juenger – Ernst's brother – put it a few years after
     the war, the struggle against nihilism and technology was still at its
     height. See his *Nietzsche* (Frankfurt am Main, 1949), p. 47. For a recent
     variation on the theme, see Gerd Begfleth (ed.), *Zur Kritik der
     Palavernden Aufklaerung* (Munich, 1984). See my *The Nietzsche
     Legacy*, pp. 269–71, 303, 306–7.

41   Martin Heidegger, 'The Recorate 1933/34: Facts and Thoughts', *Review
     of Metaphysics,* 38 (1984/85), pp. 484–485.

42   These comments are to be found in 'Herbert Marcuse and Martin
     Heidegger: An Exchange of Letters', pp. 28–32.

43   See his 'Work and Weltanschauung: The Heidegger Controversy from
     a German Perspective', *Critical Inquiry*, 15 (Winter 1989), p. 453.

44   See Hannah Arendt, 'Approaches to the German Problem', *Partisan
     Review*, Vol. XII, no. 1 (Winter, 1945), pp. 93–106. The quote appears
     on p. 97. The attraction to Nazism, Arendt contended, was 'its frank
     recognition of this vacuum.' This essay has now been reproduced in
     Hannah Arendt, *Essays in Understanding 1930–1954* (ed. Jerome
     Kohn) (New York, 1994). For elaboration of this theme see Chapter 6
     of this volume.

45   For an interesting review of these theories and their problems, see Leon
     Bramson, *The Political Context of Sociology* (Princeton, 1961).

46   See the fascinating and contentious article by Ernest Gellner, 'From
     Koenigsberg to Manhattan (or Hannah, Rahel, Martin and Elfried or
     Thy Neigbour's *Gemeinschaft*)' in his *Culture, Identity, and Politics*
     (Cambridge, 1987), p. 89. Arendt, Gellner argues, was perfectly placed
     to provide a historical account of these events. Her strange refusal, to

do so, he argues, stemmed from the fact that Nazism (amongst other things) incorporated a romanticism to which she herself remained – however critically – wedded. She sought in other words to give such traditions a clean bill of health (totalitarianism as so novel and alien was 'not really after all very much concerned with *us*' [p. 86]). Her 'daemonic' depiction, her 'mystical over-dramatisation', Gellner argues, 'is itself very much in the romantic tradition – even if here, ironically, it is used to exculpate romanticism and philosophy from having fathered the allegedly alien evil' (p. 85). There may be something to this. It is true that conventional historical explanations may be able to account for novel occurrences but they may also require entirely new, alternative articulations. This is what Arendt sought to do.

47 See the 'Preface' to Steiner's *Language and Silence: Essays on Language, Literature and the Inhuman* (New York, 1977), pp. viii-ix.

48 *Ibid*. Steiner himself is a fine example of both this self-admitted Eurocentrism as well as its saving critical capacity. 'I realize that ... barbarism and political savagery are endemic in human affairs ... But I think there is hypocrisy in the imagination that would claim universal immediacy, that would seek impartial appropriation throughout the provocations of all history and all places. My own consciousness is possessed by the eruption of barbarism in modern Europe ... I do not claim for this hideousness any singular privilege; but this is the crisis of rational, humane expectation which has shaped my own life and which I am most directly concerned' (p. viii).

49 Even before Auschwitz, Juergen Habermas writes, Fascism and National Socialism 'issued waves not only of irritation but also of fascinated excitement. There was no theory of contemporaneity not affected to its core by the penetrating force of fascism.' See his 'Between Eroticism and General Economics: Georges Bataille', *The Philosophical Discourse of Modernity*, trans. Frederick Lawrence (Cambridge, Mass. 1937) p. 216.

50 On this see Saul Friedlander, 'The Shoah in Present Historical Consciousness', in *Memory, History, and the Extermination of the Jews of Europe* (Bloomington, 1993), especially p. 50. This essay is perhaps the deepest and most suggestive piece written on the topic. I am very indebted to it.

51 The phrase 'symbolic code words' is Amery's, p. vii. Amery too exemplifies the kinds of categories that characterise this discourse and its attempts to grapple with the phenomenon. National Socialist abominations, he writes, 'took place among the German people, a people of high intelligence, industrial capability, and unequaled cultural wealth

– among the people of "Poets and Thinkers." For me this is a fact that until this day remains unclarified and, despite all the diligent historical, psychological, sociological, and political studies that have appeared and will yet appear, at bottom probably cannot be clarified./ On the one hand there is really nothing that provides enlightenment on the eruption of radical Evil in Germany, and on the other hand (despite Chile, etc. etc.) this Evil really is singular and irreducible in its total inner logic and its accursed rationality. For this reason all of us are still faced with a dark riddle. We know that it did not happen in a developing country, nor as the direct continuation of a tyrannical regime, as in the Soviet Union, nor in the bloody struggle of a revolution fearing for its existence, as in the France of Robespierre. It happened in Germany. It issued, so to speak, through spontaneous generation, from a womb that bore it as a perversion' (p. viii).

52   Once again, it was Hannah Arendt who provided an intellectually coherent articulation to this generally felt intuition. 'Radical evil', she wrote, 'had now made itself manifest even though the entire philosophical tradition of the West had not been able to really conceive of it. Christian theology had provided the Devil himself with a celestial origin while Kant – who had originated the concept – rationalized its existence by attributing it to a "perverted ill will" traceable to comprehensible motives. 'Therefore, we actually have nothing to fall back on in order to understand a phenomenon that nevertheless confronts us with its overpowering reality and breaks down all standards we know ... Until now the totalitarian belief that everything is possible seems to have proved only that everything can be destroyed. Yet, in their effort to prove that everything is possible, totalitarian regimes have discovered without knowing it that there are crimes which men can neither punish nor forgive. When the impossible was made possible it became the unpunishable, unforgivable absolute evil which could no longer be understood and explained by the evil motives of self-interest, greed, covetousness, resentment, lust for power, and cowardice.' See *The Origins of Totalitarianism*, p. 443 and p. 459. I have inverted the order of the quote here. Arendt, it is true, was talking of the overall totalitarian project, including the Soviet model. But both in this work itself as well as in her other books and personal correspondence 'Auschwitz' remained the great rupture, the most grotesque incarnation of what she took to be 'radical evil.'

53   For some general comments on this (although from a different point of view) see Yehuda Bauer, 'Conclusion: The significance of the Final Solution', in David Cesarani (ed.), *The Final Solution: Origins and implementation* (London and New York, 1994), pp. 300–9.

54 Hobsbawm made these remarks in a *The Late Show* interview (the week of October 24, 1994) with Michael Ignatieff. See 'NB' by D.S. in *The Times Literary Supplement* (October 28, 1994), p. 16. To be fair to Hobsbawm, his brilliant new book *Age of Extremes: The Short Twentieth Century 1914–1991* (London, 1994) is free of such apologetics and candidly faces the fact of Stalinist brutality. See especially chapter 13, 'Real Socialism'.

55 Culture, Adorno wrote in the lines preceding this quote, 'abhors stench because it stinks – because, as Brecht put it in a magnificent line, its mansion is built of dogshit. Years after that line was written Auschwitz demonstrated irrefutably that culture has failed.

That this could happen in the midst of the traditions of philosophy of art, and of the enlightening sciences says more than that these traditions and their spirit lacked the power to take hold of men and work a change in them. There is untruth in those fields themselves, in the autarky that is empathically claimed for them.' See *Negative Dialectics*, op. cit., pp. 366–7.

56 For a good explication of these processes – not just in Germany – see Charles S. Maier, *The Unmasterable Past: History, Holocaust, and German National Identity* (Cambridge, Mass., 1988).

57 The main documents of the *Historikerstreit* are reproduced in *Yad Vashem Studies*, XIX (1988) and *New German Critique*, no. 44 (Spring/Summer, 1988). See too my 'History, Politics, and National Memory: The German *Historikerstreit*', *Survey of Jewish Affairs* (1988), pp. 222–38.

58 Dan Diner, 'Between Aporia and Apology: On the Limits of Historicizing National Socialism', in Peter Baldwin, *Reworking the Past: Hitler, the Holocaust, and the Historian's Debate* (Boston, 1990), p. 144. See Chapter 7 for a more detailed discussion of this issue.

59 Werner Hamacher, 'Journals, Politics: Notes on Paul de Man's Wartime Journalism', in Werner Hamacher, Neil Hertz and Thomas Keenan (ed.), *Responses: On Paul de Man's Wartime Journalism*, trans. Susan Bernstein (Lincoln, Nebraska, 1989), p. 459.

60 See his 'A Past that will not Pass Away', *Yad Vashem Studies*, XIX (1988), p. 71.

61 See Alf Luedtke, '"Coming to Terms with the Past": Illusions of Remembering, Ways of Forgetting Nazism in West Germany', *Journal of Modern History*, 65 (September 1993), pp. 542–72.

62 'Auschwitz cannot be explained', writes Elie Wiesel, because 'the Holocaust transcends history', in 'Trivialising the Holocaust: Semi-Fact and Semi-Fiction', *New York Times* (April 16, 1978). The historian Nora

Levin wrote: 'The Holocaust refuses to go the way of most history, not only because of the magnitude of the destruction – the murder of six million Jews – but because the events surrounding it are in a very real sense incomprehensible.' See her *The Holocaust: The Destruction of European Jewry*, 1919–1945 (New York, 1973), pp. xi-xii.

63   Elisabeth Domansky, '"Kristallnacht", the Holocaust and German Unity: The Meaning of November 9 as an Anniversary in Germany', *History and Memory*, 4 (no. 1, Spring/Summer 1992), pp. 60–94. The quote appears on pp. 78–79.

64   On this phenomenon, see Pierre Vidal-Naquet, *Assassins of Memory: Essays on the Denial of the Holocaust*, translated by Jeffrey Mehlman (New York, 1992); Deborah Lipstadt, *Denying the Holocaust: The Growing Assault on Truth and Memory* (New York, 1993).

65   As Raul Hilberg noted in the Preface to his 1961 masterpiece (referring to common modes of perception and not realising what was to come): 'The destruction of the European Jews has not yet been absorbed as a historical event. This does not mean a general denial that millions of people have disappeared, nor does it imply a serious doubt that masses of these people were shot in ditches and gassed in camps. But acknowledgment of a fact does not signify its acceptance in an academic sense.' See his *The Destruction of the European Jews* (New York, 1973), p. v.

66   As Vidal-Naquet writes: 'There is currently no historian, to be sure, who is prepared to retain the figure of four million human beings disappearing in Auschwitz. A million deaths is a reasonable – however enormous – hypothesis. But it is true that the figure of four million is officially indicated all over Auschwitz through the auspices of the Poles, and Claude Lanzmann was wrong to write that "the most serious estimates hover around three and a half million."' See *Assassins of Memory*, pp. 139–140.

67   For a thorough multi-sided examination of this question see Saul Friedlander (ed.), *Probing the Limits of Representation: Nazism and the 'Final Solution'* (Cambridge, Mass., 1992).

68   See his *The Postmodern Condition: A Report on Knowledge* (Minneapolis, 1984), p. 81.

69   *Ibid.*, p. 82.

70   Terry Eagleton, 'Awakening from Modernity', *Times Literary Supplement* (February 20, 1987), p. 194. One should, however, dismiss absurd accusations that deconstruction is in some way itself Nazi. One should also be wary of over-simple statements that question deconstruction because it 'renders theoretically unintelligible basic moral

terms such as "good" and "evil" ... does not permit us to utter the sentence "Nazism is evil" with any theoretical justification.' See Charles L. Griswold's letter, 'Deconstruction, The Nazis and Paul de Man' in *New York Review of Books* (October 12, 1989), p. 69. For a reading of the ethical moment as essential to the deconstructive project, see Simon Critchley, *The Ethics of Deconstruction: Derrida and Levinas* (Oxford: Blackwell, 1992).

71 Lyotard, *The Post-Modern Condition*, p. 81.

72 The monumental-didactic mode that is most suited to the code's moral tone, writes Saul Friedlander, poses a fundamental dissonance to contemporary sensibility 'as the ironic mode is an essential dimension of this sensibility and as the disconnection betwen moral judgement, aesthetic norms, and intellectual analysis represents a strong component of present-day Western culture.' See his *History, Memory*, p. 55.

73 See Shoshana Felman and Dori Laub, *Testimony: Crises of Witnessing in Literature, Pyschoanalysis, and History* (New York and London, 1992), p. 194.

74 *Ibid.*, p. 201. Felman's italics. The point of prooflesness is here simply stated rather than argued. Indeed, Felman quotes Robert Faurisson a leading 'Holocaust-denier' to the effect that after perusing thousands of documents he could not find a single deportee 'capable of proving to me that he had really seen, with his own eyes, a gas chamber.' (Claude Lanzmann – whose film *Shoah* Felman incisively analyzes in terms of the problem of witnessing and recounting – did bring forward such a witness.) Paradoxically, Felman's denial of the reliability – even the possibility – of such witnessing replicates 'revisionist' logic. This aside, need one point out that the crises and 'cryptic' forms of narrative that Felman directly links to the *Shoah* took shape long before the 1940s. Indeed, they were constitutive of much-earlier modernist writers such as Kafka, James, Joyce and Proust. Felman has put the cart before the horse. The trends she describes are less a result of the Holocaust than an important prism by which that event has become to be perceived. (To be sure, the *Shoah* has reinforced such perceptions but hardly accounts for their genesis.)

75 *Ibid.*, p. 160.

76 Noel Malcolm puts the tension thus: 'To describe the Holocaust as a unique outburst of evil is to make it inexplicable, but to try to explain it is to risk reducing it to the level of ordinary events.' See 'Selective Memories', *Times Literary Supplement* (October 28 1994), p. 32.

77 'Historians', Michael Marrus writes, 'are used to tramping over their fields while suspending judgements on the fundamental issues that are

ultimately at stake . ...We simply do the best we can, knowing that our efforts are necessarily imperfect, incomplete and inadequate.' See *The Holocaust in History* (London, 1989), p. 7.

78 In general see Paul de Man, *Wartime Journalism, 1940–1942*, (ed. Werner Hamacher, Neil Hertz, and Thomas Kennan) (Lincoln, 1988) and (by the same editors and press, 1989), *Responses: On Paul de Man's Wartime Journalism*.

79 Felman and Laub, *Testimony*, p. 139.

80 *Ibid.*, p. 152.

81 See Hartman's 'Judging Paul de Man' in his *Minor Prophecies: The Literary Essay in the Culture Wars* (Cambridge, Mass., 1991), p. 125.

82 See La Capra's insightful comments in 'The Personal, the Political and the Textual: Paul de Man as Object of Transference', in *History and Memory,* 4 (no. 1, Spring/Summer 1992), esp. pp. 10–20.

83 Frederick Crews, 'The Revenge of the Repressed: Part II', *The New York Review of Books* (December 1, 1994), p. 54.

84 Felman and Laub, *Testimony*, p. 196.

85 For just one example, see Gertrude Himmelfarb's review of such post-modernist trends, *On Looking into the Abyss* (New York, 1994) and Alan Ryan's critique: 'Himmelfarb argues against the goings-on she dislikes by trotting out the Holocaust ...', in 'The Two Himmelfarbs', *TLS* (August 5, 1994), p. 7. I have discovered David H.Hirsch's, *The Deconstruction of Literature: Criticism after Auschwitz* (Hanover and London, 1991) too late to consider here.

86 For an advocacy of this kind of thinking as a way of thinking through the Holocaust and for its decidedly new relevance in (and for) Israel see the (Hebrew) article by Michal Ben-Naftali-Berkowitz, 'The Israeli Philosophers and the Holocaust', *Teoria V'Bikoret*, 4 (Autumn, 1993).

87 As Yehuda Bauer, 'Conclusion', in Cesarani (ed.), *The Final Solution* (London and New York, 1994) (p. 304) notes, the lessons of the Holocaust – and by extension, of the whole Nazi experience – are essentially open to change: 'each generation will look at the event from its own perspective and will derive different lessons. That of course means that it is not the Holocaust itself that is the lesson, but the lesson is in the eye of the beholder, depends on his or her circumstances and will be applicable in an environment that will hopefully radically differ from that of the Holocaust.'

88 See Meinecke, *The German Catastrophe* (Boston, 1950) and Gerhard Ritter, *The German Problem* (Columbus, 1965). The original German edition of Meinecke's book was published in 1946; Ritter's work was based upon his *Europe and the German Question* that appeared in 1948.

89 Karl Jaspers, *The Question of German Guilt*, translated by E.B. Ashton (New York, 1947), pp. 17ff. The quote appears on pp. 20–1.

90 A comparative perspective may be revealing here. In Japan, as Ian Buruma has recently pointed out, there is a ubiquitous indifference or denial of crimes committed. The case was quite different in Germany, he argues, where the 'war was not only remembered on television, on the radio, in community halls, schools and museums; it was actively worked on, labored, rehearsed. One sometimes got the impression, especially in Berlin, that German memory was like a massive tongue, seeking out, over and over, a sore tooth.' See his *The Wages of Guilt: Memories of War in Germany and Japan* (London, 1994) and the review by Gordon Craig in the *New York Review of Books* (July 14, 1994), pp. 43–5.

91 See James Young, *The Texture of Memory: Holocaust Memorials and Meaning* (New Haven, 1993), p. 21. He goes on to say (p. 20): 'No less industrious than the generations preceding them, German teenagers now work as hard at constructing memorials as their parents did in rebuilding the country after the war, as their grandparents did in building the Third Reich itself.' As will shortly become apparent I am deeply indebted to Young and his many stimulating ideas.

92 See Geoffrey Hartman, (ed.), *Bitburg in Moral and Political Perspective* (Bloomington, 1986).

93 See Elisabeth Domansky, '"Kristallnacht" ... ', op. cit., p. 82; Saul Friedlander, *Reflections of Nazism: An Essay on Kitsch and Death,* trans. Thomas Weyr (New York, 1984), p. 45.

94 See their *The Inability to Mourn: Principles of Collective Behavior,* trans. Beverley R. Placzek, Preface by Robert Jay Lifton (New York, 1975), pp. xxv–xxvi, xvi–xvii. The German original appeared in 1967.

95 Moses Moskowitz, 'The Germans and the Jews: Postwar Report', *Commentary* 1/2 (1946), p. 10.

96 See Steven T. Katz, 'Misusing the Holocaust Paradigm to Mis-write History: Examples from Recent Mediaeval Historiography', *Michael* XIII (1993), pp. 103–130.

97 See Emily Miller Budick, 'Some Thoughts on the Mutual Displacements/Appropriations/Accomodations of Culture in Three Contemporary American Women Writers', in *Prospects* (forthcoming, 1995).

98 Bernstein, *Foregone Conclusions*, op. cit., p. 85.

99 See Biale's review of Steven T. Katz, *The Holocaust in Historical Context*, vol. 1 (Oxford University Press, 1994), *Tikkun* (January–February 1995).

100 David Grossman, *see under: Love*, translated by Betsy Rosenberg (London, 1990). The quotes appear on pp. 29 and 51 respectively.

101 See Robert Alter's 'Foreword' to Ehud Ben Ezer (ed.), *Unease in Zionism* (New York, 1974), especially pp. 12–13. The article was first published in 1970. The other articles in this collection also provide a window into both the popular atmosphere and critical *Zeitgeist* of the time.

102 See Bernstein, *Foregone Conclusions*, p. 77 and (note 12), p. 156.

103 See Emil Fackenheim's 'Jewish Faith and the Holocaust' in *The Jewish Return Into History: Reflections in the Age of Auschwitz and a New Jerusalem* (New York, 1978), p. 32, his italics. The article appeared originally in *Commentary* (August 1968) and was as contributive to as much as it reflected the *Zeitgeist*. Both Fackenheim and Wiesel published prodigously on these themes.

104 For all kinds of reasons – some of which will be apparent from this essay – these formulations appear far less compelling today than they did when they first appeared. As Michael Bernstein writes there is a 'scarcely disguised coerciveness of Fackenheim's taking upon himself the decision who are "authentic" Jews, and then enjoining upon them the requirement to live their Jewishness to the full precisely in order to deny Hitler a "posthumous victory" ... No one can speak for those murdered, and no one can determine what would count as further betrayal of their suffering. The freedom to choose ... is precisely what Nazism made impossible for Jews ...'. *Foregone Conclusions*, p. 44.

105 The aura of holiness becomes most acute at points where it is perceived to be most under threat. Responding to a suggestion for the winners of the Nobel Peace Prize winners to attend a ceremony for the 50th anniversary of the liberation of Auschwitz, Baron Maurice Goldstein, opposed Yassir Arafat's participation on the grounds that 'we should do everything to exclude the possibility of a confrontation in such a holy place as Auschwitz.' See 'Auschwitz survivors won't invite Arafat', *The Jerusalem Post* (November 18, 1994), p. A4. (On November 16th 1994, the ex-speaker of the Knesset, a member of the Likud party, Dov Shilansky, declared that the only reason that Yassir Arafat would go there would be to learn from his master, Adolf Hitler, how to murder Jews.) Later, it was announced that the Auschwitz National Committee had 'decided not to invite the 1994 laureates because they have not yet officially received the prize.'

106 Robert Alter, 'Deformations of the Holocaust', *Commentary* (February 1981).

107 See Robert S. Wistrich's Frank Green Lecture, *Antisemitism in the New Europe* (Oxford Centre for Hebrew and Jewish Studies, 1994), p. 7.

108 Arno Mayer, *Why did the Heavens not Darken? The 'Final Solution' in History* (New York, 1990), pp. 16–17.

109 Sidra Dekoven Ezrahi, 'Revisioning the Past: The Changing Legacy of the Holocaust in Hebrew Literature', *Salmagundi* (Winter 1985/Spring 1986), p. 246.

110 See the recent highly controversial work by Tom Segev, *The Seventh Million: The Israelis and the Holocaust* (New York, 1993). See too Amos Elon, 'The Politics of Memory', New York Review of Books (October 7, 1993), p. 7; Adi Ophir, 'On Sanctifying the Holocaust: An Anti-Theological Treatise', *Tikkun* 2 (no. 1, 1987).

111 Ezrahi, 'Revisioning ...', p. 246.

112 The open espousal of such attitudes is contained in interviews with Palestinan youth visiting the memorial site of Lohamei Haghettoat in Israel as shown in the recent film 'Don't Touch My Holocaust' (see below). Information on this 1994 film scripted by Asher Tlalim may be found in the catalogue to *The 11th Jerusalem Film Festival* (Jerusalem, 1994), p. 45.

113 Ezrahi, 'Revisioning ... ', p. 246. See also pp. 269–70.

114 See Moshe Zimmerman, 'Why do they call the soldiers Nazis?', *Shishi* (Hebrew) (July 15 1994), p. 18.

115 For an upholding of the gay position see Yael Dayan, 'A right to choose the way we want to live', *The Jerusalem Post* (June 3, 1994), A5 and (in Hebrew) B. Michael, 'To whom does the Holocaust belong?' *Yediot Achronot* [supplement] (June 3 1994), p. 17.

116 See George Mosse's useful review in *Central European History* 26 (no. 3, 1993), pp. 365–8.

117 As always one should be aware of over-generalisations. Thus at least one important ultra-Orthodox rabbi declared that religious law held all Jewish victims of the Nazis to be equally holy. See *Yediot Achronot* (June 5 1994) p. 22.

118 Macy Gordon, '"Gay" Jews who are proud of sin', *The Jerusalem Post* (June 3, 1994), A5.

119 On the nationalist and bourgeois notions and appropriation of middle-class morality, see George L. Mosse's stimulating *Nationalism and Sexuality: Respectability and Abnormal Sexuality in Modern Europe* (New York, 1985).

120 See Martin Broszat's comments in his correspondence with Saul Friedlander, 'A Controversy about the Historicization of National Socialism', *New German Critique* 44 (Spring–Summer, 1988), espe-

cially pp. 90–1. Felman, *Testimony*, also stresses this arguing that many interpretations delimit as much as they reveal (see especially p. xix). The phrase 'a certain noisiness' appears on p. 123. See too Pierre Nora, 'Between Memory and History': *Les Lieux de Memoire*, translated Marc Roudebusch, *Representations* 26 (1989), pp. 13. All these are discussed in Young, *The Texture of Memory*, p. 5.

121 *Ibid.*, p. 7.

122 *Ibid.*, p. 21.

123 *Ibid.* See Chapter 1, 'The Countermonument: Memory against itself in Germany' (pp. 27–48) which discusses a whole series of these kinds of works by young artists who 'explore both the necessity of memory and their incapacity to recall events they never experienced directly' (p. 27).

124 For details of this film directed by Asher Tlalim see the catalogue of *The 11th Jerusalem Film Festival* (Jerusalem, 1994), p. 45. A German film on this group and its work, directed by Andres Veiel, entitled *Balagan*, was also made. (See p. 169 of the same catalog.)

125 I am grateful to Elisabeth Freund and John Landau for their comments.

126 It should be noted that in 1953(!) Ernst Wolfgang Toepf was awarded with a patent for an incinerator 'for the burning of skeletons, bodies and parts thereof'. See the article by Shlomo Shamir, 'Successors of Firm that Invented Incinerators for Concentration Camps Claim Return of their Property from Germany', (Hebrew) *Ha-aretz* (September 1 1994), p. A16.

127 Young, *The Texture of Memory*, p. 26.

128 Of course there are forces both within and without that resist this tendency. Thus A.M. Rosenthal of the *New York Times* wrote of Bill Clinton's October 1994 visit to President Assad of Syria: 'President Clinton has been to his Bitburg, and beyond. In Damascus, the local SS is not buried but at work every moment.' Quoted in *The Jerusalem Post* (November 4, 1994), p. A7.

129 These words, Levi reports, were written as early as 1947 and published for the first time in *The Truce* in Italy in 1963. See his chapter 'Shame' in *The Drowned and the Saved*, pp. 52–67. The quote appears on p. 54.

2 German Jews beyond *Bildung* and Liberalism: The Radical Jewish Revival in the Weimar Republic

1 Not only can this be taken as a *leitmotif* of the Weimar Jewish revival, but Rosenzweig's gnomic remark immediately following was typical of its overall paradoxical style as well. After 'pin-point', he wrote 'so

that just one man – I, that is – can occupy it.' See the letter to Gertrud Oppenheim, July 1924 in *Gesammelte Werke* 1, edited by Rachel Rosenzweig and Edith Rosenzweig-Scheinmann (Den Haag, 1979), p. 980.

2 Letter of 29 October 1937 to Zalman Schocken on his sixtieth birth-day entitled 'A Candid Word about the True Motives of My Kabbalistic Studies' reproduced in David Biale, *Gershom Scholem: Kabbalah and Counter-History* (Cambridge, Mass., 1979), pp. 74–6 in English and pp. 215–16 in German.

3 'Theologico-Political Fragment' in Walter Benjamin, *Reflections* (ed. Peter Demetz) (New York, 1978) pp. 312–13.

4 *Geist der Utopie* (Muenchen/Leipzig, 1918), p. 319.

5 Sorkin, *The Transformation of German Jewry 1780–1840* (New York/Oxford, 1987).

6 *German Jews Beyond Judaism* (Bloomington, 1985).

7 I discovered the best – and most recent – account of *Bildung* well after this paper was first written. See the illuminating study by Aleida Assmann, *Arbeit am National Gedaechtnis: Einz kurze Geschichte der deutschen Bildungsidee* (Frankfurt, 1993). See too W.H. Bruford, *The German Tradition of Self-Cultivation: 'Bildung' From Humboldt to Thomas Mann* (Cambridge, 1975).

8 See Sidney M. Bolkosky, *The Distorted Image: German Jewish Perceptions of Germans and Germany, 1918–1935* (New York, 1975). The interpretive frame in which Bolkosky sets these examples is open to question.

9 Ludwig Strauss, quoted in Mosse, *German Jews Beyond Judaism*, p. 14; on Blumenfeld, see Hannah Arendt's letter of September 7, 1952, in *Hannah Arendt–Karl Jaspers Correspondence 1926–1969*, edited by Lotte Kohler and Hans Saner (New York, 1992) p. 198.

10 Jewishness here is envisaged not as a particular community or set of con-tents but, as Walter Benjamin once put it, as 'noble bearer and repre-sentative of the intellect'. Quoted in Anson Rabinbach, 'Between Enlightenment and Apocalyse: Benjamin, Bloch and Modern German Jewish Messianism', *New German Critique*, no. 34 (Winter 1985) p. 97.

11 This appears in as yet unpublished paper 'The Ambivalence of Bildung: Jews and Other Germans'.

12 See Paul Mendes-Flohr's review of *German Jews Beyond Judaism in Studies in Contemporary Jewry*, Vol.V (1989), pp. 377–9. The quote appears on p. 398.

13 The German edition of the book is, perhaps more accurately, entitled *Juedische Intellektuelle in Deutschland* (Frankfurt, 1992).

14 There were of course differences in age as well as opinions. Bloch was
    born in 1885, Rosenzweig 1886, Benjamin 1892, Scholem 1897.
    Nevertheless they did constitute an intellectual generation. Rosenzweig
    and Benjamin died relatively young while Bloch and Scholem enjoyed
    longevity.

15 Leo Lowenthal has vividly described the way in which this worked:
    'About a year after my first meeting with [Siegfried] Kracauer [around
    the end of World War I], he introduced me to Adorno, who was then
    eighteen years old. I introduced him to my friend Ernst Simon, who,
    like myself, was studying history, *Germanistik*, and philosophy, and
    who won me over to a very messianic version of Zionism. Through
    Ernst Simon, Kracauer met Rabbi Nobel, then a revered figure in our
    Jewish circle, to whose *Festschrift*, on the occasion of his 50th birth-
    day, Kracauer contributed. Through Nobel, Kracauer first met Martin
    Buber and later Franz Rosenzweig. In the spring of 1922, I introduced
    him to Ernst Bloch, and he in turn introduced me to Horkheimer, who
    was already a good friend of Adorno's.' See his 'As I Remember
    Friedel', *New German Critique* (no. 54, Fall 1991), p. 6. Those very
    close friends Scholem and Benjamin were, of course, either in contact
    or familiar with most of these figures.

16 I am not arguing that this is the only possible legacy of Weimar (nor
    is this the legacy with which I would necessarily identify). The left
    and Marxist traditions of Kurt Tucholsky, Georg Lukács and Karl
    Korsch can be considered another, as can the writings of more liber-
    al-minded thinkers and writers discussed by Mosse. But, if present
    cultural fashions are any indication, the growing emphasis on the
    thinkers (and kind of thinking) discussed here increasingly seems to
    be regarded (together with its right-wing opposition and mirror) as
    somehow its most pertinent contemporary legacy. The dynamics of
    its reception process still need to be studied. Clearly it operates dif-
    ferently within different cultures; the American is not the same as,
    say, the Israeli or German case. The manifold psychological as well
    as intellectual functions these Jewish thinkers presently play within
    German cultural life certainly merits study. Juergen Habermas seems
    to have been one of the major early pioneers successfully promoting
    this interest. See his essays on these topics (beginning in 1961) in
    Philosophical-Political Profiles, translated by Frederick G. Lawrence
    (Cambridge, Mass., 1985).

17 While lumping these aspects together here it should be clear that these
    all have separate histories and structures. Radical utopianism is obvi-
    ously not the same as messianism. Nevertheless salvation appears at

the end of history or as an event within history but never produced by it. As such it can be discussed together with messianic strains.

18   For an attempt to define these distinctive characteristics, see Detlev J.K. Peukert, *The Weimar Republic: The Crisis of Classical Modernity*, translated by Richard Deveson (London, 1991). See especially Parts I and VI.

19   See, in this connection, Kurt Sontheimer, 'Weimar Culture', in Michael Laffan (ed.), *The Burden of German History* (London, 1989), especially p. 1.

20   Eberhard Kolb, *The Weimar Republic*, translated by P. S. Falla (London, 1988) p. 84.

21   It is a little known but telling fact that none other than Carl Schmitt arranged for the publication of Ernst Bloch's *Geist der Utopie* by Duncker & Humblot in 1918. Personal communication from Raphael Gross.

22   This holds even in the face of the apparent (and always illusory) stabilization that is supposed to have characterised the years 1924–29. Indeed, even the *Neue Sachlichkeit*, the 'new sobriety', the cultural expression of that politico-economic period, presented itself within these terms of reference, as an overt alternative to what was recognised as the prevalent revolutionary, redemptive, apocalyptic discourse of the time. As the expressionist playwright Paul Kornfeld put it in his 1924 comedy *Palme oder der Gekraenkte:* 'Let us hear no more of war and revolution and the salvation of the world! Let us be more modest and turn to other, smaller things.' Quoted in Kolb, *The Weimar Republic*, p. 85.

23   On the radicalisation of the right, see my *The Nietzsche Legacy in Germany 1890–1990* (Berkeley, 1992), especially Chapters 5 and 6; Jeffrey Herf, *Reactionary Modernism: Technology, culture, and politics in the Third Reich* (Cambridge, 1984) and Martin Greiffenhagen, *Das Dilemma des Konservatismus in Deutschland* (Frankfurt, 1986), especially pp. 241–56.

24   Karl Loewith, 'The Political Implications of Martin Heidegger's Existentialism', translated by Richard Wolin and Melissa J. Cox, *New German Critique*, no. 45 (Fall 1988).

25   George Steiner, 'Heidegger, Again', *Salmagundi*, nos.82–83 (Spring–Summer 1989).

26   See Assmann, *Arbeit am Nationalen Gedaechtnis*, pp. 9, 29–30, 74–5.

27   Rudolf Vierhaus, 'Bildung' in *Geschichtliche Grundbegriffe: Historisches Lexicon zu politisch-sozialen Sprache in Deutschland*, Vol.1, (ed. Otto Brunner, Werner Conze, Reinhart Koselleck) (Stuttgart,

1972), pp. 508–551. The quote appears on p. 508. See too especially p. 516.

28   *German Jews Beyond Judaism*, p. 7.

29   Martin Buber, '*Bildung* und Weltanschauung' (Frankfurter Lehrhaus-rede), *Mittelstelle fuer Juedsiche Erwachsenen Bildung, Reichsvertretung der Juden in Deutschland* (Frankfurt, April 1937) p. 1. Quoted in Mosse, *German Jews Beyond Judaism*, p. 36 and note 53, p. 88.

30   See 'The Influence of the Volkish Idea on German Jewry' in George L. Mosse, *Germans and Jews: The Right, The Left, And the Search For A 'Third Force' In Pre-Nazi Germany* (London, 1971) especially p. 89; Mosse, *German Jews Beyond Judaism*, p. 36.

31   See Paul Mendes-Flohr, 'Nationalism as a Spiritual Sensibility: The Philosophical Suppositions of Buber's Hebrew Humanism' in his *Divided Passions: Jewish Intellectuals and the Experience of Modernity* (Detroit, 1991), especially p. 190.

32   See the fascinating article by Anson Rabinbach, 'Between Enlightenment and Apocalypse', *New German Critique*, no. 34 (Winter 1985) especially pp. 88ff.

33   For a history of these developments, see my *Brothers and Strangers: The East European Jew in German and German-Jewish Consciousness 1800–1923* (Madison, 1982), Chapters 5, 6.

34   See respectively *Brothers and Strangers*, pp. 193–8); Reinhard Blomert, 'Das vergessene Sanitorium' in Norbert Giovannini, Jo-Hannes Bauer, Hans-Martin Mumm (eds.), *Juedisches Leben in Heidelberg: Studien zu einer unterbrochenen Geschichte* (Heidelberg, 1992, pp. 249–62; Gershom Scholem, *From Berlin to Jerusalem: Memories of My Youth* (New York, 1980) pp. 131, 146–8.

35   See Rabinbach, 'Between Enlightenment and Apocalypse ...', pp. 82–3.

36   Unpublished Loewenthal letter to Simon of April 9 1920, kindly provided to me by Guy Meron.

37   The complexity of the relationships can be gleaned from a brief look at Gershom Scholem, *Walter Benjamin: The Story of a Friendship*, translated by Harry Zohn (Philadelphia, 1981) and *The Correspondence of Walter Benjamin and Gershom Scholem 1932–1940*, (ed. Gershom Scholem) (Cambridge, Mass., 1991); Franz Rosenzweig, *Briefe* (ed. Edith Rosenzweig) (Berlin, 1935) and many other sources mentioned in this chapter.

38   There is of course another side to this – the problematic relation (yet continued attraction) to tradition that characterised these modernists. As Hannah Arendt wrote, Benjamin's choice to study baroque (in a double sense) had 'an exact counterpart in Scholem's strange decision

to approach Judaism via the Cabala which is untransmitted and untransmittable in terms of Jewish tradition, in which it has always had the odor of something downright disreputable. Nothing showed more clearly – so one is inclined to say today – that there was no such thing as a "return" either to the German or European or the Jewish tradition than the choice of these fields of study. It was an implicit admission that the past spoke directly only through things that had not been handed down, whose seeming closeness to the present was thus due precisely to their exotic character, which ruled out all claims to a binding authority.' See the 1968 essay 'Walter Benjamin' reproduced in her *Men in Dark Times* (New York, 1968), p. 195. Of all four men Benajmin, of course, was the most resistant to salvationary solutions. (see pp. 189–90).

39 Rosenzweig had extreme monarchist views, was 'outraged at the prospects of a President [*sic*] Scheidemann or an Emperor Max ...' and in November 1919 exclaimed that it is 'most natural, normal and inevitable ... to be in the reactionary camp'. See Stefan Meineke, 'A Life of Contradiction: The Philosopher Franz Rosenzweig and his Relationship to History and Politics', *Leo Baeck Institute Yearbook (LBIYB) XXXVI* (1991), p. 477.

40 See the letter to Rudolf Ehrenburg of May 5 1919 in Franz Rosenzweig, *Briefe* (Berlin, 1935) p. 359.

41 Ludwig Feuchtwanger, the editor of the Duncker and Humblot publishing house, rejected Bloch's title, Scholem writes, 'because it might scare readers away. Benjamin described to me Bloch's impressive appearance and told me that Bloch was now working on his magnum opus, *System des theoretischen Messianismus [System of theoretical messianism]*; he grew wide-eyed when he mentioned this.' See *Walter Benjamin: The Story of a Friendship*, p. 79.

42 Given the manifold, complex nature of the *Bildungs* idea, it has been pointed out (in conversation with Joel Golb), that in some of its versions it contains an epiphanic, flashing quality. It is possible that the thinkers we have considered here even drew from that particular tradition. But, even if this is so, this strain remains distinct from what Mosse regards as *Bildungs* classical core, the one to which German-Jewish intellectuals remained most steadfastly loyal.

43 On this (and related themes) see the interesting reflections by Paul Mendes-Flohr, '"The Stronger and the Better Jews": Jewish Theological Responses to Political Messianism in the Weimar Republic', *Studies in Contemporary Jewry*, Vol. VII (1991), pp. 159–85. See especially pp. 165–9.

44 See Sorkin, *The Transformation of German Jewry*, p. 15.

45   See 'Re The Theory of Knowledge, Theory of Progress', in *Benjamin:*
      Philosophy, Aesthetics, History (ed. Gary Smith) (Chicago and London,
      1989), p. 61. Characteristically gnomic, Benjamin went on to say: 'If
      one were to go by the blotter, though, nothing of what has been writ-
      ten would remain.' As for Scholem, see the remarkable letters on Kafka
      that he wrote to Benjamin (July 9,17 1934). There his insistence on
      the theological mode is completely apparent. See *The Correspondence,*
      of Walter Benjamin and Gershom Scholem pp. 122–7.

46   'Theses on the Philosophy of History', in Walter Benjamin,
      Illuminations (edited by Hannah Arendt, translated by Harry Zohn)
      (New York, 1969), p. 263.

47   Bloch, *Geist der Utopie*, p. 445.

48   Quoted in Hans Saner, *Karl Jaspers* (Hamburg, 1970) p. 33. On the
      Heidelberg experience of these 'Jewish Apocalyptics', see Eva Karadi,
      'Ernst Bloch and Georg Lukács in Max Weber's Heidelberg' in W.J.
      Mommsen and J. Osterhammel (eds.), *Max Weber and his*
      Contemporaries (London, 1987) pp. 499–514.

49   This remained a constant from 1916 on. For a late statement see his
      remarkable 1974 essay, 'Reflections on Jewish Theology' where he
      addresses the limits of Zionist 'normalization' and of secularization
      in general: 'The position of the man of the secularistic age *vis-à-vis*
      his society is more helpless than ever in his confrontation with nihilism
      (p. 293) ... I admit that this unshakable belief in a specific moral cen-
      ter, which bestows meaning in world history on the Jewish people,
      transcends the sphere of pure secularization. I would not even deny
      that in it a remnant of theocratic hope also reaccompanies that reen-
      try into world history of the Jewish people that at the same time sig-
      nifies the truly Utopian return to its own history (pp. 294–5) ... I
      consider a complete secularization of Israel to be out of the question
      so long as the faith in God is still a fundamental phenomenon of any-
      thing human and cannot be liquidated 'ideologically' (p. 297).' This
      is reproduced in Gershom Scholem, *On Jews and Judaism in Crisis:*
      Selected Essays (ed. Werner J.Dannhauser) (New York, 1976) pp.
      261–97.

50   Benjamin 'Theses on the Philosophy of History', p. 255.

51   See Paul Mendes-Flohr, '"To Brush History Against the Grain": The
      Eschatology of the Frankfurt School and Ernst Bloch', in *Divided*
      Passions (Detroit, 1991). Bloch's 'atheistic messianism' opposes reli-
      gious messianism in that the latter limits man's capacity to create his
      own future. In effect, Bloch defers to the infinite, unrealizable future.
      Still he too rejects progressive, linear development.

52 For an excellent overview of Bloch's work, see Chapter 5 of Martin Jay, *Marxism and Totality* (Berkeley, 1984); see too George Steiner, 'Sojourns in the Wondrous', *Times Literary Supplement* (4 October 1985).

53 Paul Mendes-Flohr has pointed out that although Rosenzweig failed to integrate the historical-apocalyptic ingredients of messianism into his theology he had a profound phenomenological appreciation of its role. See '"The Stronger and the Better Jews"', pp. 165–9.

54 See his *The Messianic Idea in Judaism And Other Essays on Jewish Spirituality* (New York, 1971).

55 'The utopian, messianic element', Henry Pachter writes, 'in the problematic of neo-Marxism constituted the major point of contact with Scholem, who drew attention to the Jewish source of utopian thinking in the Frankfurt School; for it is evident that messianism is the basic pattern on which both he and they built their particular methods of criticizing the present system. (Interestingly, both Bloch and Max Horkheimer at the ends of their lives recognized religion as an expression of their aspirations; Scholem was vindicated.)', 'Gershom Scholem – The Myth of the Mythmaker', *Salmagundi* (no. 40, Winter 1978), pp. 9–39. The quote appears on p. 22.

56 'On the 1930 Edition of Rosenzweig's Star of Redemption'. This appeared originally in the *Frankfurter Israelitisches Gemeindeblatt*, X (1931) and is reproduced in Gershom Scholem, The *Messianic Idea in Judaism* (New York, 1971). The quote appears on p. 323. As a Zionist, moreover, Scholem seems to have been disturbed by the historical quietism implied by Rosenzweig's conception of messianism.

57 This outline of the restorative, utopian and apocalyptic elements of messianic thought rests upon the brilliant schema and analysis of Rabinbach, 'Between Enlightenment and Apocalypse', especially pp. 84–8. Rabinbach also argues that this thinking is characterised by a profound ethical ambivalence, a mood caught between doom and hope, and the poles of contemplation and action.

58 On this theme, especially in Benjamin, see Richard Wolin, *Walter Benjamin: An Aesthetic of Redemption* (New York, 1982), especially pp. 36–44.

59 Ernst Bloch, *Geist der Utopie* (1923) (Frankfurt am Main, 1964), p. 347. Quoted in Rabinbach, 'Between Enlightenment and Apocalypse', p. 85. The first edition appeared in 1918, the second in 1923.

60 For German-Jewish modernizers, Yiddish (or the *Jargon*) was synonymous with *Unbildung*. Indeed, as Moses Mendelssohn wrote in 1782, it had 'contributed not a little to the immorality of the common

man; and I expect a very good effect on my brothers from the increasing use of the pure German idiom.' It was typical of this *Bildungs* faith in culture that it held that immorality could somehow be countered by the proper use of language. See the quote in Michael A. Meyer, *The Origins of the Modern Jew* (Detroit, 1967), p. 44. See also *Brothers and Strangers*, Chapter 1.

61 For an analysis of these developments see Allan Janik and Stephen Toulmin, *Wittgenstein's Vienna* (New York, 1973). See also Sander Gilman, *Jewish Self-Hatred: Anti-Semitism and the Hidden Language of the Jews* (Baltimore and London, 1986).

62 See the entry for October 24, 1911 in *The Diaries of Franz Kafka 1910–1913* (ed. Max Brod) (New York, 1965), p. 111.

63 For a comparative examination see Stéphane Moses, 'Walter Benjamin and Franz Rosenzweig', in Gary Smith (ed.), *Benjamin*, pp. 228–46 and Martin Jay, 'The Politics of Translation: Siegfried Kracauer and Walter Benjamin on the Buber–Rosenzweig Bible', *The Leo Baeck Institute Year Book*, XXI (1976) especially pp. 18 ff.

64 Not only in this, but in many other respects as well, the similarities between Rosenzweig and Heidegger have been variously noted. See Karl Loewith, 'M. Heidegger and F. Rosenzweig *or* Temporality and Eternity', *Philosophy and Phenomenological Research 3* (1942–1943), pp. 53–77; Steven S. Schwarzschild, 'Franz Rosenzweig and Martin Heidegger: The German and the Jewish Turn to Ethnicism' and Alan Udoff, 'Rosenzweig's Heidegger Reception and the re-Origination of Jewish Thinking' in Wolfdietrich Schmied-Kowarzik (ed.), *Der Philosoph Franz Rosenzweig (1886–1929)*, Internationaler Kongress – Kassel 1986. Band II – *Das Neue Denken und seine Dimensionen* (Freiburg/Muenchen: Karl Alber, 1988). pp. 887–9 and 923–950; Stephane Moses, *System and Revelation: The Philosophy of Franz Rosenzweig*, translated by Catherine Tihanyi (Detroit, 1992), pp. 290–3.

65 See Franz Rosenzweig, *The Star Of Redemption*, translated by William W. Hallo (Boston, 1971), especially pp. 109–11, 125–32, 141–2, 150–1.

66 See Rosenzweig's 'The Function of Translation' in Nahum N. Glatzer, (ed.), *Franz Rosenzweig: His Life and Thought* (New York, 1961), pp. 252–261. Originally Part Two from the essay 'Die Schrift und Luther' in Rosenzweig's *Kleinere Schriften*, pp. 141–66 (Berlin, 1937).

67 Quoted in George Steiner, *After Babel: Aspects of Language and Translation* (London/ New York, 1975), p. 244.

68 See 'The Task of the Translator' in Benjamin, *Illuminations*, The quote appears on p. 82. See too 'On Language as Such and on the Language

of Man', in *Reflections*, To be sure, unlike Rosenzweig, Benjamin believed that after the Fall language degenerated into the profane medium of communication. The act of translation had an almost magical reconstitutional function, revealing original truth and meaning from the obscurities of mere communication.

69 Moses, 'Walter Benjamin and Franz Rosenzweig', op. cit., especially pp. 238–9.

70 On the complex nature of the relationship, see Michael Brocke, 'Franz Rosenzweig und Gerhard Gershom Scholem' in Walter Grab and Julius H. Schoeps, *Juden in der Weimarer Republik* (Stuttgart and Bonn, 1986), pp. 127–52.

71 See Robert Alter's excellent *Necessary Angels: Tradition and Modernity in Kafka, Benjamin, and Scholem* (Cambridge, Mass., 1991), especially pp. 36–7.

72 Gershom Scholem, *'Od Davar* (Tel Aviv, 1989), pp. 58–9. The original, 'Bekenntnis ueber unsere Sprache', is reproduced in Brocke, *op. cit.,* pp. 148–50.

73 George L. Mosse, 'Gerschom Scholem as a German Jew', *Modern Judaism* 10 (1990), pp. 117–33. See especially pp. 124–5.

74 *Ibid.*, p. 129.

75 See *The Nietzsche Legacy in Germany*, especially Chapters 5 and 6.

76 On Rosenzweig's and Bloch's relation to Nietzsche, see my *The Nietzsche Legacy*, pp. 101–2, 182–4, 217–8, 288–9. On Benjamin, see R. Reschke, 'Barbaren, Kult und Katasrophen. Nietzsche bei Benjamin', in *Aber ein Sturm weht vom Paradiese her. Texte zur Walter Benjamin* (Leipzig, 1992) pp. 303–41.

77 Letter to Zalman Schocken in Biale, *Gershom Scholem*, pp. 75–6. The modernist connection here should be clear: immediately afterward Scholem commented it was in Kafka that he found 'the most perfect and unsurpassed expression of this fine line.'

78 See his letter to Rudolf Hallo of March 3 1922 where he refers to 'der boese Scholem. Warum disputierst du? ... Am wenigsten mit einem Nihilisten wie Scholem. Der Nihilist behaelt immer recht. ... In Scholem steckt das Resentiment des Asketen.' See Franz Rosenzweig, *Briefe* (Berlin, 1935) p. 431.

79 Gershom Scholem, 'The Crypto-Jewish Sect of the Doenmeh (Sabbatians) in Turkey' in his *The Messianic Idea in Judaism*, p. 164. The article was originally written in German.

80 *Keneset II* (1937), pp. 347–92. The English version, 'Redemption through Sin' is in *The Messianic Idea in Judaism*, pp. 78–141. The quote appears on p. 109.

81 In 1935 Scholem wrote to Benjamin that this essay – on 'the ideology of religious nihilism in Judaism' – could 'only be written in Hebrew ... if the author is to remain free from apologetic inhibitions.' See Gershom Scholem, ed., *The Correspondence of Walter Benjamin and Gershom Scholem 1932–1940*, p. 174. See letter 79 (December 18, 1935), pp. 172–4. While that may be so I would also argue that, at least in part, the *Fragestellung*, categories and mode of thinking were very much related to the post–1916 German cultural milieu.

82 See the interesting unpublished paper by David Biale, 'Scholem and Modern Nationalism'.

83 Mosse, 'Gerschom Scholem ...', p. 121, which notes that Scholem's notion of history had absolutely no conception of progress or organic, steady development without perceiving the concomitant undermining of the *Bildungs* ideal.

84 See the unpublished paper by Robert Alter, 'Scholem and Modernism', especially p. 5.

85 Benjamin, 'Theses on the Philosophy of History', op. cit., p. 256.

86 See the unpublished paper by Stéphane Moses, 'Benjamin, Rosenzweig, Scholem: The Critique of Historical Reason', given at the International Conference on *Walter Benjamin's Jewish Constellation* (July 14 1992), p. 147.

87 Unpublished letter to Magrit Rosenstock, 11 November 1918 quoted in Stefan Meineke, 'A Life of Contradiction ...', p. 481.

88 See the comments by Hans Meyer, 'Ernst Bloch in der Geschichte' in *Reden ueber Ernst Bloch* (Frankfurt am Main, 1989), p. 60.

89 Ernst Bloch, *Erbschaft dieser Zeit* (Zuerich, 1935) p. 58; see the translation by Neville and Stephen Plaice, *Heritage of Our Times* (Berkeley and Los Angeles, 1991), p. 62.

90 This point is nicely developed in Paul Mendes-Flohr, '"To Brush History against the Grain": The Eschatology of the Frankfurt School and Ernst Bloch', *Divided Passions*.

91 Moses, 'Benjamin, Rosenzweig, Scholem: The Critique of Historical Reason', op. cit.

92 As Benjamin put it: 'The concept of the historical progress of mankind cannot be sundered from the concept of its progression through a homogenous, empty time. A critique of the concept of such a progression must be the basis of any criticism of the concept of progress itself.' 'Theses on the Philosophy of History' in *Illuminations*, p. 261.

93 For a comparative examination, see Ulrich Hortian, 'Zeit und Geschichte bei Franz Rosenzweig und Walter Benjamin' in *Der Philosoph Franz Rosenzweig*, pp. 815–27; Stephane Moses, 'Walter Benjamin and Franz

Rosenzweig', pp. 228–46. While Bloch certainly dismisses 'progress' his eruptive, flashing moments, important as they are, do not bring ultimate redemption. This is infinitely deferred into the future.

94 For an exposition of Benjamin's view of history see Stephane Moses, 'Eingedenken und Jetzzeit: Geschichtliches Bewusstein im Spaetwerk Walter Benjamins', in *Memoria Vergessen und Erinnern: Poetik und Hermeneutik,* XV (eds. Anselm Haverkamp and Renate Lachmann) (Muenchen, 1993).

95 'Walter Benjamin' in Gershom Scholem, *On Jews and Judaism in Crisis,* pp. 194–5.

96 It is surely no accident that Rosenzweig's *Star of Redemption*, that anti-Hegelian treatise, begins in rhapsodic praise of that important founder of modernism, Nietzsche. See too Robert Alter, 'Scholem and Modernism'.

97 This applies too to Bloch's central notion in *Erbschaft dieser Zeit* of 'Ungleichzeitigkeit' in which social and cultural structures of the past are active in the present alongside aspects pregnant with the future.

98 Neville and Stephen Plaice, *Heritage of Our Times*, p. 197. But see generally pp. 195–208.

99 'One-Way Street' is reproduced in Benjamin *Reflections*, pp. 61–94. See the comments in Demetz's 'Introduction', pp. xviii–xix.

100 On this, see Ricardo J. Quinones, *Mapping Literary Modernism: Time and Development* (Princeton, 1985).

101 Neville and Stephen Plaice, *Heritage of Our Times*, p. 228.

102 See 'Revue Form in Philosophy (1928)' in *Heritage of Our Times,* op. cit., especially pp. 334–5. Bloch refers to Benjamin's style as 'photomontage'.

103 Charles Taylor, *Sources of the Self: The Making of the Modern Identity* (Cambridge, 1989) pp. 462 and 465. The whole chapter 'Epiphanies of Modernism' is relevant. Nevertheless, as Taylor, shows, this decentering process was a paradoxical way of re-establishing unity at a deeper level, reinforcing the radically reflexive (and thus inward) posture of (an always manifold) modernism.

104 'Surrealism: The Last Snapshot of the European Intelligentsia' is reproduced in Benjamin, *Reflections*, pp. 177–192. The quote appears on p. 179. The piece was originally written in 1929. The vitality of the *Bildungs* idea, as Aleida Assmann has observed, was a function of an unproblematised notion of a 'centre', whether of the person or the nation (something which in our own time is no longer conceivable.) My argument is that such problematisation was already present in the

writings we have considered here. See Assmann, *Arbeit am National Gedeachtnis*, (Frankfurt, 1993) p. 111.

105 When this paper was first presented at a conference in Madison, Wisconsin in October 1993, it was objected that these intellectuals indeed remained constant to the original *Bildungs* idea but that its emphases shifted according to the dictates of changing circumstances. The critique of reason, it was argued, was built into *Bildung* itself: when the reason of critique failed it became the critique of reason. But this provides the notion of *Bildung* with a remarkably potent protean quality – one which, at least in Mosse's book, does not appear in the original and enduring conception which informed its Jewish appropriation.

3 'The Jew Within': The Myth of 'Judaization' in Germany

1 There are innumerable examples of this. Among the better known are Jakob Fries, *Ueber die Gefahrdung des Wohlstandes und Charakters der Deutschen durch die Juden* (Heidelberg, 1816); Christian Friedrich Ruehs, *Ueber die Anspruche der Juden an das deutsche Buergerrecht* (Berlin, 1815).

2 Fries, *Gefaehrdung des Wohlstandes*, pp. 9–11. The translation here is by Mark Gelber, *The Jew in the Modern World: A Documentary History* (ed. Paul R. Mendes-Flohr and Jehuda Reinharz) (New York, 1980) pp. 258–9.

3 Hannah Arendt's still fresh comments on the nature of modern Jewish identity may be found in her *Rahel Varnhagen: The Life of a Jewish Woman* (New York, 1974) pp. 218. Heine's poem, 'The New Israelite Hospital in Hamburg' (1841), translated by Margaret Armour can be found in *The Poetry and Prose of Heinrich Heine* (ed. Frederic Ewen) (New York, 1948) p.285.

4 On the difference between pre- and post-emancipation conditions, see Reinhard Ruerup, 'Emancipation and Crisis: The "Jewish Question" in Germany, 1850–1890', *Leo Baeck Institute Year Book* (hereafter *LBIYB*) 20 (1975) pp. 13–25.

5 On the history of the term 'Judaizer', as well as a case history in which the notion is employed somewhat differently from here, see Paul Lawrence Rose, *Bodin and the Great God of Nature: The Moral and Religious Universe of a Judaiser* (Geneva, 1980), esp. pp. 5–9.

6 See the still important work by Joshua Trachtenberg, *The Devil and the Jews: The Medieval Conception of the Jews and Its Relation to Modern Antisemitism* (Cleveland, 1961) p.181. See, too, Lewis Feuer, *Spinoza and the Rise of Liberalism* (Boston, 1966) p.48. I thank Stephen Whitfield for this reference.

7   Friedrich Kluge and Alfred Goetze, *Etymologisches Woerterbuch* (Berlin, 1951) p.347.

8   See Jacob Grimm and Wilhelm Grimm, *Deutsches Woerterbuch*, 6 (Leipzig, 1855) pp. 1819–20.

9   This treatment of the relation between usury and 'Judaization' is taken mainly from Trachtenberg, *Devil and the Jews*. For the quotation from Sir Francis Bacon, see p. 192; for Bernhard of Clairvaux, pp. 191.

10 Fries, *Gefaehrdung des Wohlstandes*, in *The Jew in the Modern World*, pp. 259.

11 Friedrich Buchholz, *Moses und Jesus: Ueber das intellektuelle und moralische Verhaeltnis der Juden und Christen – Eine historisch-politische Abhandlung* (Berlin, 1803) pp.215–16, 208–9. On military life as the solution, 217ff.

12 These suggestive connections may be found in an interesting article by Orland Figes, 'Ludwig Boerne and the Formation of a Radical Critique of Judaism', *LBIYB* 29 (1984) pp. 351–82. Although the present essay does not deal specifically with Boerne, he very much fits the pattern under discussion.

13 Heinrich Heine to Christian Sethe, November 20, 1816, quoted in Jeffrey L. Sammons, *Heinrich Heine: A Modern Biography* (Princeton, 1980) pp. 38–9.

14 Quoted in Helmut Hirsch, 'Karl Marx zur Judenfrage und zu Juden: Eine weiterfuehrende Metakritik?' in Walter Grab and Julius Schoeps (eds), *Juden und Vormaerz in der Revolution von 1848* (Stuttgart and Bonn, 1983) p.207.

15 Quoted in Sammons, *Heine*, pp. 249–50.

16 Heinrich Heine, 'Moses' (1854), trans. Frederic Ewen, in *Poetry and Prose of Heine*, pp. 665–6.

17 I am not concerned here with the question of priority and influence. For a detailed discussion of the ideational links between Moses Hess and Karl Marx, see Julius Carlebach, *Karl Marx and the Radical Critique of Judaism* (London, 1978) pp. 110–24.

18 Moses Hess, 'Ueber das Geldwesen' (1845), Theodor Zlocisti (ed.), in *Moses Hess: Sozialistische Aufsaetze, 1841-1847* (Berlin, 1921) p.182. There is a good discussion of Hess in Robert S. Wistrich's excellent *Socialism and the Jews: The Dilemma of Assimilation in Germany and Austria-Hungary* (London and Toronto, 1982) pp. 36–44.

19 Bruno Bauer, *Die Judenfrage* (Braunschweig, 1843). For a translation, see Bruno Bauer, 'The Jewish Problem', in Lawrence L. Stepelevich (ed.), *The Young Hegelians: An Anthology* (Cambridge, 1983) pp. 187–97.

20 All quotations from 'On the Jewish Question' are from Tom Bottomore (ed. and trans.) *Karl Marx: Early Writings* (New York, 1964), see pp. 10–11, 31, 21.

21 *Ibid.*, pp. 34, 36, 37, 35.

22 *Ibid.*, p. 39.

23 See the analysis by Natan Rotenstreich, 'For and against Emancipation: The Bruno Bauer Controversy', *LBIYB* 4 (1959), 23–27. See also, Wistrich, *Socialism and the Jews*, pp. 25–31; Carlebach, *Marx and Judaism*, pp. 148–84.

24 See, for instance, I. Meszaros, *Marx's Theory of Alienation* (London, 1970), especially pp. 30–1; Hirsch, 'Marx zur "Judenfrage".'

25 On this general point, see Louis Dumont, *From Mandeville to Marx: The Genesis and Triumph of Economic Ideology* (Chicago and London, 1977); Joyce Oldham Appleby, *Economic Thought and Ideology in Seventeenth-Century England* (Princeton, 1978).

26 Karl Kautsky, *Are the Jews a Race?* reprint edn. (Westport, 1972) p. 246. See also the important essay by George L. Mosse, 'German Socialists and the Jewish Question in the Weimar Republic', in his *Masses and Man: Nationalist and Fascist Perceptions of Reality* (New York, 1980) pp. 284–315.

27 For this entire section on the socialist movement and the theme of *Verjudung*, I base myself upon material drawn from Wistrich's important study, *Socialism and the Jews*. See p. 47, and p. 362 note 161.

28 Eduard Bernstein, quoted in *ibid.*, p. 48.

29 Bernstein, 'Die Verjudung des Deutschen Reiches', *Der Sozialdemokrat,* January 9, 1881, pp. 1–2, quoted in Wistrich, *Socialism and the Jews,* p. 97. For a similar attack on antisemitism that also contains some ambiguous comments, see August Bebel, 'Vorschlag einer Resolution zum Thema Antisemitismus und Sozialdemokratie', in Irving Fetscher (ed.), *Marxisten gegen Antisemitmus* (Hamburg, 1974) pp. 58–76.

30 Otto Bauer, 'Das Ende des Christlichen Sozialismus', *Der Kampf* 4, no. 9 (June 1, 1911) pp. 393–8, quoted in Wistrich, *Socialism and the Jews*, p. 191.

31 For expositional accounts of Sombart, see Herman Lebovics, *Social Conservatism and the Middle Classes in Germany, 1914–1933* (Princeton, 1969); and Arthur Mitzman, *Sociology and Estrangement: Three Sociologists of Imperial Germany* (New York, 1973). Marxism, according to Sombart, had its roots in the Greek philosophy of decadence and the 'Jewish spirit'. Marx himself was 'the most rootless and contradictory of all socialists'. See Lebovics, *Social Conservatism*, pp. 62–6.

32   See Paul R. Mendes-Flohr, 'Werner Sombart's *The Jews and Modern Capitalism:* An Analysis of Its Ideological Premises', *LBIYB* 25 (1976) pp. 87–107.

33   For examples of the *voelkisch* way in which Sombart employed the term *Verjudung*, see his 'Artvernichtung oder Artverhaltung', in Hermann Bahr *et al.* (ed.), *Der Jud ist Schuld: Diskussionsbuch ueber die Judenfrage,* (Basel, 1952), esp. p. 252. See also his *Die Zukunft der Juden* (Leipzig, 1912) and *Judentaufen* (Munich, 1912).

34   Werner Sombart, *A New Social Philosophy* (New York, 1969) pp. 177, 178–9. See also p. 175ff. This is a translation by Karl F. Geiser of Sombart's *Deutscher Sozialismus* (1934).

35   This has been superbly captured by Fritz Stern in his *Gold and Iron: Bismarck, Bleichroeder and the Building of the German Empire* (New York, 1977). See also Stern, 'Money, Morals, and the Pillars of Society', in his *The Failure of Illiberalism: Essays on the Political Culture of Modern Germany* (Chicago and London, 1975) pp. 26–57.

36   Reported in *General-Anzeiger* (Frankfurt am Main), December 22, 1900, no. 300, quoted in Ruerup, 'Emancipation and Crisis', p. 23.

37   Henry Wassermann, 'The *Fliegende Blaetter* as a Source for the Social History of German Jewry', *LBIYB* 28 (1983) pp. 124–128.

38   Particularly noteworthy are Freytag's *Soll und Haben* (1855) and Raabe's *Hungerpastor* (1864). For historical context, see Ernest K. Bramsted, *Aristocracy and the Middle Classes in Germany: Social Types in German Literature, 1830–1900* (Chicago and London, 1964); George L. Mosse, 'The Image of the Jew in German Popular Literature: Felix Dahn and Gustav Freytag', in his *Germans and Jews: The Right, the Left, and the Search for a 'Third Force' in Pre-Nazi Germany* (London, 1971).

39   This is the first mention of the term that I have found. Jacob Katz, in *From Prejudice to Destruction: Anti-Semitism, 1700–1933* (Cambridge, Mass., 1980) pp. 186–7, suggests the same.

40   For an interesting treatment of Heinrich Laube, see *ibid.,* 182–84. For an analysis of the relation between the rise of 'new' assimilated Jewry and modern antisemitism, see Steven E. Aschheim, *Brothers and Strangers: The East European Jew in German and German-Jewish Consciousness, 1800–1923* (Madison, 1982) Chap. 3.

41   For this translation, see *Richard Wagner's Prose Works* (trans. William Ashton Ellis), vol. 3, *The Theatre* (London, 1907) pp. 81–2.

42   *Ibid.,* p. 84.

43   This perception of weakness and the attribution of almost uncanny powers to the 'Jewish spirit' were not, of course, limited to Germany. France

was also a center of this kind of thinking. Gougenot des Mousseaux's *Le Juif, le judaisme et la judaisation des peuples chretiens* (1869) not only influenced Edouard Drumont and other leading French antisemites but was translated by Alfred Rosenberg into German in 1921. The notion of 'Judaization' also became a key slogan in Austrian antisemitism. See Karl Tuerk, *Die Verjudung Oesterreichs: Eine Warnung fuer das deutsche Reich* (Berlin, 1889). In certain cases, as with political Zionist activity, Jews sometimes even encouraged notions of their great power and influence. For all that, it is still surprising to read empirical British statesmen dealing with the problem of the Balfour Declaration and the later British mandate. Sir Mark Sykes wrote in 1916 that it may seem 'odd and fantastic', but 'when we bump into a thing like Zionism which is atmospheric, international, cosmopolitan, subconscious and unwritten – very often unspoken – it is not possible to work and think in ordinary lines'. Of the draft mandate Lord Curzon commented that it 'reeks of Judaism' and had 'been drawn up by someone reeling under the fun-mes of Zionism.' These quotations appear in the fascinating review by Conor Cruise O'Brien, 'Israel in Embryo', *New York Review of Books,* March 15, 1984, pp. 36, 37.

44 Richard Wagner, 'Was ist Deutsch?', in *Richard Wagner's Gesammelte Schriften,* 13 (Leipzig, n.d.) pp. 166, 171.

45 See the insightful remarks by Paul Lawrence Rose in 'The Noble Anti-Semitism of Richard Wagner', *Historical Journal* 25 (1982) pp. 751–63.

46 For a recent example, see L.J. Rather, *The Dream of Self-Destruction: Wagner's Ring and the Modern World* (Baton Rouge, 1979).

47 The way in which Wagner treated his Jewish 'friends' is a matter of dispute. See Rose, 'Anti-Semitism of Wagner', pp. 754–9. See too, Peter Gay, 'Hermann Levi: A Study in Service and Self-Hatred', in his *Freud, Jews and Other Germans: Masters and Victims in Modernist Culture* (New York, 1978) pp. 189–230.

48 For just one example, see Wilhelm Marr, *Der Judenspiegel* (Hamburg, 1862) pp. 3, 11.

49 Houston Stewart Chamberlain, *Die Grundlagen des neunzehnten Jahrhunderts* (Munich, 1906), 1: pp. 544–5, 574.

50 Conrad Alberti, 'Judentum und Antisemitismus: Eine zeitgenoessische Studie', *Die Gesellschaft* 4 (1889) p. 1730.

51 Otto Weininger, *Geschlecht und Charakter: Eine Prinzipielle Untersuchung*, reprint ed. (Berlin, 1932) p. 403.

52 *Ibid.,* pp. 413, 401.

53 See Wagner's 'Erkenne dich selbst' and 'Heldentum und Christentum', in *Wagners Gesammelte Schriften*, pp. 14, 182–95, 193–203.

54 See Cosima Wagner's diary entry for December 27, 1878: 'Richard says: "Personally, I have always had the best friends among the Jews, but their emancipation and civil equality before we had become [true] Germans has been destructive. I regard Germany as annihilated."' Quoted in Rose, 'Anti-semitism of Wagner', p. 759.

55 See the anonymous *Die Verjudung des Christlichen Staates: Ein Wort zur Zeit* (Leipzig, 1865) p. 30.

56 Paul Koehler, *Die Verjudung Deutschlands und der Weg zur Rettung* (Stettin, 1880) p. 25.

57 *Ibid.,* pp. 30, 48.

58 Chamberlain, *Die Grundlagen*, 2, p. 1115 note 1.

59 For Paul de Lagarde, see his 'Ueber das Verhaeltnis des deutschen Staates zu Theologie, Kirche und Religion: Ein Versuch Nicht-Theologen zu orientieren' (1873), in his *Deutsche Schriften* (Goettingen, 1886) pp. 56–7. For Alfred Rosenberg, see his Robert Pois (ed.), *Race and Race History and Other Essays*, (New York, 1970) p. 69.

60 Friedrich Nietzsche, 'The Anti-christ', in *The Portable Nietzsche*, ed. Walter Kaufmann (New York, 1968) pp. 592–93. Nietzsche's italics here and in the following quotations.

61 Friedrich Nietzsche, *On the Genealogy of Morals* (ed. and trans. Walter Kaufmann and R.J. Hollingdale) (New York, 1969), p. 35.

62 *Ibid.,* p. 36. Nietzsche similarly did not discourage racists reading his work with statements such as these about the Jews: 'The simulation of "holiness" which has really become genius here, never even approximated elsewhere in books or among men, this counterfeit of words and gestures as an *art*, is not the accident of some individual talent or other or of some exceptional character. This requires *race*. In Christianity all of Judaism, a several-century-old Jewish preparatory training and technique of the most serious kind, attains its ultimate mastery as the art of lying in a holy manner. The Christian, this *ultima ratio* of the lie, is the Jew once more – even *three* times more.' *Anti-Christ*, no. 44, 620.

63 On the weakening, 'democratizing' effects, see Dietrich Eckart, *Der Bolschewismus von Moses bis Lenin: Zwiegespraech zwischen Adolf Hitler und mir* (Munich, 1924), esp. p. 28. On 'pity-ethics', see Hermann Rauschning, *Hitler Speaks: A Series of Conversations with Adolf Hitler on his Real Aims* (London, 1939) p. 57. We know now that Rauschning – so long considered authoritative – is a somewhat suspect source. Nevertheless the comments on 'pity-ethics' are consonant with much else that Hitler said and wrote.

64 Dietrich Eckart, *Das Judentum in und ausser uns*, in Alfred Rosenberg (ed.), *Dietrich Eckart: Ein Vermaechtnis* (Munich, 1928) p. 204. The

whole essay is pertinent to the present theme, from which it derives its title.

65   Lagarde, 'Ueber das Verhaeltnis', pp. 56–7.

66   Paul de Lagarde, 'Leopold Zunz und seine Verehrer', in Paul Fischer (ed.), *Ausgewaehlte Schriften*, (Munich, 1934) pp. 223, 224.

67   Paul de Lagarde, 'Programm fuer die konservative Partei Preussens' (1884) in *Deutsche Schriften*, pp. 367, 368. See too, his 'Juden und Indogermanen' (1887), in *Ausgewaehlte Schriften*, pp. 239, 242–46.

68   Rudolf Pannwitz, *An das Juedische Volk*, Flugblaetter 5 (Nuremberg, 1919) p. 3.

69   See Marr's rather Feuerbachian *Religioese Streitzuege eines Philosophischen Touristen* (Berlin, 1876) pp. 38, 144.

70   Katz, *From Prejudice to Destruction*, pp. 260–1.

71   See Hannah Arendt's analysis of this transformation in the chapter on 'Antisemitism as an Outrage to Common Sense' in her *The Origins of Totalitarianism* (Cleveland, 1963) pp. 3–10.

72   Wilhelm Marr, *Der Sieg des Judenthums ueber das Germanenthum: Vom nicht confessionellen Standpunkt aus betrachtet* (Bern, 1879) pp. 33, 41 45.

73   Eugen Duehring, *Die Judenfrage als Frage der Raceschaedlichkeit fuer Existenz, Sitte und Kultur,* reprint edn. (Berlin, l892) p. 138.

74   *Ibid.,* esp. p. 72.

75   See Peter Gay, *Weimar Culture: The Outsider as Insider* (New York, 1968).

76   Alfred Rosenberg, 'Der Jude' (1918), in his *Schriften aus den Jahren, 1917–1921* (Munich, 1943) p. 89.

77   Alfred Rosenberg, section entitled 'Kultur: The Volkish Aesthetic', in *Race and Race History*, especially pp. 149, 167, 173.

78   Rosenberg, 'Der Jude', p. 100.

79   See Richard von Schaukal, 'Grundsaetzliches zur Judenfrage', in *Der Jud ist Schuld*, p. 179 note 6.

80   Artur Dinter, 'Die Rassen- und Judenfrage im Lichte des Geistchristentums', in *ibid.,* p. 97. The whole essay is instructive.

81   Arthur Dinter, *The Completion of the Protestant Reformation* (London, 1937).

82   Arthur Dinter, 'Rassen- und Judenfrage', p. 96.

83   For an excellent analysis of Dinter's ideas and career see George M. Kren and Rodler F. Morris, 'Race and Spirituality: Arthur Dinter's Theosophical Antisemitism', *Holocaust and Genocide Studies*, 6 (no. 3, 1991) pp. 233–52. Dinter, they argue, was implicated in the radicalization and popularization of anti-semitism but explicitly renounced

violence against the Jews and was probably unaware of the 'Final Solution'.

84 See Max Wundt, *Deutsche Weltanschaaung. Grundzuege voelkischen Denkens* (Munich, 1926) and *Volk, Volkstum, Volkheit* (Langensalza, 1927). The quote appears in Hans Sluga, *Heidegger's Crisis: Philosophy and Politics in Nazi Germany* (Cambridge, Mass., 1993) p. 117. See Sluga's excellent treatment of Wundt and the Kantians in Nazi Germany.

85 See Hans F. K. Guenther, *Rassenkunde des Deutschen Volkes* (Munich, 1923), and his *Rassenkunde des Juedischen Volkes* (Munich, 1930).

86 George L. Mosse, *Toward the Final Solution: A History of European Racism* (New York, 1978), esp. the chapter entitled 'The Mystery of Race', pp. 94–112.

87 See Goebbels' speech in Hermann Haarmann, Walter Huder and Klaus Silberhaar (eds.), *'Das war ein Vorspiel nur. ... ' Buecherverbrennung Deutschland 1933: Voraussetzungen und Folgen* (Berlin, 1983) p. 197.

88 See 'Antrittsvorlesung in Berlin' in Alfred Baeumler, *Maennerbund and Wissenschaft* (Berlin, 1933) p. 137. Quoted in Sluga, *Heidegger's Crisis*, p. 127.

89 Quoted in Eckart, *Der Bolschewismus*, p. 46.

90 See Rauschning, *Hitler Speaks*, esp. p. 231.

91 Adolf Hitler, *Mein Kampf*, trans. Ralph Manheim (Boston, 1971), pp. 318, 246–7.

92 *Ibid.*, p. 318.

93 On this point, see the chapter entitled 'The Language of Nature', in J.P. Stern, *Hitler: The Führer and the People* (London, 1984) esp. p. 51. See, too, Ernst Nolte, *Three Faces of Fascism* (New York, 1969).

94 See the classic article by Alex Bein, 'The Jewish Parasite: Notes on the Semantics of the Jewish Problem, with Special Reference to Germany', *LBIYB* 10 (1964), pp. 3–40.

4 Nietzsche, Anti-Semitism and Mass Murder

1 I have discussed all this in great detail in my *The Nietzsche Legacy in Germany, 1890–1990* (Berkeley, 1992).

2 Walter Kaufmann (ed.), *The Will to Power* (New York, 1968), 960 (1885–1886), p. 504.

3 There are no end of supporting contemporary examples of this. At the 'higher' levels of discourse this was best illustrated by Heidegger, who initially viewed Nazism (and Fascism) as essentially Nietzschean projects, the most radical attempts to overcome Western nihilism. 'The two men', he proclaimed in his 1936 lectures on Schelling, 'who each in his own way, have introduced a counter-movement to nihilism –

Mussolini and Hitler – have learned from Nietzsche, each in an essentially different way. But even with that, Nietzsche's authentic metaphysical domain has not yet come into its own.' Quoted in Thomas Sheehan, 'Heidegger and the Nazis', *New York Review of Books* (16 June 1988).

4 *The Destruction of Reason* (trans. Peter Palmer) (Atlantic Highlands, NJ, 1981) p. 341. The work was completed in 1952 but based on essays written in the 1930s and 1940s.

5 *Nietzsche: Philosopher, Psychologist, Antichrist* (Princeton, NJ, 1950).

6 Our culture is awash with this Nietzsche. All the above-named authors works should be consulted. For typical examples of this genre amongst many, see Clayton Koelb (ed.), *Nietzsche as Postmodernist: Essays Pro and Con* (Albany, 1990); David B. Allison (ed.), *The New Nietzsche: Contemporary Styles of Interpretation* (Cambridge, Mass., 1985).

7 On Kaufmann's denaturing of Nietzsche's power-political dimensions, see Walter Sokel, 'Political Uses and Abuses of Nietzsche in Walter Kaufmann's Image of Nietzsche', *Nietzsche-Studien* 12 (1983).

8 The most relevant text in this regard is Juergen Habermas, *The Philosophical Discourse of Modernity*, trans.Frederick Lawrence (Cambridge, Mass., 1987). Habermas declared prematurely in 1968 that Nietzsche was 'no longer contagious' but subsequently spent a considerable amount of time combating the epidemic! For his mistimed proclamation, see his 'Zur Nietzsches Erkenntnistheorie' in Friedrich Nietzsche, *Erkenntnistheoretische Schriften* (Frankfurt, 1968).

9 'Nietzsche and National Socialism', *Michael* XIII (1993), pp. 11–27. See especially p. 11.

10 See *The Nietzsche Legacy in Germany*, especially Chs. 8–10 and the Afterword.

11 The full passage is filled with ambiguities, combining awe, disgust and fear. See *Daybreak: Thoughts on the prejudices of morality*, translated by R.J. Hollingdale (Cambridge, 1982) pp. 205, 124–5.

12 For some recent attempts to examine Nietzsche's views on Jews and Judaism in the relation to his whole philosophy, see Arnold M. Eisen, 'Nietzsche and the Jews Reconsidered', *Jewish Social Studies* 48, no. 1 (Winter 1986); M.F. Duffy and Willard Mittleman, 'Nietzsche's Attitude toward the Jews', *Journal of the History of Ideas* 49, no. 2 (April–June 1988); Jacob Golomb, 'Nietzsche's Judaism of Power', *Revue des etudes juives* 147 (July–December 1988).

13 See, for example, Walter Kaufmann (ed.), *On the Genealogy of Morals, Ecce Homo*, (New York, 1969), III, 14, pp. 123–4. See too Yirmiyahu Yovel, 'Nietzsche, the Jews and *Ressentiment*' in Richard Schacht

(ed.), *Nietzsche, Genealogy, Morality: Essays on Nietzsche's* On the Genealogy of Morals (Berkeley, 1994) pp. 214–36. See esp. p. 224.

14 *Ibid.,* 22, p. 144.

15 Prior to this quote the paragraph – a discarded draft for a passage from *Ecce Homo* – reads: 'Whoever reads me in Germany, has first de-Germanized himself thoroughly as I have done: my formula is known "to be a good German means to de-Germanize oneself"; or he is – no small distinction among Germans – of Jewish descent.' *Ibid.,*. p. 262, note 1.

16 I have outlined all of this in 'Nietzsche and the Nietzschean Moment in Jewish Life (1890–1939)', in *Leo Baeck Institute Yearbook* XXXVII (1992).

17 All these variations are treated in *The Nietzsche Legacy.*

18 This too was a common line. For just one example see 'Friedrich Nietzsche und die Modernen', *Deutsche Zeitung*, no. 10294 (28 August 1900).

19 Alfred Baeumler, *Nietzsche als Philosoph und Politiker* (Leipzig, 1931) p. 157.

20 Heinrich Roemer, 'Nietzsche und das Rasseproblem', *Rasse: Montaschrift fuer den Nordischen Gedanken* 7 (1940)

21 Again, for just one source, see Kurt Kassler, *Nietzsche und das Recht* (Munich, 1941) p. 74ff.

22 Franz Overbeck, 'Kirchlexicon, Nietzsche und das Judentum' (Nachlass Basel A 232), in R. Braendle and E. Stegemann (eds), *Franz Overbecks underledigte Anfragen an das Christentum* (Muenchen, 1988). I thank Hubert and Hildegard Cancik for this reference.

23 *On the Genealogy of Morals*, 7, pp. 33–4.

24 'The Anti-christ' in Walter Kaufmann (ed.), *The Portable Nietzsche* (New York, 1968) p. 593.

25 Heinrich Roemer, 'Nietzsche und das Rasseproblem', p. 61.

26 As Nietzsche wrote of the Jewish 'world-historic mission':

> The 'masters' have been disposed of; the morality of the common man has won. One may conceive of this victory as at the same time a blood poisoning (it has mixed the races together) – I shan't con-tradict; but this intoxication has undoubtedly been *successful*. The 'redemption' of the human race (from the 'masters', that is) is going forward; everything is becoming visibly Judaized, Christianized, mob-ized (what do the words matter!).' *Genealogy*, 9, p. 36.

27 See his *Nietzsche und das Christentum* (Berlin-Lichterfelde, 1937) p. 75.

28   Roemer, 'Nietzsche und das Rasseproblem', p. 63.

29   Hitler's youthful companion August Kubizek in his memoir, *The Young Hitler I Knew*, trans. E.V. Anderson (Boston, 1955), claims that the young Hitler did read Nietzsche but no work by the philosopher was found in his library (although it did contain a slim volume dedicated to him by Himmler entitled *Von Tacitus bis Nietzsche*). See Robert L. Waite, *Hitler: The Psychopathic God* (New York, 1977) p. 62.

30   Even if one disregards the many Nietzsche-inspired Hitler quotations from the now rather discredited works of Hermann Rauschning, this is patently obvious in *Hitler's Table Talk 1941–1944* (trans. Norman Cameron and R.H.Stevens) (London, 1953) esp. pp. 720–2.

31   The entire thrust of my *The Nietzsche Legacy in Germany, 1890–1990*, is to establish the multiple, often contradictory, nature of Nietzsche's influence and the impossibility of reducing it to an 'essential' political direction or position. Clearly, this should be kept in mind here. This chapter obviously deals with only *one* strand of influence.

32   See his *The Siege* (London, 1986) p. 59. See generally pp. 57–9, 85.

33   'The Antichrist', 24, pp. 593–4.

34   See his *Europe in the Twentieth Century* (London, 1974), pp. 185, 186.

35   Martin Jay, 'Should Intellectual History Take a Linguistic Turn? Reflections on the Habermas–Gadamer Debate', in his *Fin-de-Siècle Socialism* (New York, 1988), p. 33.

36   Jacques Derrida, 'Otobiographies: The Teaching of Nietzsche and the Politics of the Proper Name', in *The Ear of the Other: Otobiography Transference Translation* (ed.Christie V.McDonald, trans.Peggy Kamuf and Avital Ronell) (New York, 1985) pp. 30–1.

37   Berel Lang, *Act and Idea in the Nazi Genocide* (Chicago and London, 1990) pp. 197–8.

38   Primo Levi, 'Useless Violence', in *The Drowned and the Saved*, trans. Raymond Rosenthal (London, 1988) pp. 84–5.

39   See the whole chapter entitled 'Resentments' in his stunning *At the Mind's Limits: Contemplations By A Survivor On Auschwitz And Its Realities* (trans.Sidney Rosenfeld and Stella P. Rosenfeld) (Bloomington, 1980). The quote appears on p. 68. Amery, we should note, recast Nietzsche's theory of *ressentiment* into a *positive* virtue for the maintenance of ethical consciousness over the 'natural' processes of time and forgetfulness of crimes committed but not acknowledged.

40   Lifton, *The Nazi Doctors: Medical Killing and the Psychology of Genocide* (London, 1987), especially pp. 15–27; Chapter 21 and p. 486.

41 Nietzsche, *Genealogy of Morals,* III, 14, p. 122.

42 'Tokens of Higher and Lower Culture', *Human all too Human: A book for free Spirits* (trans.R.J.Hollingdale) (Cambridge, 1986) 224, pp. 107–108.

43 On this, see my 'Max Nordau, Friedrich Nietzsche and *Degeneration*', *Journal of Contemporary History* 28 (no. 4, October 1993).

44 See Daniel Pick, *Faces of Degeneration: A European Disorder, c.1848–1918* (Cambridge, 1989) for a sense of the politically diverse annexation of the notion and its wide dissemination.

45 'On the Gift-giving Virtue', 1, 'Thus Spake Zarathustra' in *The Portable Nietzsche*, p. 187. Italics in the original.

46 Walter Kaufman (ed.), *The Will to Power,* (New York, 1968), 246 (Jan.–Fall 1888), p. 142.

47 *Ibid.,* p. 389. These kinds of sentiments are dotted throughout Nietzsche's works. See *Will to Power*, pp. 141–142, 391–3; *Zarathustra*,pp. 183–6 (although here *freedom* to die is stressed); 'Twilight of the Idols', in *The Portable Nietzsche*, pp. 536–8; *Genealogy of Morals*, pp. 120–5.

48 For examples see *The Nietzsche Legacy*, pp. 161, 163, 243–4.

49 I am presently undertaking a study on 'Nazism and Western Consciousness, 1933–1993' which will seek to investigate and place into contextual and conceptual order these diverse analyses.

50 See his *Ordinary Men: Reserve Police Battalion 101 and the Final Solution in Poland* (New York, 1992).

51 See his *Nationalism and Sexuality: Respectability and Abnormal Sexuality in Modern Europe* (New York, 1985).

52 This has recently been interestingly explored by Saul Friedlander, in '"The Final Solution": On the Unease in Historical Interpretation' in his *Memory, History, and the Extermination of the Jews of Europe* (Indiana, 1993). See especially p. 110.

53 Lichtheim, *Europe in the Twentieth Century*, p. 186. Too often this has been exclusively and ideologically linked to the downfall supposedly inherent in Nietzsche's 'atheism' thus enabling unlimited powers to man in which, given the fact that nothing is sacred, he has total license to kill. This is not the position upheld here for it, I would argue, is the anti-Enlightenment, antihumanist impulse not secularization *per se* that is linked to these events.

54 Kurt Rudolf Fischer, 'Nazism as a Nietzschean Experiment', *Nietzsche-Studien*, 6 (1977) p. 121.

55 Nietzsche, *On the Genealogy of Morals*, p. 54, I, 16, pp. 86–7, II, 17.

56 For a good evaluation of these different sides see Hans Sluga,

Heidegger's Crisis: Philosophy and Politics in Nazi Germany (Cambridge, Mass., 1993).

57 See the translation of the original *Der Faschismus in seiner Epoche* (1963) by Leila Vennewitz (New York, 1969).

58 While Nolte noted that there were many objections to Lukács, and while his thesis was quite different, Nolte was in agreement that at the end of the nineteenth century a major change in the spiritual climate of Europe took place. Nietzsche's role was clear: 'With no immediate relevance to the political events of the day, the Nietzschean doctrine, which alone permitted the equation of socialism, liberalism, and traditional conservatism, was adopted and developed by a circle of fascistoid authors: the doctrine of the revolt of the slaves and of the impoverishment of life through Judeo-Christian resentment.' *Three Faces*, p. 22.

59 *Ibid.*, p. 555. For the phrase *Vernichtungsgedanke* see the German edition *Der Faschismus in seiner epoche* (Munich, 1963), p. 533. The choice of phrase in the post-Holocaust era is telling; far more than 'destruction' (usually rendered as *'Zerstoerung'*), *'Vernichtung'* has become associated with 'extermination'.

60 *Ibid.*, pp. 556–7. Because the translation of this passage is not entirely satisfactory I have provided my own where necessary. See the original pages in *Der Faschismus*, pp. 533–4. Other mentions of Nietzsche may be found on pp. 159; 218; 534; 551–3.

61 *Ibid.*, p. 534. In his *In Bluebeard's Castle: Some Notes towards the Re-definition of Culture* (London, 1971), George Steiner presents a not too dissimilar thesis. Although he does not name Nietzsche in this regard, Steiner's view of the Holocaust is presented as an event motivated, above all, by the rage against debilitating morality and conscience, and the belief that the latter was 'a Jewish invention' (pp. 35ff). But Steiner does not limit his respectful treatment of Nietzsche to this implicit dimension. Indeed, when he is explicitly invoked it is not as the inspirer but rather as presager and superb diagnostican of the Holocaust (pp. 38; 42), very much aware (together with Kierkegaard) of the barbarizing – rather than humanizing – qualities that can inhere in culture (pp. 63–4).

62 Ernst Nolte, *Der europaeische Buergerkrieg 1917–1945: Nationalsozialismus und Bolschewismus* (Frankfurt/Berlin, 1987) pp. 514–5.

63 Ernst Nolte, *Nietzsche und der Nietzscheanismus*, op. cit.

64 *Ibid.*, pp. 192–3.

65 *Ibid.*, pp. 193–4. Note too that Nolte included this quote in his *Der Faschismus*, p. 533. The Walter Kaufmann translation again renders

Nietzsche more genteel and less biological than a more literal translation (which I have attempted above) indicates. For instance, he translates 'schonungslose Vernichtung' as 'relentless destruction'. That, of course, is a far more impersonal, almost agentless description. 'Schnongslose Vernichtung' – precisely because it so resembles Nazi vocabulary and action – should more properly be read as 'merciless or brutal extermination'. Kaufmann, moreover, translates 'Hoherzuechtung der Menschheit' as the attempt 'to raise humanity higher' thereby leaving out entirely its breeding, biological connotation. See the translation in *On the Genealogy of Morals and Ecce Homo*, 'The Birth of Tragedy', 4, p. 274.

66 In *Three Faces of Fascism*, in a rather obscure passage, Nolte had already hinted at this theme. The positive aspect of both Hitler and Nietzsche's ideas, he wrote, 'was completely outweighed by the concrete aspect of their negative will. Many decades in advance Nietzsche provided the political, radical anti-Marxism of fascism with its original spiritual image, an image of which even Hitler never quite showed himself the equal.' *Three Faces of Fascism*, p. 557. In *Der Faschismus*, this quote appears on p. 535.

67 Nolte, *Nietzsche,* p. 195.

68 *Ibid.,* p. 269.

69 *Nietzsche,* p. 88; p. 192.

70 *Ibid,* p. 89. Nolte writes that while Marx and Nietzsche developed alternative and juxtaposed conceptions bound up with the conditions of the time, neither desired to create *'Buergerkriegskonzeptionen'*. The moment that decisive steps to realize their visions were taken, however, the end was inevitable. See p. 276.

71 Nolte, incidentally, gets caught up in precisely the kind of dubious ideological *Rezeptionsgeschichte* characteristic of its 'essentialist' history. Given his conception as to how it *ought* to have proceeded – Nietzsche as champion of the 'party of life' – he can only express surprise that 'the concept of the "party of life" does not appear anywhere and the not infrequent discussions on "Marx and Nietzsche" revolve mainly around the juxtaposition of "collectivists" and "individualists"'. See *ibid.,* p. 268.

72 See his 'A Past that will not Pass Away', *Yad Vashem Studies* XIX (1988) p. 71.

5 The German–Jewish Dialogue at its Limits: The Case of Hermann Broch and Volkmar von Zuehlsdorff

1 Hermann Broch, *Briefe ueber Deutschland 1945–1949. Die Korrespondenz mit Volkmar von Zuehlsdorff* (ed. Paul Michael

Luetzeler) (Frankfurt am Main, 1986). Henceforth, *Briefe*. I thank Gidon Reuveni for drawing my attention to this document.

2 'Germany and the Germans', in *Thomas Mann's Addresses: Delivered at the Library of Congress 1942–1949* (Washington, DC, 1963), p. 48 (his italics). See too p. 64. The lecture was delivered on May 29, 1945.

3 Various commentators have commented on the persistence of Catholic themes and emphases in Broch even after he left the Church. See, for instance, Richard Brinkmann, 'On Broch's Concept of Symbol' in Stephen D. Dowden (ed.), *Hermann Broch: Literature, Philosophy, Politics* (Columbia, SC, 1988), pp. 202ff. Broch himself was aware of its continuing – and not particularly desired – hold. As late as 1950 he wrote to Waldo Frank: 'I am in the process of weeding out the last remnants of my Catholicism; that's something that will have to happen before I die.' See Paul Michael Luetzeler (ed.), *Hermann Broch Briefe 3 (1945–1951), Kommentierte Werkausgabe, Band 13/3*, (Frankfurt am Main, 1981), Letter 684, p. 413.

4 Hermann Broch, *The Sleepwalkers*, translated by Will and Edwin Muir (New York, 1964), pp. 525–6. This was yet another species of the Judaization thesis we have examined previously. 'It looks as though the current of the absolute Abstract which for two thousand years has flowed through the ghettoes like an almost imperceptible trickle beside the great river of life should now become the main stream.' At the same time, Broch's thesis was (rather simplistically) meant to account for the prevailing anti-semitic tenor of the times. Fear of the future, he wrote, was constantly active but it found 'expression merely in a fear of the Jews, whose spirit and mode of living are felt, if not recognized to be a hateful image of the future.'

5 See Saul Friedlander, 'West Germany and the Burden of the Past: The Ongoing Debate', *The Jerusalem Quarterly* (Number 42, Spring 1987), p. 17.

6 See the collection of articles in Will Schaber (ed.), *Aufbau. Reconstruction Dokumente einer Kultur im Exil* (New York and Koeln, 1972).

7 The directness of Broch's letters hardly indicate the complexities of his lifelong philosophical and literary preoccupation with death, his ambiguous relation to 'irrationalism' ('when reason becomes autonomous', he wrote in *The Sleepwalkers* [p. 627], 'it is radically evil'), his analyses of unified civilizations and their disintegration, his emphasis on mythos and longing for absolutes – whether of a religious nature (as at the beginning of his career) or an 'earthly' secular one (with which he ended his career).

8 *Briefe*, No.1, 24 July 1945, p. 21.

9 *Ibid.,* No.3, 9 August 1945, p. 26; No.5, 21.8.45, p. 32.

10 *Ibid.,* No.29, 28.8.47, p. 99.

11 *Ibid.,* No.21, 21 November 1946. The quotes appear on pp. 72–3 and 75 respectively.

12 *Ibid.,* No.22, 24 December 1946, p. 80. Broch was not consistent in this. He was at times attracted to a *Sonderweg* metaphysic of the German mind in which the extreme possibilities of evil and redemption were fused. While indifference, he wrote, was a general human characteristic, it was 'the German *Volk*, in matters good as in evil the most extreme people of the West, that served again as the concave mirror of the world-spirit.' This very indifference could be transformed into an instrument of deliverance. 'The actual practical solution will – of this I am convinced – emerge out of Germany, *for it was there that guilt was most accentuated* and there that the mystical connection between guilt and atonement is most tangibly manifest. Germany will play the leading role in the regeneration of the world as soon as the Germans grasp the meaning of guilt by virtue of indifference.' (No.3, 9 August 1945, pp. 25, 26.)

13 *Ibid.,* No.22, 24 December 1946, pp. 80–1.

14 *Ibid.,* No. 25, 27 May 1947, p. 90.

15 *Ibid.,* see for instance Broch's letters 22 and 24.

16 *Ibid.,* No. 28, 21 July 1947, p. 97.

17 On the overall ramifications of this disjunction, see my *Brothers and Strangers: The East European Jew in German and German Jewish Consciousness, 1800–1923* (Madison, 1982).

18 *Briefe*, No. 42, 28 December 1948, p. 133. For another example see Ernst von Salomon, *The Answers: To the 131 Questions in the Allied Military Government 'Fragebogen'*, Preface by Goronwy Rees, translated by Constantine Fitzgibbon (London, 1954), p. 508: 'During my whole time in camp and prison', Salomon quotes an inmate as saying, 'the only antisemitic remarks I heard were all made by Americans.'

19 *Ibid.,* No.4, 19 August 1945, pp. 27–8.

20 He wrote to Kurt Wolff that the slogan under which the book appeared – '*the* prophetic novel, demonstrating the predestination of the German people to Hitlerism' was 'no empty interpretation: the book was really prophetic and precisely as a result of the "disintegration of values" completely maintained its full meaning.' See Letter 543 (11 August 1946), Paul Michael Luetzeler (ed.), *Hermann Broch Briefe* 3 (1945–1951), (Frankfurt am Main, 1981), p. 115. In *The Sleepwalkers* he had written about the insanity of war thus: 'Is it to be referred to a

mere indifference to others' sufferings? to the indifference that lets a citizen sleep soundly next door to the prison yard in which someone is being hanged by the neck or guillotined? the indifference that needs only to be multiplied to produce public indifference to the fact that thousands of men are being impaled on barbed wire? Of course it is that same indifference, but it goes further than that; for here we have no longer merely two mutually exclusive fields of reality, that of the slayer on one side and of the slain on the other; we find them co-existing in one and the same individual. ... it is a split in the totality of life and experience ... a split that cuts right into the individual himself and his integral reality.' See Hermann Broch, *The Sleepwalkers: A Trilogy*, translated by Willa and Edwin Muir, with an Introduction by Hannah Arendt (New York, 1964), pp. 374–5.

21   *Briefe,* No.3, 9 August 1945, p. 25.

22   'Rundfunkansprache an das deutsche Volk', in Hermann Broch, Paul Michael Luetzeler (ed.), *Politische Schriften. Kommentierte Werkausgabe,* Vol.11 (Frankfurt am Main, 1978) p. 241.

23   *Briefe,* No.4, 19 August 1945, pp. 28–9. See also Zuehlsdorff's letter No. 34, 16 March 1948, pp. 109–114 where he quotes from William L. White's 1947 *Report on the Germans* which claimed that most Germans did not know of the Final Solution and that in 1939 'at least 70 per cent of the German people opposed Hitler's Jewish policy and would give help to the Jews even at risk to themselves' and that as late as 1943 'At least half the German people were glad to help the Jews when they could.'

24   For the most recent and comprehensive examination of this subject, see David Bankier, *The Germans and the Final Solution: Public Opinion under Nazism* (Oxford, 1992).

25   'A. borrowed a copper kettle from B. and after he had returned it was sued by B. because the kettle now had a big hole which made it unusable. His defence was: "First, I never borrowed a kettle from B. at all; secondly, the kettle had a hole in it already when I got it from him; and thirdly, I gave him back the kettle undamaged." ' See Sigmund Freud, *Jokes and Their Relation to the Unconscious*, translated by James Strachey (New York, 1963), p. 62.

26   *Briefe,* No.4, 19 August 1945, p. 30.

27   *Ibid.,* No.6, 31 August 1945, p. 38.

28   *Ibid.,* No.34, 16 March 1948, p. 110.

29   *Briefe,* No.9, 29 October 1945, p. 44.

30   *Ibid.,* No.34, 16 March 1948, p. 112.

31   The pages of Will Schaber (ed.), *Aufbau*, reflect this.

32 What was needed, Arendt wrote, was a form of control over German industry, she wrote, or rather a European form of cooperation (that in effect formed the nucleus of the present European Union.) See her 'Approaches to the German Problem', *Partisan Review*, 12 (no. 1, 1945), p. 102.

33 *Briefe*, No.44, 20 March 1949, p. 139.

34 *Ibid.,* No.6, 31 August 1945, p. 38.

35 Zuehlsdorff enunicated an ongoing line of argument not only in terms of comparative relativisation but also in terms of his fury against Morgenthau. As recently as 1985 the editor of the mass circulation *Der Spiegel*, Rudolf Augstein, wrote that as far as Morgenthau was concerned Hitler had missed a good follower. The same article also argued for the comparative relativisation of atrocities. See Rudolf Augstein, 'Auf die schiefe Ebene zur Republik', *Der Spiegel 2*, 1985, pp. 31–2.

36 *Briefe,* No.43, 28 February 1949, pp. 134–135.

37 Jean Amery, *At the Mind's Limits: Contemplations by a Survivor on Auschwitz and its Realities* trans. by Stanley Rosenfeld and Stella P. Rosenfeld (Bloomington, 1980) p. 65.

38 *Briefe*, No.9, 29 October 1945, p. 45.

39 *Ibid.,* No.10, 5.11. 45, pp. 46–47.

40 *Ibid.,* No.15, 14 February 1946, p. 53.

41 Letter of January 22, 1946 to Thomas Mann (who did the italicising). See *An Exceptional Friendship: The Correspondence of Thomas Mann and Erich Kahler*, translated by Richard and Clara Winston (Ithaca, 1975) p. 113. In the rest of the letter while Kahler indicated his concern about the German relationship to its own recent past he also made extremely critical comments concerning Allied post-war behaviour.

42 See Ronald Webster, 'American Relief and Jews in Germany, 1945–1960: Diverging Perspectives', *Leo Baeck Institute Yearbook* XXXVIII (1993), pp. 293ff.

43 *The Patton Papers, 1940–1945, ed. Martin Blumenson* (Boston, 1974, entry for September 17, 1946). Quoted in Stern, *ibid.,* pp. 81–2. Here again the disparity between Jewish and German perceptions could not have been greater as one internee – Ernst von Salomon – under Patton's authority made clear: 'And what happened to Patton? The Americans accused our generals of having collaborated with the Hitlerite lunacy. What happened to the one American general who refused to collaborate with the Morgenthau lunacy? Patton was kicked out, fired because of his humane, decent and politically sensible attitude towards the internees – and for no other reason. ... when he was killed in a car

smash, there were very few people who were not firmly convinced that he had been murdered by Jews.' Ernst von Salomon, *The Answers,* pp. 505–6.

44 For a detailed examination of both German and American perceptions, see Frank Stern, *The Whitewashing of the Yellow Badge: Antisemitism and Philosemitism*, trans. Willam Templer (Oxford, 1992). Stern traces the zig-zags of attitudes in the field as well as official policy. At the beginning there was an official instruction not to provide special treatment for the Jews as this would replicate Nazi practices! Though this was rescinded, attitudes in the field continued to be decidely ambivalent if not outright negative.

45 *Ibid.,* p. 89.

46 *Briefe,No.34,* 16 March 1948, p. 111.

47 *Ibid.,* No.42, 28 December 1948, pp. 132–133.

48 *Ibid.,* No.15, 15 February 1946, p. 56.

49 *Ibid.,* No.18, 16 February 1946, pp. 65–66.

50 *Ibid.,* No.42, 28 December 1948, p. 132.

51 *Ibid.,* No.7, 5 September 1945, p. 41.

52 *Ibid.,* No.19, 8 March 1946, pp. 68ff.

53 *Ibid.,* No.42, 28 December 1948, pp. 132, 133.

54 *Ibid.,* No.43, 28 February 1949, p. 137.

55 This was clearly not always – or only – a German–Jewish divide. Thus Thomas Mann's comments about the Germans in a letter to Erich Kahler: 'They have learned nothing, understand nothing, regret nothing, have not the slightest sense ... that their sacred German soil long ago ceased to be sacred and has instead been desecrated again and again by injustice and the utmost baseness. ... Frau Elsa Bruckmann ... curses the Americans fearfully; they deliberately and systematically bomb German children's hospitals. Some persons expressed mild doubt and incidentally asked even more mildly about the dreadful mass killings of children by the Germans. "But you cannot compare that", she replied. "Those were Jewish children."' It should be noted that this was written before the end of the war when Mann refused to believe that there would ever be a German surrender. See his letter of 20 October 1944, in *An Exceptional Friendship*, p. 90.

56 The commentaries on the novel are legion. But for this reading, see especially George Steiner, 'The Hollow Miracle' in *Language and Silence: Essays on Language, Literature and the Inhuman* (New York, 1977) p. 103. In the Preface (p. xi) Steiner comments that 'Broch's life and works are of themselves an exemplary form of civilization, a refusal of cheapness and chaos.'

57 Gisela Brude-Firnau, 'Broch's Spell and the Present' in Dowden (ed.), *Hermann Broch,* pp. 125–33. See especially p. 131.

58 Thus many of Broch's ongoing literary and philosophical concerns were (problematically) integrated into his study of mass psychology, that sought simultaneously to scientifically analyse Nazism and search for ways of overcoming the kinds of attraction it exerted. This uncompleted project obsessed him ('The mass psychology is worth suicide', he wrote in his first letter to Zuehlsdorff [No.1, 24 July 1945, p. 21]) but never aroused much interest nor did it exert the influence that he sought. See his *Massenwahntheorie: Beitraege zu einer Psycholgie der Politik* (Franfkurt am Main, 1979). This appears as Vol. 12 in Paul Michael Luetzler (ed.), *Hermann Broch Kommentierte Werkausgabe,* Analyses of all the above themes may be found in Dowden (ed.), *Hermann Broch.*

59 'Hermann Broch: 1886–1951', in Hannah Arendt, *Men in Dark Times* (New York, 1968) pp. 126–7.

6 Hannah Arendt and Karl Jaspers: Friendship, Catastrophe and the Possibilities of the German–Jewish Dialogue

1 Hannah Arendt and Karl Jaspers, *Correspondence 1926–1969,* edited by Lotte Kohler and Hans Saner, translated from the German by Robert and Rita Kimber (New York, San Diego, London, 1992).

2 This is the title of a review of the correspondence by Richard A. Schweder, *The New York Times* (September 20, 1992) p. 1.

3 Gordon A. Craig, 'Letters on Dark Times', *The New York Review of Books* (May 13, 1993) p. 10.

4 Amongst the many other issues discussed, the most important include ruminations on American society, McCarthyism, the Vietnam war and so on. Moreover, given the intimate nature of the correspondence, the letters reveal fascinatingly unguarded opinions about intellectual peers ranging from Theodor Adorno to Gershom Scholem and Walter Kaufmann.

5 Judging from this correspondence (as well as her public pronouncements) Arendt remained deeply ambivalent about Heidegger to the very end, torn between attraction to, and admiration for, her former lover-teacher and her scorn for his Nazi past and his actions thereafter. The relationship has been much discussed in the literature but see the *Correspondence,* pp. 47–8, 142, 457, 459–60, 629–30, 634.

6 Thus, as just one example, Arendt demonstrated a continuing, quite conventional German-Jewish disdain for *Ostjuden* (East European Jews). See Letter 285, Arendt to Jaspers, *Correspondence,* April 13,

1961, pp. 434–6). Jaspers too demonstrated a similar and equally traditional, if at times qualified, non-Jewish German attitude. See Letter 56, Jaspers to Arendt, April 19, 1957, especially p. 82 and the comments by Jaspers and Arendt respectively on Kurt Blumenfeld's Russian-Jewish wife, Jenny. See Letters 159, August 29, 1964 and 160, October 6, 1954, especially pp. 246 and 248.

7 See Elisabeth Young-Bruehl, *Hannah Arendt: For Love of the World* (New Haven and London, 1982) p. 127. Unfortunately, Young-Bruehl supplies no explanation for this quite remarkable action. In general, unorthodox couplings characterised Arendt's circle of friends. This is illustrated by the case of Lotte Sempell who, despite the fact that she had lost Bluecher to Arendt, remained within the circle. 'At a 1938 performance of a Yiddish theater troupe, Chanan Klenbort acted as interpreter for Arendt, Bluecher, and Lotte Sempell. Lotte Sempell ended the evening with Klenbort, and eventually the unlikely match between a German bourgeois Protestant and a Polish *shtetl* Jew, which resulted in marriage and two children, was made' (Young-Bruehl, p. 136).

8 Letter No. 34, Arendt to Jaspers, January 29, 1946, *Correspondence*, p. 29.

9 For overviews of this question see Jeremy Noakes, 'The Development of Nazi Policy towards the German-Jewish "Mischlinge" 1933–1945' and Ursula Buettner, 'The Persecution of Christian-Jewish Families in the Third Reich', *Leo Baeck Institute Yearbook* XXXIV (1989).

10 For details, see Hans Saner, *Karl Jaspers In Selbstzeugnissen und Bilddokumenten* (Hamburg, 1970) pp. 47–8.

11 Karl Jaspers, *Erneurung der Universitaet. Reden und Schriften 1945–1946* (Heidelberg, 1986) pp. 96–9. This translation comes from Frank Stern, *The Whitewashing of the Yellow Badge*, pp. 205–6.

12 Anson Rabinbach has argued that Jaspers *Die Schuldfrage* ingeniously applied Arendt's Jewish categories to contemporary German experience, rendering the Germans as latterday pariahs. See this (as yet unpublished) essay, 'The German as Pariah: Germans and Jews in Karl Jaspers' *Die Schuldfrage*', in *Reader for the Symposium on Jewish Identity in the German World: Emancipation, Assimilation and Thereafter* (Berkeley, 16–17 March, 1990) pp. 183–220. Jaspers was probably also aware of the pariah category through his familiarity with the work of his intellectual model, Max Weber.

13 Hannah Arendt, 'The Jew as Pariah: A Hidden Tradition' appeared originally in *Jewish Social Studies*, Vol. VI, No. 2, April 1944, pp. 99–122. It is reprinted in Hannah Arendt, *The Jew as Pariah: Jewish*

Identity and Politics in the Modern Age (ed. Ron H. Feldman) (New York, 1978). The quote appears on p. 67.

14 See the English version, *The Question of German Guilt*, translated by E.B. Ashton (New York, 1947).

15 Typical of such responses was Ernst Robert Curtius's comments on Jaspers' talk 'Unsere Zukunft und Goethe' given on the occasion of receiving the Goethe Prize in 1947: 'Jaspers hat seit 1945 deutlich bekundet, dass er den vielunworbenen Posten eines praeceptor Germaniae anstrebt. Er hat unsere Kollektivschuld so sonnenklar erwiesen, dass wir nur noch mit schlechten Gewissen weiterleben. Ein Wilhelm von Humboldt unserer Zeiten, hat er den deutschen Universitaeten Richtlinien gegeben, bis er ihnen den Ruecken kehrte. Ein kommender praeceptor Helvetiae. Als Reformator hat er sodann einen neuen Glauben entdeckt, den er "biblische Religion" nennt und dessen Pointe darin besteht, dass Judentum und Christentum ungefaehr dasselbe seien. Er kroent diese volkserziehersichen Leistungen durch eine "Kampagne in der Schweiz" die sich gegen Goethe richtet. Habemus papam!' Ernst Robert Curtius, 'Goethe oder Jaspers?', *Die Tat* (2 April 1949). Quoted in Saner, pp. 58–9.

16 See Arendt, *The Jew as Pariah*, Part II: 'Zionism and the Jewish State' for five such critical essays written between 1942 and 1950.

17 Hannah Arendt, *Eichmann in Jerusalem: A Report on the Banality of Evil* (New York, 1963).

18 For a comprehensive survey and analysis of the extreme responses Arendt's Eichmann evoked and the reasons for this see Richard I. Cohen, 'Breaking the Code: Hannah Arendt's *Eichmann in Jerusalem* and the Public Polemic – Myth, Memory and Historical Imagination' in *Michael* XIII (1993) pp. 29–85. The literature on this question is voluminous.

19 Stephen Whitfield, *Into the Dark: Hannah Arendt and Totalitarianism* (Philadelphia, 1980) p. 172.

20 'Eichmann in Jerusalem', 'An Exchange of Letters between Gershom Scholem and Hannah Arendt' (1963), reproduced in *The Jew as Pariah*, pp. 240–5. See especially p. 241.

21 *Ibid.*, pp. 246–7.

22 To be sure, Arendt added, on a personal and individual (as opposed to public-political) level the question of whether she was a German or a Jew was unimportant. Letter 50, Arendt to Jaspers, December 17, 1946, *Correspondence*, p. 70.

23 *Ibid.*, Letter of 7 October 1967, quoted in Young-Bruehl, *Hannah Arendt*, p. 139 (see too note 23, p. 508).

24 Apart from *Die Schuldfrage*, Jaspers was constantly concerned with specifically German questions. See, for instance, *Hoffnung und Sorge: Schriften zur deutschen Politik 1945–1965* (Munich, 1965); *Wohin treibt die Bundesrepublik? Tatsachen – Gefahren – Chancen* (Munich, 1966); *Antwort. Zur Kritik meiner Schift 'Wohin treibt die Bundesrepublik?'* (Munich, 1967).

25 See Michael Walzer, *Interpretation and Social Criticism* (Cambridge, Mass., 1987).

26 '"What remains? The language remains": A conversation with Guenter Gaus' in Hannah Arendt, *Essays in Understanding 1930–1954*, (ed. Jerome Kohn) (New York, 1994) p. 14.

27 'On Humanity in Dark Times: Thoughts about Lessing' (Address on accepting the Lessing Prize), in Hannah Arendt, *Men in Dark Times*, translated by Clara and Richard Winston (New York and London, 1968) pp. 17–18, 23.

28 This kind of thought was typified by his *Die Geistigen Situation der Zeit* (1931) in which the Nazis are not even mentioned. See the English translation by Eden and Cedar Paul, *Man in the Modern Age* (London, 1951). For an analysis of these tendencies in Jaspers' early thought see Rabinbach, 'The German as Pariah'.

29 Karl Jaspers, *Schicksal und Wille. Autobiographische Schriften* (Munich, 1967) p. 35. (Quoted in Saner, p. 44.)

30 This admiration persisted throughout Jaspers' life. Although Weber 'was no genius and inferior to both Nietzsche and Kierkegaard', Jaspers wrote as late as 1966, 'he is nonetheless in comparison with those eternal adolescents and dubious figures, plainly and simply a man.' Letter 396, Jaspers to Arendt, *Correspondence*, April 29, 1966, pp. 635–9. The quote appears on p. 637.

31 Karl Jaspers, *Max Weber: Deutsches Wesen im politischen Denken, im Forschen und Philosophieren* (Oldenburg, 1932). For the quote see p. 7.

32 Letter 24, Arendt to Jaspers, *Correspondence*, January 6, 1933, pp. 18–19.

33 *Ibid.,* Letter 22, Arendt to Jaspers, January 1, 1933, p. 16.

34 This quote and the one above both appear in *ibid.,* Letter 24, Arendt to Jaspers, January 6, 1933, pp. 18–19.

35 *Ibid.,* Letter 23, Jaspers to Arendt, January 3, 1933, pp. 17–18.

36 *Ibid.,* Letter 138, Jaspers to Arendt, December 29, 1952, p. 204. In 1946, Jaspers wrote to her: 'Aren't you too, as Heine was, according to your characterization, both a Jew *and* a German? For me you are, unavoidably, but whether you want to be is another question.' Letter 46, Jaspers to Arendt, October 19, 1946, p. 63.

37 To be sure, as he wrote to Arendt, in 1947, he was prepared to concede that: 'The "German essence" – it is indeed the language and only the language. I quite agree with you. But that is no small thing and it would be wonderful if German were still spoken and somewhere in the world in future centuries. That is no longer a sure thing.' *Ibid.*, Letter 52, Jaspers to Arendt, January 1, 1947, pp. 71–2. See too his 1965 radio talk 'Was ist deutsch?' reproduced in Karl Jaspers, *Hoffunung und Sorge: Schriften zur Deutschen Politik 1945–1965* (Muenchen, 1965) pp. 346–65.

38 Jaspers to Arendt, Letter 83, January 26, 1949, *Correspondence*, p. 128. As Jaspers wrote to Heidegger as late as 1953, proper philosophy could only be true 'when the ground (soil) is true [*wenn der Boden wahr ist*], and for both of us it is German.' See Letter 151, Jaspers to Heidegger, 3 April 1953 in Martin Heidegger/Karl Jaspers, *Briefwechsel 1920–1963*, edited by Walter Biemel and Hans Saner (Frankfurt am Main, 1990) p. 214. Heidegger, it will be remembered, also privileged the depth of German and Greek cultures but conspicuously omitted that of the Jews.

39 For the latest revised edition, see Hannah Arendt, *Rahel Varnhagen: The Life of a Jewish Woman*, translated by Richard and Clara Winston (New York and London, 1974). The work was first published in German in 1959. For details of the book's history, see Arendt's 'Preface'. On the importance of Rahel to Arendt's overall thinking, see Dagmar Barnouw, *Visible Spaces: Hannah Arendt and the German-Jewish Experience* (Baltimore and London, 1990), especially Chapter 2.

40 Arendt insisted on the selective nature of such incorporation. She told Jaspers: 'Whatever of the straightforward historical insights I still consider relevant are contained in shorter form and devoid of all "psychology" in the first part of my totalitarianism book.' Letter 135, Arendt to Jaspers, *Correspondence*, p. 201. That may be so, but the nature of the incorporated historical insights were so striking precisely because of their psychological penetration (although their relation to the totalitarian project of mass extermination was never really made clear). See for instance the brilliantly suggestive section in Chapter 3 'The Jews and Society' of *The Origins of Totalitarianism* (Cleveland and New York: The World Publishing Company, 1951) where Arendt delineates the newly forged structure and dilemmas of modern Jewish identity. 'The behavior patterns of assimilated Jews, determined by this continuous concentrated effort to distinguish themselves, created a new Jewish type that is recognizable everywhere. Instead of being defined by nationality or religion, Jews were being transformed into a social

group whose members shared certain psychological attributes and reactions, the sum total of which was to constitute 'Jewishness'. In other words, Judaism became a psychological quality and the Jewish question became an involved personal problem for every individual Jew.' (p. 66 of *The Origins*). See too pp. 84–7.

41 Letter 83, Jaspers to Heidegger, 20 June 1929 in the *Briefwechsel 1920–1963,* pp. 121–2.

42 Thus as late as 1957 – upon the publication of the revised *Rahel* – he wrote that 'it will probably please no one, not the Jews or the anti-Semites or even me (except that in one way or another I like everything you do, even if I disagree with it).' Letter 205, Jaspers to Arendt, February 24, 1957, *Correspondence,* pp. 310–13. The quote appears on p. 312.

43 *Ibid.,* Letter 138, December 29, 1952, pp. 204–5.

44 *Ibid.,* Letter 14, March 30, 1930, p. 10.

45 *Ibid.,* Letter 15, pp. 11–12. It is dated, presumably incorrectly, as March 24 a week *before* Jaspers penned his comments. The letter was presumably written on April 24, 1930.

46 Ibid. Letter 134, August 23, 1952, pp. 192–6.

47 *Ibid.,* Letter 135, September 7, 1952, pp. 196–201.

48 *Ibid.,* Letter 135, September 7, 1952, pp. 200–1. She added: 'Whatever of the straightforward historical insights I still consider relevant are contained in shorter form and devoid of all "psychology" in the first part of my totalitarian book. And there I'm content to let the matter rest.'

49 Jaspers' writings on these questions are volumnious. The most important and representative of these writings are *The Origin and Goal of History,* translated by Michael Bullock (New Haven, 1953) and 'The Atom Bomb and the Future of Man', *Evergreen Review* (no. 5, 1958) pp. 37–57.

50 On this, see Arendt's essay, 'Karl Jaspers: Citizen of the World?', in *Men in Dark Times,* pp. 81–94.

51 See the interesting review and assessment of her thought in David Miller, 'The nagging glory: Hannah Arendt and the Greek polis', *Times Literary Supplement* (July 9, 1993) pp. 6–7. See also Maurice Cranston, 'Hannah Arendt', *Encounter* (March 1976) 46 (3).

52 The number of such studies keeps on growing. See, for instance, Margaret Canovan, *The Political Thought of Hannah Arendt* (New York and London, 1974) and her recent *Hannah Arendt: A reinterpretation of her political thought* (Cambridge, 1992); Bhikhu Parekh, *Hannah Arendt and the Search for a New Political Philosophy* (London

and Basingstoke, 1981); George Kateb, *Hannah Arendt: Politics, Conscience, Evil* (Totowa, N.J., 1983); Leah Bradshaw, *Acting and Thinking: The Political Thought of Hannah Arendt* (Toronto Buffalo London, 1989); Jeffrey C. Isaac, *Arendt, Camus and Modern Rebellion* (New Haven, 1993); David Watson, Arendt (London, 1992).

53 See, in this respect, the important essay by Martin Jay, 'The Political Existentialism of Hannah Arendt' in his *Permanent Exiles: Essays on the Intellectual Migration From Germany to America* (New York, 1985) pp. 237–56.

54 As she later put it: 'I was interested neither in history nor in politics when I was young. If I can be said to "have come from anywhere", it is from the tradition of German philosophy.' See her letter to Gershom Scholem in Feldman, *The Jew as Pariah*, pp. 245–6.

55 These 'positive' aspects are most apparent in her *The Human Condition* (Chicago, 1958) and *On Revolution* (London, 1963). Both the 'negative' and 'positive' aspects are couched in terms of Arendt's ongoing 'existential' predilection to view human malleability in (rather ahistorical) almost unlimited ways. See Jay, 'The Political Existentialism of Hannah Arendt', p. 244.

56 Letter 141, Jaspers to Arendt, *Correspondence*, April 3, 1953, p. 208. Jaspers was referring specifically to the last chapter of *The Origins of Totalitarianism*, 'Ideology and Terror'. In the 'Preface' to her *Visible Spaces*, Dagmar Barnouw also stresses the interdependence between these destructive and regenerative elements in Arendt's thought.

57 *Ibid.,* Letter 135, pp. 197–8. Here Arendt acknowledged the influential role in her thought of the German Zionist Kurt Blumenfeld.

58 Thus: 'The interpretation given by society to the fact of Jewish birth and the role played by Jews in the framework of social life are intimately connected with the catastrophic thoroughness with which antisemitic devices could be put to work. The Nazi brand of antisemitism had its roots in these social conditions as well in political circumstances. And though the concept of race had other and more immediately political purposes and functions, its application to the Jewish question in its most sinister aspect owed much of its success to social phenomena and convictions which virtually constituted a consent by public opinion. / The deciding forces in the Jews' fateful journey to the storm of the events were without doubt political; but the reactions of society to antisemitism and the psychological reflections of the Jewish question had something to do with the specific cruelty, the organized and calculated assault upon every single individual of Jewish origin, that was already characteristic of the antisemitism of the Dreyfus Affair. This

passion-driven hunt of the "Jew in general", the "Jew everywhere and nowhere", cannot be understood if one considers the history of anti-semitism as an entity in itself, as a mere political movement. Social factors ... changed the course that mere political antisemitism would have taken if left to itself, and which might have resulted in anti-Jewish legislation and even mass expulsion but hardly in wholesale extermination.' *The Origins of Totalitarianism*, p. 87.

59 For a good exposition of the place of anti-semitism in her overall scheme see Ben Halpern, 'The Context of Hannah Arendt's Concept of Totalitarianism' in *Totalitarian Democracy and After* (Jerusalem, 1984) pp. 386–98. Arendt's totalitarianism was a product of the breakdown of nation-states and essentially international. As Halpern puts it: 'For it was the *Protocols of the Elders of Zion* that became the model the fascists followed; taking the exterritorial survival of the Jewish people as their example, the fascists developed an essentially anti-national, global conspiracy of their own, with anti-Semitism as its essential base.' Both Jaspers and Arendt were very critical of Halpern (*Correspondence*, pp. 121–3, 162). Halpern was aware of this hostility and prefaces his article by stressing that he would 'perform the task with all the empathy she deserves' (p. 387).

60 Irving Howe, *The Decline of the New* (New York, 1970) pp. 244–5.

61 Some Israeli critics have gone so far as to suggest that Arendt's views on the Jews were influenced by anti-Semitic thinking and echoed *Mein Kampf*. A leading Israeli analyst of political thought (in a 1993 conversation) told me that he regarded Arendt's view of the determinative centrality of the Jewish role within the State as the same as the Nazi view.

62 The sources of anti-Semitism, Leon Wieseltier argued against Arendt, were 'to be found in certain aspects of German history, and French history, and Russian history. Not in Jewish money but in German industry; not in Rahel Varnhagen's attic, but in the drawing rooms of the Faubourg-St-Germain ... not in Jewish achievement, but in the pitiful inability of certain political cultures to tolerate it; not in the Jewish insistence upon difference, but in the non-Jewish insistence upon sameness. Study the *goyim*, in short, not the Jews. ... There is something morally quite simple about totalitarianism ... the victims were, in these systems of slavery and murder, simply powerless.' See his 'Understanding Anti-Semitism: Hannah Arendt on the origins of prejudice', *The New Republic* (October 7, 1981) pp. 29–32. The quote appears on p. 32.

63 See the 'Conclusion' of Whitfield, *Into the Dark*, especially p. 254.

64 Barnouw, *Visible Spaces*, p. 162 (see also pp. 28–9).

65 'Organized Guilt and Universal Responsibility', *Jewish Frontier* (January 1945) pp. 19–23. Reprinted in Arendt, *The Jew as Pariah.*

66 For an excellent critical analysis, see Rabinbach's 'The German as Pariah', op. cit.

67 Arendt to Jaspers, August 17, 1946, *Correspondence*, pp. 51–6. The quote appears on p. 54.

68 *Ibid.,* Jaspers to Arendt, October 19, 1946, pp. 60–3. The quote appears on p. 62.

69 *Ibid.,* December 17, 1946, pp. 68–70. The quote appears on p. 69.

70 *Ibid.,* Arendt to Jaspers, March 4, 1951, pp. 165–8. The quote appears on p. 166.

71 'Total Domination', *The Origins of Totalitarianism*, pp. 437–59. The quote appears on p. 437.

72 *Ibid.,* p. 277. See the whole chapter, 'The Decline of the Nation-State and the End of the Rights of Man'.

73 These weaknesses are by now well enough known not to require elaboration here. But, for an interesting defence of Arendt's work, see Bernard Crick, 'On Rereading *The Origins of Totalitarianism*', *Social Research* 44 (no. 1, Spring 1977) pp. 106–26. He concludes (p. 126) thus: 'Rereading her, I am convinced that even yet her stature has been underestimated. There is a view of political and social man just as comprehensive as those of Hobbes, Hegel, Mill, and Marx; and, to my mind, one far more flattering to humanity.' This whole issue of *Social Research* is devoted to Arendt.

74 See Gellner, 'From Koenigsberg to Manhattan (or Hannah, Rahel, Martin and Elfried or Thy Neighbour's *Gemeinschaft)' in his Culture, Identity, and Politics* (Cambdridge, 1987). For a more detailed discussion of this question, see Chapter 1 of this book, especially footnote 46.

75 See Volume I, *The Spell of Plato* of *The Open Society and its Enemies* by K.R. Popper (London, 1945).

76 Arendt to Jaspers, March 4, 1951, *Correspondence*, p. 166.

77 *Ibid.,* Jaspers to Heinrich Bluecher, July 21, 1952, p. 186. Jasper's clearly did not go along with this view, expressing as he did in numerous places in this correspondence a visceral hatred for Marx (pp. 186–7): 'Marx's thinking and his personality with its sense of outrage, its violence, and its dictatorial character filled with hate, have not only had, I think, an influence that can hardly be overestimated but also bear responsibility for what has happened. I have not up to now been able to meet this man with anything but hatred on my own part (as I do Luther and Fichte). I hate his unique insight into an incredibly influ-

ential, though also limited, realm of reality, and I hate his penetrating intelligence. He uses his insight and his intelligence to satisfy his will for justice, a will that from the beginning was both a will to power and a desire for vengenance. Marx does not use his hate and his love as organs of cognizance and then put them on ice, turn away from them, play them off against each other in order to achieve through self-criticism a maximum of truth. Instead, he falls victim to his own hatred and follows it, in the name of justice, into an abominable vision. So I see in him a distortion of philosophy and absurdities that are both glaring and pernicious.' In a letter of December 29, 1952 (p. 205), Jaspers wrote to Arendt: 'I harbor the hope that you will in the end find Marx the intellectually responsible originator of what prepared the way for totalitarianism. Intolerance, indeed terror are exemplified in his personal character.' For critical remarks on Arendt's approach to Marx, see Jay, 'The Political Existentialism of Hannah Arendt'.

78 *Ibid.,* Letter 373, Arendt to Jaspers, (received on) April 13, 1965, especially pp. 592–3 and Letter 399, Arendt to Jaspers, July 4, 1966, p. 644 and notes 2 and 3 on pp. 793–4. Arendt's dislike for Adorno had early roots. Her first husband, Guenther Stern, was encouraged by Adorno to submit a *Habilitationschrift* on the philosophy of music which he then promptly found unsatisfactory – on the grounds that it was not sufficiently Marxist. After having met Adorno, she told Stern: 'Der kommt uns nicht ins Haus! (*That one's not coming into our house!*).' See Young-Bruehl, *Hannah Arendt*, p. 80.

79 Gerhard Ritter, *The German Problem: Basic Questions of Political Life* (Columbus, 1965). The work was published originally in 1962. This was a revised, expanded version of his 1948 treatise *Europe and the German Question.*

80 Friedrich Meineke, *The German Catastrophe*, translated by Sidney B. Fay (Boston, 1950). The original appeared in German in 1946.

81 Hannah Arendt, 'Approaches to the German Problem', *Partisan Review*, Vol. XII, no. 1 (Winter, 1945) pp. 93–106. The quote appears in p. 95.

82 *Ibid.,* p. 96.

83 *Ibid.,* p. 96.

84 *Ibid.,* p. 97. Given Arendt's general predisposition to deny national essences this may have been a little disingenuous. See her previous comments about her own inability to find in herself a 'German character'.

85 *Ibid.,* Letter 14, Jaspers to Arendt, January 12, 1952, p. 174.

86 See Arendt's, 'Karl Jaspers: A Laudatio', in *Men in Dark Times*, translated by Clara and Richard Winston (New York and London, 1968) pp. 71–80.

87 See Letter 267, Jaspers to Arendt, *Correspondence*, October 14, 1960, p. 404.

88 'On Humanity in Dark Times', especially pp. 26–31.

89 Letter 140, Arendt to Jaspers, February 19, 1953, pp. 206–7. The entire correspondence is filled with similar mutual celebratory passages.

90 Hannah Arendt, 'What remains? The language remains', p. 22.

91 Letter 46, Jaspers to Arendt, October 19, 1946, pp. 60–1.

92 *Ibid.,* Letter 88, Jaspers to Arendt, March 15, 1949, p. 134.

7 Small Forays, Grand Theories and Deep Origins: Current Trends in the Historiography of the Holocaust

1 For the most recent example see the masterly article by Michael Marrus, 'Reflections on the Historiography of the Holocaust'. [Paper presented for the symposium 'L'année 1942 et les Juifs en France', Ecole des Hautes Etudes en Sciences Sociales, Paris, 15–17 June 1992.] This essay is very much indebted to it. His comprehensive *The Holocaust in History* (London, 1989) is also very useful. For earlier analyses see Lucy S. Dawidowicz, *The Holocaust and the Historians* (Cambridge, 1981) and Otto Dov Kulka, 'Major Tendencies and Trends of German Historiography on National Socialism and the "Jewish Question" (1924–1984)', *Leo Baeck Institute Yearbook* XXX (1985). Ian Kershaw's *The Nazi Dictatorship: Problems and Perspectives of Interpretation* (London, 1985) provides an excellent overview. It has now been updated into a third edition (1993).

2 I am, furthermore, limiting the scope of this essay to issues related to German and 'perpetrator' history and shall not deal with other important problems such as Jewish responses, the role of non-Germans in the destruction process and Western governmental policies and popular attitudes.

3 Given the sheer horror and scale of the event, Elie Wiesel's argument that 'Auschwitz cannot be explained' because 'the Holocaust transcends history' may, at times, be a tempting and sobering one: 'The dead are in possession of a secret that we, the living, are neither worthy of nor capable of recovering.' See his 'Trivialising the Holocaust: Semi-Fact and Semi-Fiction', *New York Times* (April 16, 1978, section 2.) Historians too have been known to argue in this vein. Nora Levin, author of a widely-read history of the Holocaust, writes: 'The Holocaust refuses to go the way of most history, not only because of the magnitude of the destruction – the murder of six million Jews – but because the events surrounding it are in a very real sense incomprehensible. No one altogether understands how mass murder on such a scale could have happened or

could have been allowed to happen. The accumulation of facts does does not yield this understanding; indeed comprehensibility may never be possible.' Nora Levin, *The Holocaust: The Destruction of European Jewry, 1919–1945* (New York, 1973), pp. xi–xii. But surely 'comprehensibility' must be understood as a finite and changing rather than a single, final state. As Michael Marrus puts it: 'Historians are used to tramping over their fields while suspending judgements on the fundamental issues that are ultimately at stake ... We simply do the best we can, knowing that our efforts are necessarily imperfect, incomplete and inadequate.' See his *The Holocaust in History*, p. 7. See too Dan Magurshak, 'The "Incomprehensibility" of the Holocaust: Tightening up Some Loose Useage' in the useful anthology edited by Alan Rosenberg and Gerald E. Meyers, *Echoes from the Holocaust: Philosophical Reflections on a Dark Time* (Philadelphia, 1988).

4   For summaries and evaluations of this debate, see Juergen Kocka, 'German History before Hitler: The Debate about the German *Sonderweg*', *Journal of Contemporary History* 23 (1988) pp. 3–16 and my 'Nazism, Normalcy and the German *Sonderweg*', *Studies in Contemporary Jewry* 4, *The Jews and the European Crisis*, edited by Jonathan Frankel (New York and Oxford, 1988) pp. 276–92.

5   The literature on this is vast. For convenient overviews see Charles S. Maier, *The Unmasterable Past: History, Holocaust, and German National Identity* (Cambridge, Mass., 1988) and Richard Evans, *In Hitler's Shadow: West German Historians and the Attempt to Escape the Nazi Past* (London, 1989). See too my 'History, Politics, and National Memory: The German *Historikerstreit*', *Survey of Jewish Affairs* (1988), pp. 222–38.

6   Friedlander's contribution, it seems to me, lies mainly in his role as a critic, a kind of cultural seismometer, consistently identifying, and opening for discussion, emergent interpretive issues surrounding the historiography and memorialization of the Holocaust. A critical monographic assessment would surely be welcome. For a few examples, see 'Some Aspects of the Historical Significance of the Holocaust', *Jerusalem Quarterly* (no. 1, Fall 1976); 'From Anti-Semitism to Extermination: A Historiographical Study of Nazi Policies towards the Jews and an Essay in Interpretation', *Yad Vashem Studies*, 16 (1984) pp. 1–50; *Reflections of Nazism: An Essay on Kitsch and Death* (New York, 1984); 'West Germany and the Burden of the Past: The Ongoing Debate', *Jerusalem Quarterly* 42 (Spring 1987).

7   'Introduction', Saul Friedlander (ed.), *Probing the Limits of Representation: Nazism and the 'Final Solution'*, (Cambridge, Mass.,

1992) pp. 4–5. Friedlander is undoubtedly correct in his analysis of the problem raised by post-modernism. However, his evaluation of its more positive potential – as well as the intrinsic opaqueness of Holocaust historiography – is more open to question: ' ... the very openness of postmodernism to what cannot yet be formulated in decisive statements, but merely sensed, directly relates to whoever considers that even the most precise historical renditions of the Shoah contain an opaqueness at the core which confronts traditional historical narrative.' (p. 5).

8   'Of Plots, Witnesses, and Judgements' in *Probing the Limits*, p. 103.

9   Hayden White's assertions, in effect, constitute the unifying problematic of most of the essays. See, his 'Historical Emplotment and the Problem of Truth' in *Probing the Limits*. It should be pointed out here that for all of post-modernism's denial of 'objectivity' and its problematization of historical truth it (perhaps self-contradictorily) affirms the reality and monstrousness of the Nazi genocide against the Jews, something the so-called 'revisionists' are not prepared to do. Nevertheless, as various essays in *Probing the Limits* suggest, postmodernism has created the kind of free-wheeling cultural and epistemological climate that provides, if not direct legitimation, an atmosphere conducive to the Holocaust-denying revisionist agenda.

10 Carlo Ginzburg, 'Just One Witness', *Probing the Limits*.

11 A translation of Broszat's piece 'A Plea for the Historicization of National Socialism' appears in Peter Baldwin (ed.), *Reworking the Past: Hitler, the Holocaust, and the Historian's Debate* (Boston, 1990) pp. 77–8.

12 'Unter der Herrschaft des Verdachts' in *'Historikerstreit': Die Dokumentation der Kontroverse um die Einzigartigkeit der nationalsozialistichen Judenvernichtung* (Munich, 1987) p. 45.

13 See Saul Friedlander, 'Some Reflections on the Historicization of National Socialism' as well as the correspondence between Broszat and Friedlander, 'A Controversy about the Historicization of National Socialism' in Baldwin, *Reworking the Past*, pp. 88–134.

14 'Between Aporia and Apology: On the Limits of Historicizing National Socialism', in *ibid.*, p. 144.

15 Mayer, *Why did the Heavens not Darken?* (New York, 1990) p. xiii.

16 For a classic illustration of all these themes, see Lucy Dawidowicz *The War against the Jews* (New York, 1975). In his 'Reflections on the Historiography of the Holocaust', Michael Marrus has a long list of writings that adopted this approach. It should be clear that in this paper we are talking about a trend not an iron-clad law. Studies advocating

the centrality of anti-Semitism as the moving force continue to appear and will be considered in the course of this essay.

17   Arendt, *The Origins of Totalitarianism* (New York, 1951) p. 7.
18   The historiography of the 1960s – at least in the work of Norman Cohn – sought to do this not in terms of wider circumstances but by speculative recourse to a psychologically based, specific strain of what was called 'exterminatory anti-Semitism'. While Cohn's comparative discussion of the differences between Jew-hatred and Black racism remains highly illuminating, the psychological links and motivations connecting this imputed form of anti-Semitism to Nazi genocidal impulses have not been definitively established. See his *Warrant for Genocide* (London, 1967), especially the Conclusion: 'A Case-Study in Collective Psychopathology'.
19   Marrus, 'Reflections on the Historiography of the Holocaust', op. cit., p. 12.
20   George Mosse has regularly talked in this vein about France. See, for instance, *Towards the Final Solution: A History of European Racism* (New York, 1978) p. 168.
21   See George L. Mosse, 'Die Rechte und die Judenfrage', in Werner E. Mosse (ed.), *Entscheidungsjahr 1932* (Tuebingen, 1964) pp. 183–249.
22   See the divergent interpretations of Peter Pulzer, 'The Beginning of the End', Peter Gay, 'At Home in Germany: The Jews during the Weimar Era' and Werner E. Mosse, 'German Jews: Citizens of the Republic' in Arnold Paucker (ed.), *The Jews in Nazi Germany 1933–1943* (Tuebingen, 1986) and Donald L. Niewyk, *The Jews in Weimar Germany* (Baton Rouge, 1980), Chapter III.
23   Geoffrey Pridham, *Hitler's Rise to Power: The Nazi Movement in Bavaria 1923–1933* (New York, 1973) pp. 237–44; William Sheridan Allen, *The Nazi Seizure of Power: The Experience of a Single German Town 1930–1935* (Chicago, 1965),p. 77; Jeremy Noakes, *The Nazi Party in Lower Saxony 1921–1933* (London ,1971) pp. 209–10.
24   Oded Heilbronner, 'The Role of Nazi Antisemitism in the Nazi Party's Activity and Propaganda – A Regional Historiographical Study', *Leo Baeck Institute Yearbook* XXXV, (1990) pp. 397–439.
25   David Bankier, *The Germans and the Final Solution: Public Opinion Under Nazism* (Oxford, 1992) p. 115.
26   'The German Jewish Population and the Jews in the Third Reich: Recent Publications and Trends in Research on German Society and the "Jewish Question"', *Yad Vashem Studies* 16 (1984) 421–35.
27   Bankier, *The Germans and the Final Solution*, p. 156.
28   Ian Kershaw, 'German Popular Opinion and the "Jewish Question", 1939–1943: Some Further Reflections' in Paucker (ed.), *The Jews in*

Nazi Germany, pp. 365–85. Against Kershaw, Bankier argues (in agreement with Martin Broszat) that this indifference was not a relatively 'normal' response, a function of energy sapped in the concerns of daily life but, rather, prompted by an explicit awareness of being accomplices who shared responsibilities for crimes (p. 145). Significantly, however, as he says elsewhere, this indifference was not separate from but rather an integral part of the brutalizing continuum to which this paper refers, a wider inuring process in which one could talk casually of the death of *millions of Russians* who would perish of starvation as a result of the scorched earth policy. 'Awareness', writes Bankier, 'of the magnitude of atrocities against Poles and Russians created a psychological framework in which the public submerged the specific annihilation of the Jews' (pp. 106–7).

29 Raul Hilberg, *The Destruction of the European Jews* (Chicago, 1961) pp. 653–62.

30 Hannah Arendt, *Eichmann in Jerusalem: A Report on the Banality of Evil* (New York, 1963).

31 Stanley Milgram, *Obedience to Authority: An Experimental View* (New York, 1974).

32 Christopher R. Browning, *The German Foreign Office and the Final Solution: A Study of Referat DIII of Abteilung Deutschland* (New York, 1978).

33 Christopher R. Browning, *Ordinary Men: Reserve Police Batallion 101 and the Final Solution in Poland* (New York, 1992).

34 See Browning's 'German Memory, Judicial Interrogation, Historical Reconstruction' in Friedlander (ed.), *Probing the Limits of Representation,* p. 27.

35 'The full weight of this statement, and the significance of the word choice of the former policeman', Browning comments, 'cannot be fully appreciated unless one knows that the German word for "release" (*erloesen*) also means to "redeem" or "save" when used in a religious sense. The one who "releases" is the *Erloeser* – the Savior or Redeemer!' *Ordinary Men,* p. 73.

36 I know of no more graphic, personalised account of the way in which dehumanization works than that contained in Gitta Sereny's interview with Franz Stangl, the commandant of Treblinka. See her insightful and deeply disturbing study *Into That Darkness: From Mercy Killing to Mass Murder* (New York, 1974), especially pp. 200–2.

37 For an interesting analysis of the universal and particular ingredients, see Yehuda Bauer's finely nuanced essay 'The Holocaust in Contemporary History', *Studies in Contemporary Jewry* I (1984) pp.

201–24. There is, he writes, 'a dialectical tension between the universal and the particularistic aspects of that watershed event: holocuast has to be seen as a general category, as the outermost pole on a continuum of evil; yet at the same time, as an event which has (so far) overtaken Jews alone. ... Being general as well as specific, the term holocaust carries with it the implication that, because it happened once, it may happen again – to any group if the conditions are right.' (p. 217) On the same problem – and for an analysis of the ideological implications of this question – see Adi Ophir, 'On Sanctifying the Holocaust: An Anti-Theological Treatise', *Tikkun* 2 (no. 1, 1987) pp. 61–7.

38 Of course, there is also not unanimity here. 'Moderate' functionalists would not go so far as some of their more radical colleagues who have suggested that the Holocaust was the (almost accidental) outcome of lowly-placed functionaries responding to immediate field problems and uncertain signals from above. For a sympathetic view of functionalism and the 'functionalist-intentionalist' debate see Tim Mason, 'Intention and Explanation: A Current Controversy about the Interpretation of National Socialism', in G.Hirschfeld and L.Kettenacker (ed.) *The Fuehrer State: Myth and Reality* (Stuttgart, 1981).

39 See the brilliant analysis in Chapter 9, 'The Decline of the Nation-State and the End of the Rights of Man' of *The Origins of Totalitarianism* (Cleveland, 1958). The quote appears on p. 277. For a general history, see Michael R. Marrus, *The Unwanted: European Refugees in the Twentieth Century* (New York, 1985).

40 For the German case, see the chapter on 'The Brutalization of German Politics' in George L. Mosse, *Fallen Soldiers: Reshaping the Memory of the World Wars* (New York, 1990).

41 Andreas Hillgruber, *Zweierlei Untergang, Die Zerschlagung des Deutschen Reiches und das Ende des europaischen Judentums* (Berlin, 1986), p. 67.

42 Istvan Deak, 'Strategies of Hell', *New York Review of Books* (October 8, 1992) pp. 8–10.

43 For one criticism locating Mayer's work within the broader revisionist context of the *Historikerstreit*, see Dominick La Capra's review in *New German Critique* (no. 53, Spring/Summer 1991).

44 Mayer, *Why did the Heavens Not Darken?* (New York, 1990) pp. 16–17. This new edition contains the author's 'Afterword'.

45 *Ibid.*, p. 226. Mayer, to be sure, acknowledges a fundamental difference betwen these two events. In the first Crusade Jews were given the choice of baptism – whereas in the Nazi case Jewish life was in principle pollutive, unamenable to any redemptive action. Nevertheless he

insists upon the homology arguing that both were concomitants 'of a socially grounded project of comprehensive retrogression.'

46 *Ibid.,* p. 12.
47 Mayer's claim in the 'Afterword' (p. 464) that foootnotes seemed superfluous in a work of synthesis is unconvincing especially given the plenitude of factual – as well as interpretive – problems that critics have identified in this work.
48 For a detailed discussion of this debate see Marrus, *The Holocaust in History*, pp. 45–6.
49 See Christopher Browning, *Fateful Months: Essays on the Emergence of the Final Solution* (New York, 1985).
50 Mayer, *Why did the Heavens,* p. 201. The same, Mayer argues, applied to the original crusade: 'In 1095 it was the popular crusaders who in their impatience rallied to the idea of making local Jews tangible surrogates for the Moslem infidels, who were beyond their immediate reach' (p. 228).
51 The pitfalls of such scapegoat theories have been known for a long time. Hannah Arendt's own views on this are controversial to say the least but her overall observations are nevertheless illuminating. The notion, she writes, 'implies that the scapegoat might have been anyone else as well. ... .The scapegoat explanation ... remains one of the principal attempts to escape the seriousness of antisemitism and the significance of the fact that the Jews were driven into the storm centre of events' (*The Origins of Totalitarianism,* pp. 5–7). George Mosse put it even more succinctly. Such views, he wrote, 'would maintain that anti-Semitism could have been eliminated by redirecting the psychic drives of Germany's maladjusted people. But there is a greater failing inherent in the psychological interpretation: it denies the endemic nature of anti-Semitism and regards it as a transitory phenomenon fulfilling certain psychological needs which could have been gratified by any other minority had the Jews not existed.' *The Crisis of German Ideology: Intellectual Origins of the Third Reich* (New York, 1964) p. 301.
52 See my 'Caftan and Cravat: The Ostjude as a Cultural Symbol in the Development of German Anti-Semitism' in S. Drescher, D. Sabean and A. Sharlin (eds.), *Political Symbolism in Modern Europe* (New Brunswick, 1982) and Chapter 3 of my *Brothers and Strangers: The East European Jew in German and German–Jewish Consciousness, 1800–1923* (Madison, 1982).
53 While Mayer's work purports to replace the ethnocentric and ideological understanding of the Holocaust with a new, open historical

interpretation, writes Daniel Jonah Goldhagen, 'it is itself an artful construction of half-truths, itself in the service of an ideology. And it is riddled with extraordinary factual errors, which amount to a pattern of falsification and distortion.' See too especially Goldhagen's very critical comments concerning Mayer's treatment of the initial activities of the *Einsatzgruppen* in 'False Witness', *The New Republic* (April 17, 1989), pp. 39–44. The quote appears on p. 39.

54 Eugen Weber, 'Revolution, Counterrevolution? What Revolution?', *Journal of Contemporary History*, 9 (1974) p. 33.

55 Jeffrey Herf, *Reactionary modernism: Technology, culture, and politics in Weimar and the Third Reich* (Cambridge, 1984).

56 'False Witness', p. 40.

57 Mayer, *Why did the Heavens*, p. 313.

58 Michael Burleigh and Wolfgang Wippermann, *The Racial State: Germany 1933–1945* (Cambridge, 1991) p. 22.

59 R.W. Darre, 'Marriage Laws and the Principles of Breeding' (1930) in *Nazi Ideology before 1933*, translated by Barbara Hiller and Leila J.Gupp (Manchester, 1978) p. 115.

60 See Chapter 3 of Burleigh and Wippermann, *The Racial State*, for details of these programmes such as *Ahnenerbe, Lebensborn* etc. Even the putative social welfare measures of the Nazis flowed from these collective biological assumptions. The authors quote Joseph Goebbels (p. 69) to the following effect: 'Our starting point is not the individual, and we do not subscribe to the view that one should feed the hungry, give drink to the thirsty or clothe the naked – those are not our objectives. Our objectives are entirely different. They can be put most crisply in the sentence: we must have a healthy people in order to prevail in the world.'

61 See the illuminating essay by Robert-Jam Van Pelt, 'A Site in Search of a Mission', in Yisrael Gutman and Michael Berenbaum, eds., *Anatomy of the Auschwitz Death Camp* (Bloomington, 1994), especially p. 103

62 Gisela Bock, *Zwangssterilisation im Nationalsozialismus* (Opladen, 1986). For the figures see pp. 230ff. Sterilisation, it is true, was not limited to Germany but was also lamentably carried out in the USA. The relevant figures are, however, as Burleigh and Wippermann point out (p. 253), very different. Thirty states in the USA with comparable laws sterilised 11,000 people between 1907 and 1930.

63 For a valuable survey of the literature, see Michael Burleigh, 'Euthanasia in the Third Reich', *Social History of Medicine (1991)*, 4. See too Ernst Klee, *'Euthanasie' im NS-Staat. Die 'Vernichtung lebensunwerten Lebens'* (Frankfurt am Main, 1983); Goetz Aly, Peter Chroust and

Christian Pross, *Cleansing the Fatherland: Nazi Medicine and Racial Hygiene,* translated by Belinda Cooper (Baltimore and London, 1994); Manfred Kluepel, *'Euthanasie' und Lebensvernichtung am Beispiel der Landesheilanstalten Haina und Merxhausen. Eine Chronik der Ereignisse 1933–1945* (Kassel, 1984); Walter Schmuhl, *Rassenhygiene, Nationalsozialismus, Euthanasie* (Goettingen, 1987).

64 Quoted in Burleigh and Wippermann, *The Racial State,* p. 142. Hitler made the massive scope of his bio-political conceptions eminently clear. He told a party rally in August 1929 that: 'If Germany were to get a million children a year and was to remove 700,000–800,000 of the weakest people, then the final result might even be an increase in strength' (p. 142).

65 See Benno Mueller-Hill, 'The Idea of the Final Solution and the role of Experts,' in David Cesarani (ed.), *The Final Solution: Origins and implementation* (London and New York, 1994) p. 62.

66 For a description of this process and the people involved see Henry Friedlander, 'Euthanasia and the Final Solution', in Cesarani (ed.), *The Final Solution,* pp. 51–61 and Gitta Sereny, *Into that Darkness,* especially Part One.

67 Burleigh and Wippermann correctly reject what have come to be the pejorative terms 'Gypsy' and 'Ziegeuner' and use the name Sinti and Roma. The prejudice against Gypsies, obviously did not begin with the Nazis. The authors note (Chapter 5) that while they were not explicitly mentioned in Nazi racial laws the commentaries argued that it applied to them as well as Jews. Moreover, their sterilisation took place without any 'legal' basis whatever. If they formed part of a continuum there were nevertheless important differences from the Jews – distinctions were made between 'pure' and 'impure' Gypsies with the former receiving a degree of protection (while being rigorously controlled) and their deportations halted to give priority to Jewish deportations. For an explication of this view, see Yehuda Bauer, 'Jews, Gypsies, Slavs: policies of the Third Reich', *UNESCO Yearbook on Peace and Conflict Studies 1985* (Paris 1987) pp. 73–100. But this position has been recently questioned by Henry Friedlander who argues that while Nazi killings in terms of political affiliations (communists, socialists, Soviet POWs), behaviour (criminals, homosexuals) or activities (resistance members) did not amount to genocide – 'the mass murder of human beings because they belong to a biologically defined group' – such a definition indeed applies equally to Nazi policies toward the handicapped and the Gypsies as it does the Jews. See Friedlander, 'Euthanasia and the Final Solution', especially p. 51.

68 The classic study here is Robert Koehl, *RKFDV German Settlement and Population Policy 1939–1945: A History of the Commission for the Strengthening of Germandom* (Cambridge, 1957).

69 See Benno Mueller-Hill, 'The Idea of the Final Solution and the Role of Experts', pp. 62–70.

70 See the very early work by Max Weinreich, *Hitler's Professors: The Part of Scholarship in Germany's Crimes against the Jewish People* (New York, 1946). More recent work includes Till Bastian, *Von der Eugenik zur Euthanasie. Ein Verdraengtes Kapitel aus der Geschichte der deutschen Psychiatrie* (Woerishofen, 1981); Michael Burleigh, *Germany Turns Eastwards: A Study of 'Ostforschung' in the Third Reich* (Cambridge, 1988); Peter Weingart, 'Eugenik, eine angewandte Wissenschaft im Dritten Reich', in Peter Lundgreen (ed.), *Wissenschaft im Dritten Reich* (Frankfurt am Main, 1985) pp. 314–49.

71 Michael. H. Kater, *The Nazi Party: A Social Profile of Members 1919–1945* (Cambridge: Mass, 1983) p. 73.

72 One member of Reserve Police Batallion 101 described the role of the batallion physician thus. The doctor explained 'precisely how we had to shoot in order to induce the immediate death of the victim ... he outlined the contour of a human body, at least from the shoulders upward, and then indicated precisely the point on which the fixed bayonet was to be placed as an aiming guide.' See Browning's *Ordinary Men*, p. 60.

73 The literature on this is now extensive. For some English-language sources see Benno Mueller, *Murderous Science: Elimination by Scientific Selection of Jews, Gypsies, and Others, Germany 1933–1945* (Oxford, 1988); Robert N. Proctor, *Racial Hygiene: Medicine Under the Nazis* (London, 1988); Robert Jay Lifton, *The Nazi Doctors: Medical Killings and the Psychology of Genocide* (London, 1986).

74 See Lifton, op cit., especially pp. 15–27, Chapter 21.

75 On the German background of these influences, see Paul J. Weindling, *Health, Race and German Politics between national unification and Nazism, 1870–1945* (Cambridge, 1989); Peter Emil Becker, *Zur Geschichte der Rassenhygiene in Deutschland: Wege ins Dritte Reich* (Stuttgart, 1988); Peter Weingart, Juergen Kroll and Kurt Bayertz, *Rasse, Blut und Gene. Geschichte der Eugenik und Rassenhygiene in Deutschland* (Frankfurt am Main, 1988).

76 Daniel Pick, *Faces of Degeneration: A European Disorder c. 1848–1918* (Cambridge, 1989); George L. Mosse, *Towards the Final Solution: A History of European Racism* (New York, 1978). Mosse has made a masterly statement on the connection between the doctor's role in

European society in general and genocide in his review of Lifton, 'Medicine and Murder', *Studies in Contemporary Jewry* VI (1990) pp. 315–20.

77 For a general survey of the field of eugenics in this context, see Robert A. Nye, 'The Rise and Fall of the Eugenics Empire: Recent Perspectives on the Impact of Biomedical Thought in Modern Society', *The Historical Journal* 36, 3 (1993) pp. 687–700. Nye examines the divergent modes of permeation of eugenic thought within mainstream European and American science and medicine and while his article contains 'echoes of the murderous racism of the World War II era' it also stresses 'aspects of biological and racial thought that did not end in holocaust' (p. 687).

78 See his 'Response' in *George Mosse: On the Occasion of his Retirement* (Jerusalem: The Hebrew University of Jerusalem, n.d.) p. xxviii.

79 For an instance of such a 'general' indictment of medicine and science, see Mario Biagioli, 'Science, Modernity and the "Final Solution"', in Friedlander (ed.), *Probing the Limits of Representation*, pp. 185–205.

80 For a different perspective from the one outlined here see my 'Between Irrationality and Irrationalism: George L. Mosse, the Holocaust, and European Cultural History', *Simon Wiesenthal Center Annual* 5 (1988) pp. 187–202.

81 Mosse, *The Crisis of German Ideology: Intellectual Origins of the Third Reich* (New York, 1964).

82 This was (and may still be) a prevailing view. Thus Fritz Stern's important *The Politics of Cultural Despair: A Study in the Rise of Germanic Ideology* (Berkeley, 1961) enunciated the same conviction.

83 See his 'Der erste Weltkrieg und die Brutalisierung der Politik: Betrachtungen ueber die politische Rechte, den Rassimus, und den deutschen Sonderweg', in Manfred Funke *et al.* (ed.), *Demokratie und Diktatur* (Duesseldorf, 1987) pp. 127–39. See also Chapter 8 of Mosse's *Fallen Soldiers*.

84 Mosse, *Toward the Final Solution*, p. 168.

85 This analysis is contained in *Nationalism and Sexuality: Respectability and Abnormal Sexuality in Modern Europe* (New York, 1985).

86 See his *Nazism: A Historical and Comparative Analysis of National Socialism* (New Brunswick, 1978) p. 43.

87 'The Jewish stereotype', Mosse argues, 'is not unique. It's the same as the stereotype of all outsiders: sexual deviants, gypsies, the permanently insane, people who have hereditary diseases. ... these are all the people whom Hitler wanted to exterminate and whom he did exterminate. They all look the opposite of the middle-class, self-controlled idea of beauty, energy, all of this sort of thing. What you have here

is something quite new, a new kind of magnitude, where the Jew becomes an integral part of the enemies of society. And it's no accident that Hitler wanted to eliminate all these people. ...'. See the interview 'Antisemitism' in *The Jerusalem Post* (September 17, 1991) p. 8.

88 I have examined one avenue of this mediated radicalizing process in Nazism and the Holocaust in Chapters 8 and 9, and the 'Afterword' of my *The Nietzsche Legacy in Germany, 1890–1990* (Berkeley: University of California Press, 1992). See also Chapter 4 of this book.

89 Arendt, *The Origins of Totalitarianism*, p. 456.

90 See his 'Useless Violence' in *The Drowned and the Saved* translated by Raymond Rosenthal (London, 1988) p. 83.

91 Raul Hilberg, 'German Motivations for the Destruction of the Jews', *Midstream* (June 1965) p. 36. I believe that Hilberg later regretted the speculative nature of his comments.

92 See Friedlander's '"The Final Solution": On the Unease in Historical Interpretation' in his *Memory, History, and the Extermination of the Jews of Europe* (Indiana, 1993) p. 110.

93 *Ibid.*, Friedlander explains the difficulty thus: 'The historian can analyze the phenomenon from the "outside", but, *in this case, his unease cannot but stem from the noncongruence between intellectual probing and the blocking of intuitive comprehension*' (his italics), p. 111.

94 Berel Lang, *Act and Idea in the Nazi Genocide* (Chicago, 1990) pp. 168–9.

95 *Ibid.*, p. 190.

96 For instance, just as Lang indicts Kant, he entirely absolves Nietzsche, arguing that that thinker's use by the Nazis must be regarded as entirely a case of 'misappropriation', irrelevant to the genocidal project (pp. 197–8). For a different view see the 'Afterword' in my *The Nietzsche Legacy in Germany*, and Chapter 4 of this book.

97 See the review by Laurence Thomas, 'Characterizing and Responding to Genocide: A Review Essay', *Modern Judaism* 11 (1991) pp. 371–9. As he argues (p. 276), 'the very reason why we find what the Nazis did so morally heinous and inexcusable is that humanity admits of a universalist and ahistorical rendering.'

98 For a superb exposition of the essentially tolerant nature of Kant's moral (rather than empirical or historical) concept of humanity, see Leszek Kolakowski, 'Why do we Need Kant?' in his *Modernity on Endless Trial* (Chicago, 1990) pp. 44–54.

99 Emil L. Fackenheim, *To Mend the World: Foundations of Post-Holocaust Thought* (New York, 1989) pp. 272–3.

100 Although the argument for Nazism as anti-modernity was particularly strong during the 1960s and 1970s this counter-emphasis has always been present. Theorists of 'totalitarianism' consistently held that Nazism was a peculiarly 'modern' form of rule while the German sociologist Ralf Dahrendorf argued that National Socialism brought about the social revolution that never really occurred in Imperial or Weimar Germany. See 'National Socialist Germany and the Social Revolution' in his *Society and Democracy in Germany* (New York, 1969) pp. 381–3. More directly Hannah Arendt argued that the concentration camps constituted the site where the peculiarly modern totalitarian conviction – that everything was possible – could be verified. *The Origins of Totalitarianism*, p. 437. See generally Chapter 12, Section III. Furthermore no account of the Holocaust and modernity would be possible without Raul Hilberg's remarkable analysis of the 'destruction process' in terms of the workings and dynamics of an essentially modern, impersonal bureaucratic machinery.

101 Thus Allan Cassells in his *Fascism* (New York, 1975), p. 169 argued that because Germany's 'problem was one of maladjustment to the modern world, fascism there took the form of a blind, nihilistic fury directed against modernism in nearly all its forms.' This was typical of a whole welter of scholarship during the 1960s and 1970s.

102 Steiner, *In Bluebeard's Castle* (London, 1971) p. 38.

103 Wolfgang Sauer, 'National Socialism: Totalitarianism or Fascism?', *American Historical Review*, 78 (1967) p. 418.

104 Zygmunt Bauman, *Modernity and the Holocaust* (Oxford, 1989) pp. x, xiii and p. 8.

105 *Ibid.,* p. xiii. Bauman's italics.

106 Hannah Arendt, 'Approaches to the "German Problem"', *Partisan Review*, 12 (no. 1, 1945) p. 97.

107 Burleigh and Wippermann, *The Racial State*, p. 2.

108 The 'Shoah', Saul Friedlander has commented, 'does not teach us anything about modern industrial society as such, notwithstanding some linkages established between modernity and the attempt at total extermination. *A priori*, the "Final Solution" poses many questions concerning modernity, but either the linkages are kept at such a level of generality that they are irrelevant or the contradictions become insuperable.' See his essay 'The "Final Solution": On the Unease in Historical Intepretation' reprinted as Chapter VI in his *Memory, History, and the Extermination of the Jews of Europe*, p. 112.

109 Current German discussions concerning this issue (especially those by Rainer Zitelman) focus on the essential rationality and progressive

nature of National Socialism's social and economic policies. Because
the dark underside of Nazism is omitted the effect is apologetic. For
reasons that we must leave for another occasion, in the German context focus upon such 'modernity' (and the workings of a technologi-
cally advanced capitalist system) somehow renders the National
Socialist experience more palatable and 'acceptable'. For a useful discussion see Norbert Frei, 'Wie modern war der Nationalsozialismus?',
Geschichte und Gesellschaft 19 (1993) pp. 367–87. In the work of
Baumann, Mosse, Lang and others, critical views on 'bourgeois morality', Enlightenment universalism and technological-bureaucratic structures are intended to deepen rather than smooth over the indictment.
Nevertheless, the discussion concerning 'modernity' seems always to
be ideologically permeated and an awareness of its manifold implications need to accompany all attempts at academic useage. This remains
so despite Christopher Browning's correct admonition that the suggestion 'that the potential to commit such crimes is latent in modern
society in no way denies that so far Nazi Germany alone has realized
this potential ...'. See his review of Burleigh and Wippermann,
'Barbarous Utopia: The terrible uniqueness of the Nazi State', *Times
Literary Supplement* (March 20, 1992) p. 5.

110   In addition to those addressed below, see W.Schneider (ed,)
      *Vernichtungspolitik. Eine Debatte ueber den Zusammenhang von
      Sozialpolitik und Genozid im nationalsozialistischen Deutschland*
      (Berlin, 1991). See too the related work of K.H. Roth. Roth edited
      *Redationskollektiv 'Autonomie', Erfassung zur Vernichtung. Von der
      Sozialhygiene zum 'Gesetz ueber Sterbhilfe'* (Berlin, 1984) and, togeth-
      er with G. Aly, *Die restlose Erfassung. Volkszaehlen, Identifizieren,
      Aussondern im Nationalsozialismus* (Berlin, 1984).

111   See their *Sozialpolitik und Judenvernichtung. Gibt es eine Oekoenomie
      der Endlosung?* (Berlin, 1987) and *Vordenker der Vernichtung.
      Auschwitz und die deutschen Plaene fuer eine neue europaische
      Ordnung* (Hamburg, 1991). See also their collection of documents
      *Bevolkerungstruktur und Massenmord. Neue dokumente zur deutschen
      Politk der Jahre 1938–1945* (Berlin, 1991).

112   As far as I am aware their only English-language publication to date
      is 'The Economics of the Final Solution: A Case Study from the General
      Government', *Simon Wiesenthal Center Annual*, 5 (1988) pp. 3–48.
      The quotes appear on pp. 3–4.

113   *Ibid.*, p. 6 and pp. 36–7.

114   For general critiques, see H. Graml, 'Irrgeleitet und in die Irre fuehrend.
      Widerspruch gegen eine "rationale" Erklaerung von Auschwitz',

Jahrbuch fuer Antisemitschforschung 1, 1992, pp. 286–95; D. Diner, 'Rationalisierung und Methode. Zu einem neuen Erklaerungsversuch der "Endloesung"', *Vierteljahrheft fuer Zeitgeschichte* 10, 1992, pp. 359–82; and the contributions by C. Browning and U. Herbert in W. Schneider (ed.), *Vernichtungspolitik.*

115 Paul Lawrence Rose, *Revolutionary Antisemitism in Germany: From Kant to Wagner* (Princeton, 1990).

116 See the critical reviews by Anthony Quinton, 'Idealists Against the Jews', The *New York Review of Books* (November 7, 1991) pp. 38–40 and James F. Harris, *American Historical Review* (April 1992) pp. 571–2. See too Christopher Munro Clark, 'Three Books about Antisemitism', *Historical Journal* 34 (1991) p. 993.

117 See her 'Die geschriebene und das gesprochene Wort. Uber Kontinuitaet und Diskontinuitaet' in her *Juedisches Leben und Antisemitismus im 19. und 20. Jahrhundert* (Munich, 1990) pp. 54–75.

118 For the still-definitive presentation of this, see Eberhard Jaeckel, *Hitler's World View: A Blueprint for Power*, translated by Herbert Arnold (Cambridge, 1981).

119 Quoted in Burleigh and Wippermann, *The Racial State*, p. 44.

120 Jacques Derrida, 'Otobiographies: The Teaching of Nietzsche and the Politics of the Proper Name' in *The Ear of the Other: Otobiography Transference Translation*, edited by Christie McDonald, translated by Peggy Kamuf and Avital Ronell (New York, 1985) pp. 30–1.

Index

Contents

Acknowledgements

I am most grateful to the following friends and colleagues for help and advice: David T-D. Clarke, Alison Colchester, Maggie Cox, Philip and Nina Crummy, Francis O. Grew, Jenny Hall, Vivienne Holgate, Tim Malim, B. R. K. Niblett, Ros Palmer, Professor D. P. S. Peacock, Tim Thorpe and Colin R. Wallace, as well as the late and much missed Tony Gregory. Dr John A. Davies kindly allowed me to read his important survey of the iron age of Norfolk before its publication. My wife, Julia, and Ernest W. Black suggested many constructive changes to the text. It is a pleasure to acknowledge the advice of James Dyer, Series Editor of Shire Archaeology.

4

List of illustrations

1

Icenian grievances

The Roman invasion of Britain in AD 43 by the emperor Claudius
started with an attack on the Catuvellauni, a tribe based in what is now
Hertfordshire and which had conquered extensive territories in south-
eastern England. After defeating them, the Roman invasion force divided
into separate armies and moved into the Midlands and southern and
western England. The progress of these armies was not always contested
because some tribes saw the sense of coming to terms with the new
order. One such tribe was the Iceni, who entered into a treaty relationship
with Rome and became her allies; this meant that they retained their

1. A silver coin of the Icenian
king Antedios, c.AD 25-50.
Scale x 2. (By courtesy of the
Trustees of the British
Museum.)

own government without a Roman military presence. On the Icenian
throne in AD 43 was a king called Antedios, known to us only from his
coinage, and who presumably negotiated this treaty (figure 1). Such
allied kingdoms were called client states and the Roman administration
(but not necessarily the client states themselves) regarded the
arrangement as a prelude to eventual full incorporation into the empire.

The Iceni lived in East Anglia (figure 2), separated from the Corieltauvi
of Lincolnshire by the Wash, which in the first century AD extended
further south than nowadays. In Suffolk their border with the Trinovantes
to the south can be fixed with a precision unique for the tribal land
frontiers of late iron age Britain, because the archaeology of the two
tribes is quite distinct.

One major area of difference in the archaeology of the two nations
was their pottery. The Trinovantes used wheel-thrown pottery called
Belgic; among the Iceni more traditional hand-made wares remained in
use right up to the time of the Boudican revolt. In both regions the
forms of the vessels are also distinct, although on some Icenian
settlements there is a gradual adoption of Belgic pottery in the fifty
years or so before AD 60. These developments are illustrated by the

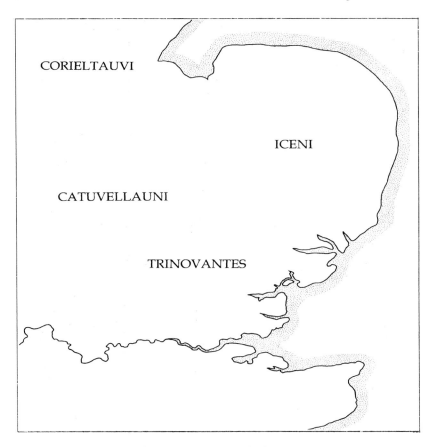

2. The Iceni and their neighbours.

pottery from the Icenian farmstead at West Stow, Suffolk (figures 3-4).
   The Trinovantes and Catuvellauni had important trade links with the
Roman world in the century before AD 43. Icenian participation in this
exchange was negligible. The tribe apparently denied access to Roman
merchants in the late iron age, a policy also followed by some tribes in
Gaul and Germany who believed that wine and other imports
undermined traditional values. This reluctance to have any dealings
with the Roman world increased the culture shock to the Iceni after AD
43 and contributed to the uneasy relationship between the tribe and
Rome after the invasion.
   The coinage of the Iceni is the most important single archaeological

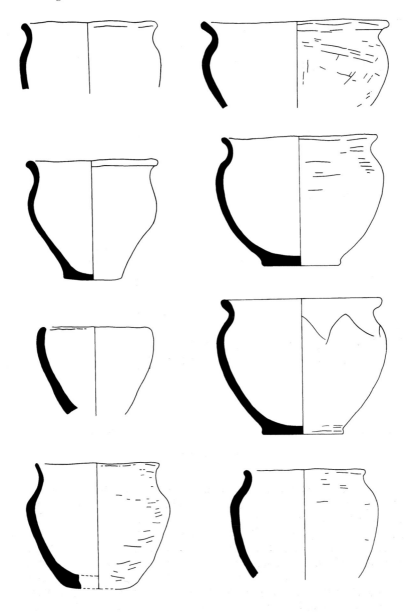

3. Traditional hand-made pottery from the Icenian farmstead at West Stow, Suffolk, *c*.AD 1-60. Scale 1:4. (After West 1989.)

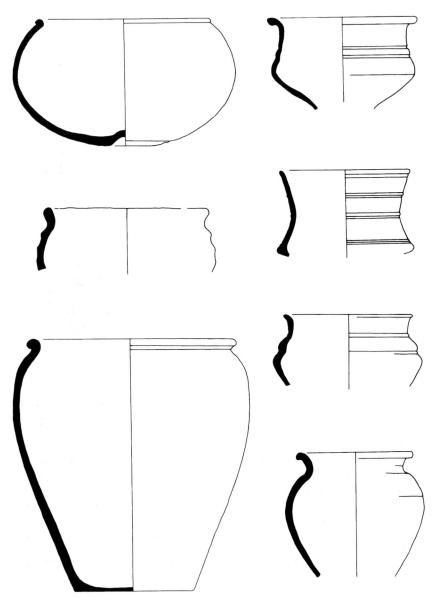

4. Wheel-thrown Belgic pottery from the Icenian farmstead at West Stow, *c*.AD 1-60. Scale 1:4. (After West 1989.)

5. The main categories of the Icenian silver coinage: boar horse (top), pattern horse (middle) and face horse (lower). Scale x 2. (By courtesy of the Trustees of the British Museum.)

source material for the tribe and is crucial in defining the extent of their territory. In the late first century BC the tribe abandoned gold but continued to strike coins in silver, sometimes with a smaller denomination called a minim. The only subsequent exceptions were king Antedios, who minted a very few gold coins about the time of the Roman invasion, and a few gold coins with the tribal name (see page 10). Standards of quality control and integrity in the Icenian mints were unimpressive: at around only 48 per cent silver, the precious metal content of the coins was lower than that of other tribes; the use of worn or broken dies is much in evidence; and plated coins (contemporary forgeries consisting of a base metal core under a silver coating, and produced by corrupt moneyers) were not uncommon.

The standard design on Icenian coins is a horse. The designs on the other side fall into three groups, showing a boar, a pattern, and a face (figure 5). It used to be thought that these three streams of coinage reflected the identity of subgroups within the tribe, but no geographical clusters that would support this are now apparent. In the first century AD inscriptions appear on the coins. Their interpretation is difficult because the names are abbreviated and it is not clear if one is reading the name of the place where the coin was minted or that of the issuer. A series of inscriptions reading ECEN and ECE is apparently a shortened version of the tribal name, making the Iceni the only tribe in Britain to put its name on coinage

6. Enlarged drawings of Icenian coins with a horse and the abbreviated tribal name, ECE. (After Allen 1970.)

(figure 6). Coins of Prasutagus show that the Iceni continued to mint coins after AD 43. Confirmation comes from two Norfolk sites, Needham and Thetford, which have produced fired clay moulds for the production of coins in early Roman contexts. Nevertheless the worn state of many of the Icenian coins found in hoards buried at the time of the Boudican revolt suggests that the output of the mints was in decline after AD 43. The Iceni are remarkable for having produced four sites with coin moulds, more than for any other tribe in Britain (figure 7). This unusual pattern suggests the kingdom had a decentralised, if not a federal structure.

The first rift between the Iceni and Rome came in AD 47. The governor of the province, P. Ostorius Scapula, decided to disarm suspect communities and to tighten control of Britain with a new programme of fort construction. Despite their nominal independence, the Iceni found themselves included in these repressive measures and they rose in revolt. They chose a place for battle defended by earthwork defences. Ranged against them were forces consisting of Britons drawn from other allied tribes in the island, led by Roman officers. There followed a fierce fight in which the Iceni were routed. The best suggestion for the site of the battle is Stonea Camp, an iron age fort on a former island in the Cambridgeshire fens occupied from the first century BC until *c*.AD 40-60. Its ditch had been filled

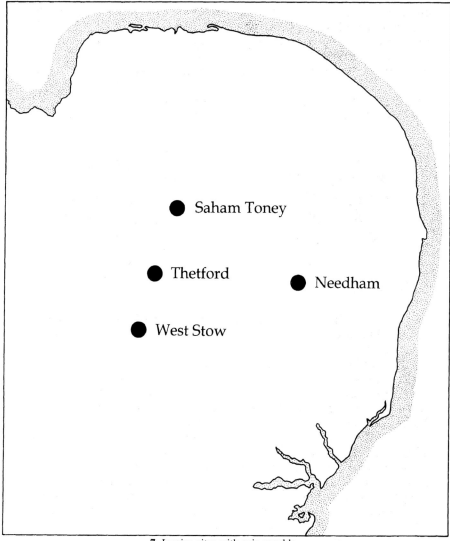

7. Icenian sites with coin moulds.

with turves from the rampart, an operation that looks like the deliberate slighting of the defences by the victorious Romans. To keep a watchful eye on the tribe, a fort was built at the major Icenian site of Saham Toney, 45 kilometres to the east. No excavations have taken place on the site of the fort but its presence can be demonstrated by a concentration of Roman military equipment and the semi-official coins of Claudius struck by the army. It is clear that the whole tribe was not involved in the events of AD 47 because otherwise its status as an allied nation would have been terminated there and then.

The garrison of the Saham Toney fort did not interfere with the rebuilding of a major religious and ceremonial site at Thetford, 16 kilometres to the south. In the 50s AD a grandiose rectangular enclosure of 32,000 square metres was constructed there. Inside an outer perimeter ditch was another ditched rectangular enclosure; the 35 metre gap between both ditches was filled with a series of nine parallel fences. Both ditches had corresponding inner ramparts. Access was through a single entrance, central on the east side of the enclosure. It was a straight corridor that ran between stout wooden fences of upright posts leading into an inner enclosure some 80 metres wide and 140 metres long. There was a massive timber gateway where the entrance joined the inner enclosure. Anyone entering the inner precinct would be faced by a largely empty arena, to the rear of which stood a two-storeyed building which the complex had inherited from a previous enclosure on the same spot.

The open layout of the inner enclosure would have been well suited to public assembly, whether for secular or religious purposes. Forty-seven brooches found on the site presumably represent accidental losses from the clothing of the people who congregated there. Thetford may well have been the scene of a tribal meeting that decided to follow Boudica in her crusade against the Romans in AD 60.

The revolt of Boudica was precipitated by the death of her husband, Prasutagus. Silver coins of the king have a high-relief portrait bust, quite unlike earlier heads on Icenian coins because they were copied from a Roman coin of Nero, who became emperor in AD 54. Its inscription reads SVBRIPRASTO. The other face has a traditional horse design with the inscription ESICO FECIT. Taken together both inscriptions mean 'Under King Prasutagus, Esico made [this coin]'. PRASTO must be the abbreviated name of the monarch and RI is short for *ricon*, a Celtic word for 'king'. Esico is either the name of the man in charge of the mint or the die-cutter. Otherwise the use of the Latin words *sub* and *fecit*, coupled with the copying of a Roman coin portrait, shows how Roman culture was starting to pervade the royal family and the mint.

In his account of the revolt, the great Roman historian Tacitus makes two errors of dating: he says that it lasted for only one year, and that it broke out in AD 61. Most people now take the view that

Prasutagus died – and that the revolt broke out – in AD 60 and that the war lasted until the following year.

The death of Prasutagus meant the end of the client kingdom of the Iceni. In his will the king hoped to safeguard at least some of his estates and property by naming the emperor Nero joint heir with his own daughters, but the Romans treated the Iceni as if they were a nation that had been defeated and forced to surrender. The financial management of the province was in the hands of the procurator, Catus Decianus. His staff descended on the Iceni and proceeded to pillage the countryside as well as the royal household. Estates of the aristocracy were confiscated and the owners evicted. The widow of Prasutagus, Boudica, was flogged and her two daughters were raped. Catus Decianus claimed that money presented to leading figures in Britain by the late emperor Claudius was in fact only loans, which he attempted to reclaim. One of the most influential figures at court in Rome, Seneca, chose this moment to call in the huge sums he had lent the Britons. Loans and gifts of money to the Iceni and their neighbours go some way to account for the Roman coins in the hoards buried at the time of the revolt. It may also explain large early hoards of Roman silver coins such as those from Sutton, Suffolk, and Woodham Mortimer, Essex, buried on or near native settlements. Hatred of Rome was not confined to the aristocracy. As an allied state, the Iceni were expected to surrender quotas of young men to serve in the auxiliary regiments of the army. This was widely resented and goes a long way to account for the enthusiastic popular response to the call to arms made by Boudica. The time seemed opportune for action because the Roman army was far away in north Wales; nor were there any troops in East Anglia itself as the Saham Toney fort had been abandoned by *c*.AD 58.

The name of this famous warrior queen of the Iceni is not without interest. In Celtic, the name *Boudica* meant 'victory' and was the equivalent of our modern Victoria. Two variant spellings, *Boudicca* and *Boadicea*, are incorrect.

There are two striking images of the queen. The historian Cassius Dio describes her as she rallied her nation: she was a tall woman with a mass of red hair that fell down to her waist; around her neck there was a ceremonial gold neck-ring called a torc. In her hand she clutched a spear; secured by a brooch to her multi-coloured tunic was a thick cloak. A later and equally powerful image of the queen is the huge bronze statue of Boudica and her daughters standing in their war chariot on the Thames embankment, near the Houses of Parliament in London. Its creator was Thomas Thornycroft, a sculptor and engineer who died in 1885. With scythes fitted to the wheels and rearing horses uncontrolled by reins, the statue bears little connection with historical reality. But it captures perfectly the perception that Boudica was a prophetic hint of the imperial greatness her successor Britons eventually achieved under Queen Victoria. On the plinth are inscribed the words of the poet William Cowper:

Regions Caesar never knew
Thy posterity shall sway.

2

Trinovantian collaboration

The Trinovantes of Essex and the south of Suffolk were the southern neighbours of the Iceni. On the west, they were flanked by the powerful Catuvellauni tribe. The Trinovantes have the distinction of being the first community in Britain to enjoy treaty relationships with Rome, going back to 54 BC when Julius Caesar attacked the island.

But recognition by Rome was not sufficient to protect the Trinovantes indefinitely against powerful enemies. Eventually Cunobelinus, a king of the Catuvellauni, conquered the Trinovantes and moved his capital from Verulamium (St Albans, Hertfordshire) to Colchester, Essex, c.AD 10. This effectively amalgamated both tribes, but after AD 43 the Romans reverted to the situation before Cunobelinus and treated both tribes as separate entities. Cunobelinus had a long reign until his death c.AD 40, only a few years before the Roman invasion. Under him the Catuvellauni won control of much of south-eastern England. It was at Colchester that Cunobelinus minted the gold coins for which he is so famous. On them appears the ancient name of Colchester, *Camulodunum* (meaning 'fortress of the war god Camulos'). Iron age Colchester itself was defended by a series of linear earthwork ramparts with outer ditches. Most of this land was agricultural and Camulodunum should be thought of as the royal estate and seat of Cunobelinus, rather than as a town or capital city in any modern sense.

Trade between the Trinovantes and the Roman world was significant in the century before the invasion of AD 43. Wine arrived in large pottery storage jars called amphoras, made in Italy; other amphoras brought olive oil, grape syrups and fish sauce from Spain. Table crockery came from Italy and Gaul. The impact of this trade with Rome was out of all proportion to its relatively modest scale because it helped Britons gain some perception of the great Mediterranean power whose rule now extended to the English Channel and the North Sea. A rich grave dated c.AD 20-30 from the Stanway cemetery outside Colchester had a set of twenty-four imported Roman pots, with no local wares at all: at Stanway, people were buried for whom only the best was good enough, and the best was Roman. This was a quite different (and more positive) outlook on the Roman world from that of the Iceni, who stood aloof from these developments.

When Claudius invaded Britain in AD 43, the emperor entered Colchester in person. Its capture, and the defeat of the Catuvellauni, marked the end of the first stage in the conquest of the island. A legionary fortress was built to house Legion XX on the site of the modern town centre. A smaller fort outside the town at Gosbecks dominated a concentration of native settlement in the Colchester dyke system. One of the first tasks of the army was to destroy the mint of the Catuvellauni; its obliterated remains have been excavated at Sheepen on the outskirts of the town. The dyke that protected it was also demolished and thrown into the ditch.

The legionary fortress at Colchester lost its garrison in AD 49 when Ostorius Scapula moved Legion XX west to fight the Silures of south Wales. To safeguard his rear, the governor founded a *colonia* at Colchester. A *colonia* was a settlement of newly retired legionaries; veterans will have been drawn from one or more of the four legions serving in Britain. The townsfolk of the new *colonia* were all Roman citizens because only they were eligible for service in the legions. Understandably the tone of a *colonia* would have had a paramilitary air, quite unlike that of an ordinary town with civilian origins. The Colchester *colonia* was intended to be the capital of the new province of Britain.

Coloniae were a time-honoured way of fastening Roman control on conquered and allied territories. They were intended to serve as urban centres from which surrounding peoples would be introduced to Roman culture and law. Claudius himself ordered the establishment of the Colchester *colonia*, a decision that reflected his conviction that *coloniae* in newly conquered territories promoted security. As former soldiers of unimpeachable loyalty, the citizens of a *colonia* could be relied upon to defend Roman interests against any local opposition. By making satisfactory provision for legionaries in their retirement, the foundation of *coloniae* avoided the unrest that had plagued the Roman state a century earlier in its civil wars, and helped to integrate retired soldiers into civilian life. Veterans were happier in *coloniae* on newly conquered territory at the frontiers of the empire because they felt more at home there with old army friends than if they were repatriated to their original homes.

Events were to show that the *colonia* at Colchester would fail dismally to fulfil the hopes of its founders. What so outraged Trinovantian feelings was the scale of land seizure around the town. Each veteran of a *colonia* was given a grant of land, typically in the order of fifty *iugera* (12.59 hectares). If the citizen body at Colchester was three thousand veterans, this would have meant the confiscation of some 37,750 hectares, an area equivalent to a circle around the town with a radius of 9 kilometres. Tacitus describes the land taken from the Trinovantes as captured territory, *agri captivi*. If the *agri captivi* were deemed to have been won by expelling the enemy, an authorised Roman could help himself

8. A section through Gryme's Dyke at Colchester, an earthwork erected by Romans in connection with land seizure from the local population AD 49-60. (Copyright Colchester Archaeological Trust.)

to as much land as he wished, when he wished. This is what happened at Colchester. Natives were driven from their lands and treated as captives and slaves; there was no one act of land seizure in AD 49, when the *colonia* was founded, but a continuing haphazard appropriation of land that went on until AD 60, when the storm broke. Roman soldiers turned a blind eye because they hoped to do the same when they retired. The existing dyke system was extended as part of this land allotment; such was the case with a stretch of Gryme's Dyke which excavation showed to have been erected after the Roman invasion (figure 8).

The ditch of the Colchester legionary fortress produced graphic evidence of the rough treatment of the local Trinovantian population. Six human skulls were found. One had a deep gash from a sword blow; another had a fracture caused by a blunt instrument such as a sword pommel (figures 9-10). These are the remains of Britons

9. The decapitated skull of a Briton executed *c*.AD 55 at Colchester. Note the gash from a sword at the base. (Copyright Colchester Archaeological Trust.)

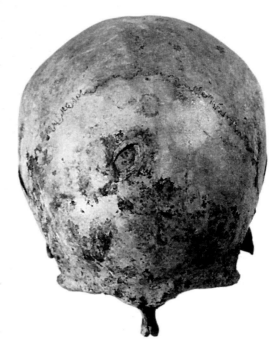

10. The decapitated skull of another Briton executed *c*.AD 55 at Colchester. Note the oval fracture in the centre. (Copyright Colchester Archaeological Trust.)

11. The vaults of the temple of Claudius at Colchester. (Copyright Colchester Archaeological Trust.)

executed by the Romans. Their heads were presumably impaled on stakes as a warning to others; eventually they rolled into the ditch of the legionary fortress sometime before it was backfilled *c.* AD 55. These executions show how relationships between the two communities at Colchester deteriorated in the years before the Boudican revolt and the skulls hint at the old scores that were settled in AD 60.

Another tribulation that led the Trinovantes to join the Boudican revolt was the temple of Claudius. After the death of Claudius in AD 54, the senate at Rome declared him a god and the construction of a temple for him began at Colchester. One of Seneca's writings has been taken to mean that Claudius was worshipped there as a god in his own lifetime (a distinct anomaly), but this view is no longer held because the language Tacitus used to describe the temple shows that it was unfinished and unconsecrated at the time of the revolt. But even this unfinished temple was a source of grave offence to the Trinovantes; they saw it as the citadel of an everlasting tyranny. Moreover the expenses of the cult were such that people appointed as priests faced bankruptcy and abused their position to extract funds from their reluctant fellow countrymen.

The podium (platform) on which the temple stood has miraculously survived, preserved by the Norman castle built around it in the middle ages. It measures some 23.5 by 32 metres and stood in a rectangular walled precinct 160 by 180 metres. Even by Roman standards, this was a large and imposing structure. The podium was made of septaria, a stone found on the Essex and Suffolk coasts. But the podium is not solid masonry throughout (there was not enough); instead the architects built a series of four adjacent vaults. Originally they were completely filled with sand; we can explore them nowadays because a tunnel was cut into them from the outside in the eighteenth century and part of their sand fill was removed (figure 11). On parts of the interior of the vaults the impressions of the timber shuttering that had been used to form their arches are still visible. On the podium stood the temple proper, fronted by eight columns and approached by a flight of steps. Marble found on the site did not come from the temple destroyed by Boudica but from the refurbishment of the building in late antiquity. The only components of the temple superstructure to have survived are some fragments of terracotta columns, about 90 centimetres in diameter; some were covered with a thick white stucco decorated with concave fluting.

Just outside the Colchester dyke system at Stanway was a group of five enclosures, four of which had nailed timber mortuary chambers. Other cremations were also discovered. Typical of the splendours of the cemetery is the warrior buried in Enclosure IV *c.*AD 45-50. The deceased had been laid to rest with his spear and shield; other grave goods included a gaming board with glass counters, imported Roman pottery and bronze and glass vessels, a gridiron for cooking food, and a wine amphora from the Pompeii region of Italy. Funerals took place at Stanway from the late first century BC until the time of the Boudican revolt (figure 12). The small number of graves, their wealth and the

12. A rich native grave dated *c*.AD 50 from the Stanway cemetery, just outside Colchester. (Copyright Colchester Archaeological Trust.)

elaborate funerary rituals show that Stanway was the cemetery of a rich native family that found favour with the new Roman order after AD 43. Otherwise their ancestral cemetery would have been a victim of the land seizures perpetrated by the veterans of the *colonia*. It was from just such a background that the natives appointed to serve as priests at the temple of Claudius were recruited.

3

Colchester destroyed

The first target of the Iceni and their Trinovantian sympathisers was Colchester. Their attack came in the late spring, with the campaigning season already underway. When the townsfolk got wind of impending trouble they appealed to Catus Decianus to reinforce the few troops still based there, but the procurator was able to spare only two hundred inadequately armed men. Preparations for the defence of the town were hindered by secret supporters of the rebel cause. No attempt was made to erect any defences, nor were women and the elderly evacuated. Tacitus says the town was not defended by a rampart and ditch; archaeology confirms this because the rampart of the former legionary fortress had been demolished and shovelled into its ditch *c.* AD 55. Q. Petillius Cerialis, the courageous but impetuous commander of Legion IX, marched south to the rescue of the town from his base in the east Midlands with a detachment of his legion, but he was ambushed and his entire force of some 1500 infantry was killed. Cerialis fled with his cavalry back to the fort at Longthorpe in Peterborough, Cambridgeshire. Excavations there have shown that he hastily built a smaller fort (whose ramparts could be defended with reduced manpower) inside the original base, where he awaited developments behind these new fortifications. Unnerved by the outbreak of the revolt, Catus Decianus escaped to Gaul. Meanwhile at Colchester the last stand of the Roman soldiers and veterans took place in the temple of Claudius, where they held out for two days. The destruction of Colchester was total: the whole town was destroyed by fire and the population annihilated. The only hint in the archaeological record of the Icenian war band at Colchester are two terrets (oval bronze rings which held the reins used to control horses), decorated in a style typical of Norfolk and north Suffolk.

The layer of burnt debris at Colchester created by the sack of the town is called the *Boudican destruction horizon*. It ranges in depth from a few centimetres to (exceptionally) as much as one metre. In places the lower parts of buildings are preserved to a height of up to 60 centimetres, allowing the architecture and plan of the legionary fortress and early *colonia* to be reconstructed in detail. Most of the Boudican destruction horizon is burnt daub. Normally daub does not survive because it reverts to the clay from which it was made, but the high temperatures reached when the town was torched turned it into a more durable substance akin to pottery. Molten glass that had subsequently solidified also testifies to the ferocity of the inferno. Broken tiles, wall plaster and smashed pottery are also common.

The Boudican destruction horizon is found right across those parts of the town and its suburbs that were occupied in AD 60. It is absent from much of the eastern area of the later walled town because those parts were not built over until after the revolt. But even in those parts of the town destroyed by Boudica, the anticipated burnt layer can be missing where the excavated area lay in gardens behind the houses that fronted the streets. At the west end of the town, burnt levels are found outside the area of the later town wall, showing urban expansion beyond the former legionary fortress in the years before AD 60. An industrial suburb 750 metres north-west of the town at Sheepen was also destroyed in the revolt. Military scrap metal there had been thought to indicate a frantic last minute rearmaments drive, but it is now felt that it was simply the raw materials of bronze workers supplying the civilian market of the *colonia.* An early cemetery just outside the town was also ransacked. Destruction extended into the countryside, to judge by the burnt levels found at the Somerford site, 1.5 kilometres west of Colchester.

Some groups of pottery from the Boudican destruction horizon represent warehouses or shops. At North Hill a building thought to have been a government store had more than thirty identical and unused *mortaria,* bowls with grits on the inside for grinding foodstuffs. Another room and adjacent corridor had over eighty flagons, again all very similar to each other. In the next room there were twenty smashed amphoras, most of which had come from southern Spain filled with olive oil. On the High Street there were two shops that sold samian ware, the famous red-slipped pottery from Gaul. Pottery Shop II was a small timber building; most of its pottery was found close to one wall. Pottery Shop I was at the other end of the High Street.

The Boudican destruction horizon is important for archaeology because it provides a fixed point for the chronology of Romano-British pottery and other artefacts. In the case of samian ware, which was traded throughout the Roman world, it is a fixed point of international significance. But a study of the samian ware from the Boudican destruction horizons at London, Verulamium and Colchester has revealed some discrepancies in the material and led to the conclusion that Pottery Shop I at Colchester is earlier than Pottery Shop II. It is now thought therefore that, although Pottery Shop II is indeed Boudican, its companion shop was destroyed in another, earlier fire *c.*AD 50-5.

The destruction of the town by fire has preserved remains of foodstuffs that would otherwise have decayed and become difficult or impossible to recognise in the archaeological record. Seven sites have produced carbonised grain, the staple food. Most of these caches of grain were

13. Dates burnt in the sack of Colchester. (Copyright Colchester Archaeological Trust.)

dominated by wheat. One of these seven deposits was unusual because about a tenth of it was made up of barley. These Culver Street grains had started to germinate: the sprouts were even, showing the damp responsible was deliberate and not the result of poor storage conditions. This was grain that had been treated to make malt for beer, the earliest example in Britain. Other foodstuffs were more exotic. At Lion Walk there was a deposit of twenty-two dates imported from the Mediterranean world (figure 13); a single plum was present as well. Another Mediterranean import is represented by the figs from Pottery Shop II. The same shop produced lentils, horsebeans and the spice coriander. Other perishable organic material preserved for study by fire includes burnt timber beams from buildings and a pair of textile mattresses tucked neatly in the corner of a room at Lion Walk.

Other finds from the Boudican destruction horizon shed further light on daily life in the town in AD 60. The Gilberd School produced a gridiron for cooking (figure 14). At Sheepen a leaded bronze dice-shaker with two dice was found; left behind in a timber-lined cellar was

14. A complete cookery gridiron from the Boudican deposits at Colchester. (Copyright Colchester Archaeological Trust.)

a leaded gunmetal stamp for embossing leather; elsewhere on the site there was a glass cameo showing a sea nymph. Lamps and moulds for their production were found at the Telephone Exchange site. Mixed up with a few complete artefacts like these are all manner of damaged or incomplete domestic items such as brooches and latch-lifters.

But above all the character of the horizon testifies to the thoroughness with which Colchester had been looted: no gold or silver has been found in the burnt levels, apart from the odd Roman coin. The same story is told by the few hoards of Roman coins present. All three consist of small numbers of relatively low-value copper or brass coins of Claudius and Agrippa (an earlier member of the imperial family). Some of these coins are burnt; the hoards had not been buried in the ground for safety but represent instead purses lying above ground when the town was sacked. Intact material that could be reused was rescued by the Romans after the revolt and this salvage operation has also affected the composition of the destruction horizon. Tiles with burn marks from AD 60 have been found recycled in the footings of later buildings. Pits were dug into the horizon in the search for valuables; they were immediately refilled with the burnt daub extracted from them. Levelling of the debris as a prelude to rebuilding must also have involved an element of salvage.

Two tombstones in the west cemetery along the south side of the main road to London had been vandalised by the rebels. One of them is a memorial to an officer called Longinus from the First Thracian cavalry regiment, the *Ala I Thracum*. The sculpture on the tombstone shows a mounted cavalryman; below the horse crouches a naked and defeated Briton on his shield (figure 15). When it was discovered, the tombstone had been smashed into six main pieces and lay face down in the ground. It must have given the Boudican rebels a grim satisfaction to flatten this image of a cowering Briton at the feet of his Roman enemy. Another tombstone found nearby had also been smashed and buried face down in the soil. It commemorated an officer in Legion XX, the centurion M. Favonius Facilis (figure 16). There is no trace of weathering on either sculpture and it is clear they had not been exposed to the elements for long before their destruction.

One casualty of the revolt was discovered on the Telephone Exchange site, where the charred and disarticulated remains of an adult lay on a verandah fronting the street. In the industrial suburb to the west of the town at Sheepen, fragments of one or more human skulls were found in Pottery Kiln XXVI and they too may represent victims of the revolt.

No other victims of the holocaust have been found at Colchester, or indeed at London or Verulamium. This is remarkable because Tacitus says that seventy thousand perished in the sack of these three towns. The Britons did not take prisoners to be sold as slaves but slaughtered everyone who fell into their hands, regardless of age or sex, through crucifixion, hanging, fire and the sword. This was not just gratuitous carnage, but the sacrifice of victims to the gods of war in time-honoured Celtic fashion.

What may have been loot from the town has been found in East

15. The tombstone from Colchester of the Roman cavalry officer Longinus, smashed in the revolt. (Copyright Colchester Archaeological Trust.)

Anglia. The most famous piece is a bronze head of the emperor Claudius from the river Alde at Rendham, Suffolk (figure 17). A jagged line around the neck showed where it had been wrenched from the body. A

16. The tombstone from
Colchester of the Roman
centurion Facilis, smashed
in the revolt. (Copyright
Colchester Archaeological
Trust.)

slight backward tilt of the head suggests the original statue had shown
the emperor mounted on horseback; we are dealing with an equestrian
statue that was on public view in the town. Part of the same statue was
found at Ashill, Norfolk, 60 kilometres away. The Ashill fragment is

17. Bronze head of the emperor Claudius from the river Alde, looted from Colchester by the Iceni. (By courtesy of the Trustees of the British Museum.)

the knee of the horse, hollow-cast like the head of Claudius. What links the two fragments is their alloy, because both pieces have low lead levels. In antiquity lead was usually added to bronze to make it flow more easily when it was cast. Alloys like that represented by the Rendham and Ashill fragments were rare and this suggests that they had indeed come from the same statue.

4
London and Verulamium sacked

When the Iceni and Trinovantes attacked Colchester, the military governor of the province, C. Suetonius Paullinus, was on a campaign far away in north Wales. His objective was the capture of Anglesey, an island whose already significant population had been swollen by refugees; their antagonism to Rome was sustained by the Druid priesthood resident there. The Roman army managed to make the crossing from the mainland and was engaged in extinguishing resistance on the island when news of the destruction of Colchester reached the governor. Suetonius broke off the Anglesey campaign at once. Accompanied by a detachment of cavalry, he hastened south through disaffected country to London, the legions and auxiliaries following behind. There Suetonius made the hard decision to abandon London to its fate and rejoin his army on its long march south-east from north Wales. Despite the entreaties of the population, London was left to its own devices. Those Londoners who were able accompanied Suetonius on the retreat. Women, the elderly, and those who were particularly attached to the place stayed behind.

London

London was a Roman creation: there was no prehistoric settlement on its site. It was built on a key position at the lowest bridging point of the Thames, on the hub of the new Roman trunk road network (figure 18). *Londinium* (its Roman name) came into being *c.*AD 50 as a town founded by immigrant craftsmen, financiers and merchants. Its population included a potter from western Switzerland called Caius Albucius, a manufacturer of blown glass and a cutter of intaglio sealstones, all newcomers to Britain bringing new skills. Despite its strategic importance, no fort was apparently placed at Londinium for its protection. The nucleus of the first London lay east of the Walbrook stream, on the hillock at Cornhill where the road from the Thames crossing met the east-west road that led to Verulamium (to the north-west), and Colchester (to the north-east). Just north of this T-junction was the first forum or market square of the new town, a small gravelled open space. By AD 60 buildings had spread west across the Walbrook towards Ludgate Hill. There was a small suburb south of the Thames at Southwark. Although London was not an officially sponsored town, it had a rectilinear planned street grid, with amenities such as piped water. This suggests that the expatriate Roman citizen traders and dealers

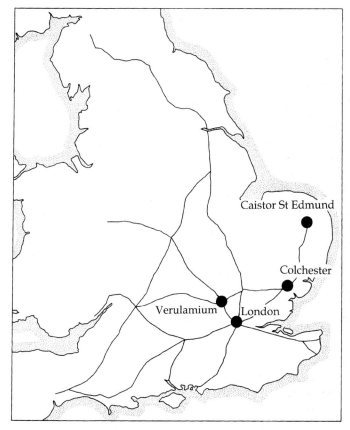

18. The nodal position of London on the road network of Roman Britain, showing cities mentioned in the text.

based there had already formed their own town council. A British contribution to Londinium is apparent in the round houses (a traditional native architectural form) found on the outskirts of the town. Otherwise the architecture consisted of rectangular structures built in a style widespread in Gaul and Italy, with walls made of sun-dried clay blocks (figure 19). Just outside the built-up zone of the first London were the cemeteries of its population. The London that Boudica destroyed in AD 60 was a city one can still recognise today: lively, cosmopolitan, and with a strong financial sector.

The departure of Suetonius from a defenceless London was not long followed by its destruction at the hands of Boudica. As at Colchester,

19. A building at 160-2 Fenchurch Street in London destroyed by Boudica. Dried bricks rest on a flint and mortar foundation. (Copyright the Museum of London.)

the destruction and slaughter were universal; the same Boudican destruction horizon found there is repeated at London. Excavations have revealed a layer of bright red burnt daub, typically 30-60 centimetres deep. Sometimes the burnt debris had accumulated in open pits to make it (exceptionally) as much as 1.5 metres deep. The depth of the horizon at Colchester, London and Verulamium suggests that most of the buildings destroyed were only single-storeyed. The distribution of sites with this burnt debris is important evidence for the extent of the town in the early Roman period. Destruction extended south of the river to include the suburb at Southwark. Structures preserved in the destruction horizon allow the architectural history of the first London to be reconstructed in some detail. But it is quite wrong to think that the remains buried in these burnt levels are a kind of Pompeii or Herculaneum: like Colchester before it, London had been thoroughly looted by its attackers. But among the portable wealth overlooked by them was a cache of four sealstones concealed in a pot at Eastcheap, presumably from a jewellery workshop to judge by their similarity of style, and a hoard of seventeen fire-blackened bronze coins of Claudius from King William Street.

An important find at 160-2 Fenchurch Street sheds some light on the background to the revolt. There a large mass of cereal burnt in AD 60 was discovered which included einkorn (figure 20). Britain lies north of those parts of Europe where einkorn was cultivated and this shows that at least some of the grain from Fenchurch Street had been imported from overseas. This was confirmed by the presence of bitter vetch and lentils (as weeds), indicating a source in the Mediterranean world. Clearly one or more poor harvests in southern Britain had caused a shortage of grain on the eve of the Boudican revolt. As the native

20. A granary in London destroyed by Boudica. The burnt grain is the black mass behind the scale. (Copyright the Museum of London.)

population had to pay some of their taxes in grain, crop failure and hunger must have contributed to the tensions that erupted so violently in AD 60.

More than one hundred human skulls have been found in the bed of the Walbrook stream. It has been suggested that they represent the decapitation of Londoners in AD 60, but an examination of the surviving skulls reached the conclusion that they had no connection with the atrocities of the revolt. None bear any signs of the sort of injuries that one might have expected of victims of Boudica. Moreover most of the skulls came from young to middle-aged adults. Tacitus says that women and the elderly were especially reluctant to flee the city in the face of Boudica, yet these are the very groups that are so under-represented in the surviving skulls. The lack of jaw bones shows the skulls had been deposited in the river unfleshed. We know the Boudican hordes did not spend long in London and, as it can take months (even in summer) for a jaw to separate from its skull, the Walbrook heads can hardly be linked with the revolt. It is now clear that they were cast in the river after the revolt, as part of ritual practices unconnected with Boudica; the decisive evidence takes the form of detached skulls found elsewhere in London until at least the mid second century AD.

Verulamium

After the sack of London, Boudica and her war host moved north along Watling Street towards Verulamium, the Roman town outside the modern St Albans in Hertfordshire that served as the capital of the Catuvellauni. Like Colchester, Verulamium was a settlement with an important late iron age predecessor. Pre-Roman Verulamium is known as *Verlamion*, after the spelling of the place found on coins of Tasciovanus, who reigned from *c*.15 BC to *c*.AD 10. A series of larger and smaller earthwork ramparts with outer ditches defended the settlement. Some mark out the sites of individual farmsteads, while others demarcate whole tracts of the countryside. Pollen analysis shows the landscape was only sparsely wooded, with most of the land devoted to pasture and arable cultivation. Finds of iron age coin moulds are widely spread across the site of the later Roman town. They concentrate around a small rectilinear ditched enclosure beneath the site of the later forum and basilica complex; it is possible this was the site of a royal residence or mint. A large cremation cemetery in use from *c*.AD 1 to 60 at King Harry Lane, with a wealth of material imported from the Roman world, testifies to the high standard of living and far-flung connections of the population. A more chilling find is a skull fragment from a house in Insula XII (an insula was one of the blocks into which a Roman town was divided), a reminder of the head hunting practised in iron age Britain.

Such was the importance of Verlamion that when the Romans built the main road that linked London and the Midlands, Watling Street, it was routed through the town. By the late 40s AD, iron age Verlamion was transforming itself into Roman Verulamium, a settlement on more truly urban lines. It did this spontaneously, with minimal Roman input. This early progress at Verulamium so impressed the Romans that it was created a *municipium*, a class of urban site second only in status to a *colonia* like Colchester, with privileges bestowed on it by law.

Understandably the architecture of early Verulamium was a blend of native and Roman. Many of the buildings were rectangular structures built on timber sleeper beams in iron age style; occasionally post-built structures are found. Roman influence is apparent in Insula XIV, where a terrace of rectilinear buildings was fronted by a colonnaded walkway, the whole block being best interpreted as a row of shops owned by an entrepreneur who leased out individual premises. Elsewhere two other early buildings destroyed by Boudica were built in masonry, a Roman innovation.

Verulamium was no match for the Boudican hordes. Like Colchester

21. The burnt deposits of AD 60 at Verulamium, clearly visible as the dark band at the bottom of the trench. (Copyright St Albans Museums.)

and London, it was razed to the ground. Sites with burnt layers from its sack are concentrated in the heart of the later city. Their geography is important because they indicate the extent of the town in AD 60. It emerges that Verulamium extended over only some 8 hectares, far smaller than used to be thought, but much more in keeping with the size of contemporary towns. At Verulamium the Boudican destruction horizon consists of the same clean red daub and ash found at London and Colchester, ranging here up to a maximum of about 50 centimetres, in Insula XVII (figure 21). Unlike London and Colchester, the destruction of standing structures was not total. Some buildings in the south-west corner of Insula XIV escaped, as well as some of the outbuildings of the shops in the opposite, north-east corner of the same insula, which fronted Watling Street, even though the shops themselves were burnt. Evidently the shops had been set alight from the Watling Street side by arsonists at a time when the wind was blowing from the south-west. One of the shops sold samian ware, to judge by the thirty-seven unused vessels spilled across the verandah fronting the street. In another shop were the burnt remains of a water tub set in the ground; it had filled with burnt daub and the carbonised sides of the tub could be seen rising

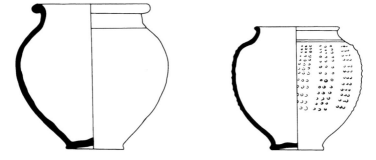

22. Two complete pots from a building at Verulamium destroyed by Boudica. Scale 1:4. (After Frere 1972.)

above the floor level. Two complete pots (figure 22) stood on the floor of another room; when the buildings were torched they had filled with burnt daub. Nearby was a pit which held a chest filled with textiles. A lump of bronze drapery from the same insula in a context dated *c.*AD 75-85 must be scrap collected from the destruction of a statue in AD 60. The character of the destruction horizon at Verulamium differs from that of London and Colchester by the absence of any parcels of coins or burnt grain deposits. Although this might reflect the thoroughness with which the town was looted, the likelihood instead is that at least some of the inhabitants escaped with their portable belongings.

Destruction was not confined to the town of Verulamium. 5 kilometres south-east of the town centre, a house at Park Street was destroyed in the revolt. When it was burnt down, it left a spread of burnt daub over the clay floor. Park Street is only 475 metres east of Watling Street and would have been an easy target for the Boudican war band using the road as it advanced on Verulamium. At Gorhambury, 2 kilometres to the north-west of Verulamium, another farmstead was destroyed in the revolt. Gorhambury was a large rectangular enclosure defended by a ditch and rampart; inside there were two rectangular buildings and one round house. These sites were not the homes of Roman oppressors, but homesteads of the native population. Their destruction shows that existing ethnic hatred – in this case Trinovantian resentment at their conquest by the Catuvellauni under king Cunobelinus – was a significant ingredient in the revolt, a factor overlooked in antiquity by historians of the revolt.

5
Boudica defeated

When Suetonius decided to abandon London and rejoin his army on its march south-east down Watling Street, his predicament was desperate. But he was an experienced and resourceful general who kept his nerve. His difficulties were compounded by the refusal of the acting commander of Legion II in Exeter, Poenius Postumus, to join forces with him. Moreover Legion IX under Petillius Cerialis had already been badly mauled by the Iceni and was immobilised in the east Midlands. The army Suetonius had at his disposal consisted of the whole of Legion XX, part of Legion XIV and those auxiliaries he was able to summon from nearby bases, in all a force of some ten thousand men.

His only hope was that the Boudican hordes would be foolhardy enough to risk a pitched battle. What Suetonius must have feared above all was a protracted guerrilla war with the prospect of surprise attacks in wooded countryside where the Britons could use a knowledge of the terrain to their advantage. But elated by their earlier victories, the Iceni and Trinovantes staked all on one battle. Suetonius was allowed to choose his own ground: his rear was protected by a wood; the plain before him in which the Britons milled around was open ground where there was no possibility of an ambush. Suetonius placed his legionaries in the centre of his battle line, with auxiliary infantry alongside; the flanks were protected by cavalry (figure 23).

When battle was joined, the legionaries discharged their javelins into the oncoming hordes. Then they pressed forward in close formation, battering at the enemy with their shields and doing murderous work with their short stabbing swords. In disciplined formations such as this, the lack of body armour among the Iceni and Trinovantes told. The Britons had even brought along their womenfolk to watch the spectacle from wagons positioned around the battle ground. This overconfidence recoiled on them because it denied them mobility and in the Roman advance the Britons found themselves trapped by their wagon train. Even the women and draught animals were killed in the Roman fury: the slaughter was immense and the Roman victory total. Tacitus says eighty thousand of the enemy fell, for the loss of only four hundred Romans.

The battle between Boudica and Suetonius settled the fate of Britain for the next 350 years. Yet the site of this most decisive of struggles remains unlocated. Tacitus gives no clues to its whereabouts. But one may assume that as the Roman army pressed south-east on its march from

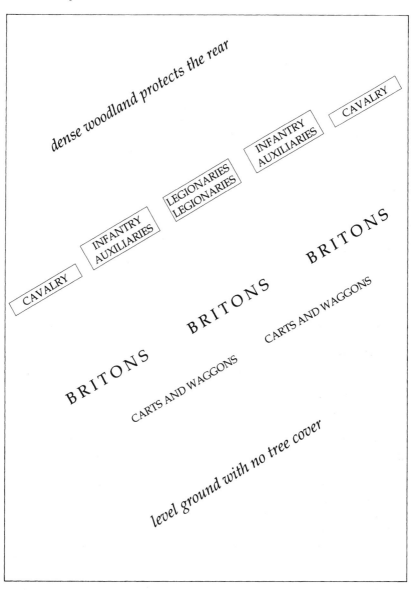

23. The layout of the battle between Suetonius and Boudica.

Anglesey, the Britons made their way up Watling Street into the Midlands towards the approaching Romans. Suetonius is unlikely perhaps to have strayed far from Watling Street itself and the scene of the final encounter may be sought somewhere along the route. A case can be made for Mancetter in Warwickshire (figure 24), where high ground approaches the road to give a terrain that fits the meagre topographical sketch of the battlefield in Tacitus.

Not long after the battle, Boudica either took her own life or died from natural causes. When Poenius Postumus learnt of the victory, his earlier refusal to obey orders and join Suetonius led him to fall on his own sword. As for Suetonius, he was hailed as the greatest general of his day.

The whole might of the Roman army was now concentrated against the Iceni and Trinovantes, and their territory was laid waste by fire and the sword. To make good Roman casualties, reinforcements of two thousand legionaries, eight auxiliary infantry cohorts and two auxiliary cavalry regiments were sent from Germany. The rebels had not sown a crop that year because they were confident of victory, and a dire famine followed their defeat. Little is known of the military bases in Essex and East Anglia that crushed the revolt. In Essex one of the two forts suspected at Chelmsford is presumably Boudican; a larger base at Great Chesterford played a still more important role. There were forts in Suffolk at Pakenham, Coddenham and possibly Stuston. The grave of a soldier from the Coddenham garrison has been found, complete with a mirror case showing Nero addressing his troops. The picture can be eked out in Norfolk with forts at Horstead, Worthing and apparently Caistor St Edmund. A pit at Baldock, Hertfordshire, dated *c.*AD 50-70, had the remains of ninety-eight sheep butchered in the winter months. This might well be the work of a Roman army unit on the march towards East Anglia in the winter of AD 60/61, provisioning itself with mutton and fleeces.

There are signs of the impact of the revolt on Icenian and Trinovantian settlements in rural Norfolk and Suffolk, although nothing yet that is comparable to the burnt destruction layers at the towns destroyed by Boudica. This is a gap in the archaeological record that is difficult to explain, particularly as the documentary evidence leaves no doubt as to the stern measures taken against both tribes.

At West Stow in Suffolk, on the edge of the tract of sandy countryside called the Breckland, there was an Icenian farmstead occupied until the mid first century AD. The settlement consisted of round houses, distinguished by their irregular plans. Brooches show occupation continued until *c.*AD 40-60. No pre-Boudican Roman pottery or coins were recovered from the site. The site was abandoned after the middle

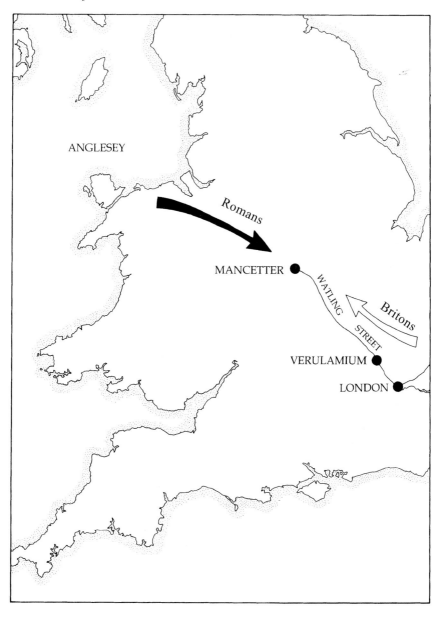

24. The movement of British and Roman forces before the final battle in the Midlands.

of the century and it is tempting to connect this with the revolt. But there is no destruction horizon at West Stow and presumably the inhabitants had left the site in the revolt, never to return, or had starved to death in its aftermath. Occupation did not resume until after c.AD 70 and within ten years an important pottery industry had emerged on the site.

A Trinovantian site that may have suffered in the revolt was Burgh-by-Woodbridge, Suffolk. It was a rectangular enclosure defended by a double ditch and rampart built in the first century BC. Just before the Roman invasion a smaller defended enclosure was built inside the main defences. About AD 60 part of these inner defences was destroyed. Two finds of unstratified Roman military equipment – an artillery bolt and a bent (and therefore used) javelin head – point to an attack on the site. If Burgh was not attacked in AD 43, it too may have been a casualty of the Boudican revolt.

The great ceremonial and religious complex at Thetford, Norfolk, is another site in East Anglia where the stern hand of Rome is evident. After the revolt the site was abandoned and it saw no resumption of activity for two hundred years. Its end was dramatic, although a lack of burnt daub from its buildings shows there was no destruction by fire. Instead the site experienced a systematic and relentless demolition. Excavation revealed little sign of rotted timber in its many postholes and post settings. Instead the larger post settings had ramps or pits cut into the ground alongside them for their removal. Smaller postholes were often oval where the posts had been rocked backwards and forwards to loosen them before extraction. Ditches were at least partially backfilled with rampart material. Scattered across the site were five pieces of Roman military equipment, suggesting the presence of the army: after the revolt, a detachment of Roman soldiers had descended on Thetford and obliterated it.

By now C. Julius Alpinus Classicianus had been sent to the province to replace Catus Decianus as procurator. Relationships between the procurator and the military governor of a province could be strained and this was certainly so with Classicianus and Suetonius. Classicianus was alarmed at the ferocity with which Suetonius was conducting the war. His concern was based not just on humanitarian considerations, but on pragmatic ones as well; the heavy casualties inflicted on the Iceni and Trinovantes would inevitably affect tax revenues from the province. Classicianus expressed his misgivings to the emperor and a civil servant called Polyclitus was sent to Britain to give an independent assessment of the situation. Although Suetonius was retained, the loss of a few ships and their crews on the coast in AD 61 provided a pretext to replace him with a new governor, P. Petronius Turpilianus.

25. The reconstructed tombstone from London of the financial governor of Britain, C. Julius Alpinus Classicianus. (By courtesy of the Trustees of the British Museum.)

His arrival meant the end of the revolt.

Classicianus died during his term of office and was buried at London. His tombstone was a large monument in the shape of an altar (figure 25). In the late Roman period it had been smashed and used as building material for a bastion on the town wall. Fragments of the tombstone were discovered on two separate occasions. Inscriptions are one of the most important categories of source material for Roman history and the Classicianus tombstone is no exception. Its inscription tells us that the tomb was erected by his wife, Julia Pacata. She was the daughter of an aristocrat from Gaul who had helped put down a revolt there in AD 21.

The tombstone also gives the full name of the procurator. From this it can be deduced that he too had come from a Celtic region of the empire and that his family had been awarded citizenship between fifty and a hundred years earlier by Julius Caesar or the emperor Augustus. Classicianus was a Gaul who had been recruited into the imperial service; his background helps explain the clemency he urged at the end of the war he experienced in Britain.

6
Native wealth hoarded

A significant feature of the archaeology of East Anglia is the large number of hoards buried early in the Roman period. They fall into two groups: coin hoards and metalwork hoards. Most of these hoards were buried at the time of the Boudican revolt in an effort to save portable wealth from the Romans. At least some of the hoards from the Fens may have been buried by people on the move trying to escape Roman vengeance in AD 61. Many hoards were never recovered because their owners died in the war or in the reprisals that followed.

The coin and metalwork hoards described in this chapter are not only major source material for the revolt, but they also allow us to build up a detailed picture of Icenian life in the heyday of tribal independence. The scale of this hoarding explains why we have more coins of the Iceni than of any other tribe in Britain. In the metalwork hoards one finds the last products of local craftsmen before traditional Icenian national life was destroyed. There is a dearth of comparable hoards in south Suffolk and Essex; evidently the Trinovantes (even allowing for the sack of Colchester) were less passionately involved in the war than their northern neighbours.

Coin hoards

Apart from a suspect report of an Icenian silver coin hoard from Battle, East Sussex, the coin hoards thought to have been buried at the time of the Boudican revolt are confined to Norfolk, north-west Suffolk and north-east Cambridgeshire. It is difficult to establish how many such hoards have been found because publication inevitably lags behind discovery, but the total now exceeds twenty-five. The hoards are dominated by silver coins of the Iceni and often consist of nothing else. The people who assembled the hoards took care to avoid collecting the plated coins so prevalent in the kingdom; such coins are more common as finds from settlement sites. The only hoard with a gold coin of the tribe is Lakenheath, Suffolk, where a solitary gold issue of king Antedios was present. Coins from other tribes are rare. The only foreign coins in the hoards in any quantity are Roman. In the Santon Downham, Suffolk, hoard there were worn brass *dupondii* of the emperor Claudius minted in AD 41-3; otherwise Roman issues consist of the silver coins called *denarii*. Occasionally one or more small amorphous blobs of silver are also found in the hoards.

Understandably, the size of the hoards varies. The largest is Field

Baulk from March, Cambridgeshire, with 872 silver Icenian coins buried in a red pot (figure 26). A more typically sized hoard consisting exclusively of Icenian silver – 153 coins – came from Fring, Norfolk. It too had been buried in a pot; the mouth had been covered with a textile cloth of vegetable fibre, possibly flax or hemp. The largest of the mixed hoards is Lakenheath, made up of one Icenian gold issue, two Catuvellaunian gold coins of king Cunobelinus, 410 Icenian silver coins and sixty-seven Roman denarii.

A few hoards were buried in pots. Without exception, they are typical of the decades around AD 50. The vessel in which the Fring hoard (for instance) was buried is a British form but in the hard fabric typical of wares fired in Roman-style kilns after AD 43. The latest closely dated

26. The hoard of Icenian coins buried in the Boudican revolt at Field Baulk, March, Cambridgeshire, with its container pot. (By courtesy of the Trustees of the British Museum.)

pot is the *c.*AD 60-70 jar in which the Field Baulk hoard had been buried.

Inevitably it is the Roman coins that offer the greatest help in dating the hoards. Details of the latest Roman coins found in the Icenian coin hoards are given in the table.

Weston Longville	Republican (before 31 BC)
North Creake	Republican (before 31 BC)
Lakenheath	Gaius (Caligula), AD 37
East Dereham	Gaius (Caligula), AD 37
Santon Downham	Dupondii of Claudius, AD 41-3
Eriswell	Nero, AD 54-5
Joist Fen	Nero, AD 55-60
Scole	Nero, AD 59-61

The latest Roman coins in the Icenian hoards. All the Roman coins are denarii, unless indicated otherwise.

Roman coins did not circulate in iron age Britain, so any hoard containing them must have been buried after the invasion of AD 43. The latest coin is a denarius of Nero from the Scole, Norfolk, hoard. The part of its inscription that gives the date cannot be read, but it is certain the coin was minted between October or December AD 59 and October or December AD 61, with AD 61 as the most likely year of issue. At first sight the date range of the Roman coins suggests that these hoards may have been buried on a number of occasions between AD 43 and the Boudican revolt. But the Romans minted very few denarii between the reign of Tiberius (who died in AD 37) and the AD 64 currency reform of Nero. Their scarcity was such that a Boudican date for all the hoards is possible because it took them so long to get into circulation. Some hoards might have been buried in the revolt of AD 47, but this was a less dramatic insurrection than the Boudican revolt and involved only part of the tribe.

Metalwork hoards

There are six metalwork hoards of early Roman date from Norfolk and Suffolk that may also have been buried in the Boudican revolt

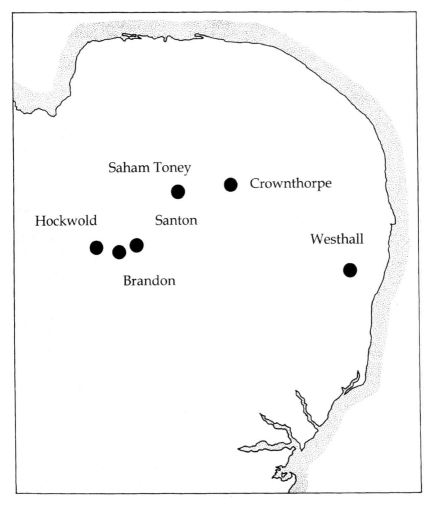

27. Metalwork hoards from East Anglia buried in the Boudican revolt.

(figure 27). There are no associated coins or pottery, so they cannot be as closely dated as the coin hoards, but in view of the scale of the revolt burial then rather than earlier is more likely. Four of these six hoards lie within 20 kilometres of Thetford and give the impression that the Breckland and its surrounding countryside were parts of the Icenian homeland that were particularly closely involved in the revolt. Each of these hoards is described in the following pages.

28. A Roman silver wine cup from the Hockwold hoard decorated with olives and vine leaves. (By courtesy of the Trustees of the British Museum.)

The hoard from Hockwold-cum-Wilton, Norfolk, is the only one of these hoards to consist exclusively of Roman material. At least seven silver wine cups are attested in this scrap hoard, although not every part of each vessel was present. All but two of the cups had handles. What is artistically the finest vessel is decorated with sprigs of olive and vine leaves in high relief; the other cups are plainer but have handles (figures 28 and 29). Each cup had been detached from its handles and base; the bowls were beaten out of shape. Their reduction to scrap metal shows they were bullion destined for recycling. We are now able to appreciate their original appearance following conservation and restoration at the British Museum.

Another hoard of drinking utensils was found at Crownthorpe, Norfolk. All are bronze and include native and Roman products. There are two small bowls with tinned interior surfaces and a pair of Roman handled-pans. Two cups are unique local copies of the kind of Roman cups found in the Hockwold hoard. They stand on pedestal bases; both have handles, perched on the top of which are tiny ducks. Most of the hoard components had been packed inside another native vessel, a large strainer bowl, complete with a dog's head spout and an internal perforated panel.

At Brandon, Suffolk, three vessels had been hidden beneath a large bronze cauldron buried upside down as a cover for them. One of them was a bronze saucepan imported from Gaul, stamped with the name of its maker, Julius. The two other vessels (like the cauldron itself) are local, native work. One is a small stave-built pail held together with plain bronze bands. The other is a spouted bronze strainer bowl, similar to the strainer in the Crownthorpe hoard. Additives in the Celtic beer which would have been prepared in the cauldron were removed by decanting the drink through bowls fitted with perforated panels and spouts. Although pottery versions of these strainer bowls lasted until the second century AD elsewhere in Britain, production of the bronze versions ended with the Boudican revolt.

The bronzework hoards from Westhall, Suffolk, and Saham Toney,

29. A plain Roman silver wine cup with handles from the Hockwold hoard. (By courtesy of the Trustees of the British Museum.)

Norfolk, illustrate another facet of Icenian life, chariot warfare and horsemanship. The Westhall find includes a harness mount, six linchpin terminals and eight terrets decorated with red enamel (glass). The Westhall terrets include a complete set of five from a chariot drawn by a pair of horses. Four of identical size were mounted on the yokes of the horses, while a larger fifth terret was placed on the actual chariot where the driver stood. When Caesar invaded Britain in 55 and 54 BC he was impressed by the chariot warfare that met him. Although its importance declined in the century after his attack on Britain, chariots were still used by some British tribes, including the Iceni, after AD 43. Six more terrets, this time brightly decorated with red, yellow and blue enamel, and another harness mount, make up the smaller hoard from Saham Toney.

The largest and most varied of the hoards is Santon, Norfolk. Most of the hoard is bronze; the little ironwork present includes a knife and a set of smith's tongs. Material in the hoard can be broadly divided into Roman and native. However, the distinction is difficult to maintain because some items, such as the steelyard with weight and pan, are Roman introductions to Britain but decorated in a local style. Native horse gear, chariot and wagon fittings include a linchpin, part of a bridle bit and harness mounts. The mounts are decorated with the abstract curvilinear patterns typical of late iron age art and inset with red enamel inlay. Bronze strips with embossed patterns presumably came from furniture. A fitting from a spouted strainer bowl has two of the ducks that are so typical and endearing a feature of Icenian metalwork. The largest item is the bronze cauldron in which the hoard had been buried; repair patches show it was an antique. Purely Roman finds include a jug and a handle from a handled-pan. Unlike the other metalwork hoards described here, Santon can be more securely and closely dated to the Boudican revolt on the basis of its brooches and fragments of Roman military armour. The miscellaneous character of this collection of new and scrap material suggests it had belonged to a metalworker.

7

Aftermath and rebirth

So traumatic had been the Boudican revolt that the Romans postponed new conquests in Britain for ten years, until they were confident that Essex and East Anglia had been pacified. Indeed Nero had contemplated a complete withdrawal from Britain. We are not told when, but the period after the suppression of the revolt seems likely. In AD 61 the replacement of Suetonius by P. Petronius Turpilianus marked the end of the revolt. Turpilianus himself undertook no military operations in the province. His successor from AD 63 until 69 was M. Trebellius Maximus. Trebellius had conducted a census and tax assessment of Gaul in AD 61 and had been promoted to Britain because of this experience of aggrieved provincials in testing circumstances. His administration was courteous and conciliatory; no military campaigns were undertaken and consolidation was the order of the day. Policy did not change until the appointment in AD 71 of Petillius Cerialis (who himself had so nearly lost his life in the Boudican revolt), when there was a resumption of wars of conquest in western and northern Britain under the new Flavian dynasty. Such is the background to the archaeological evidence for provincial recovery after the Boudican revolt.

Colchester

The destruction of the *colonia* at Colchester and the annihilation of its citizen body was regarded by the Romans as a major catastrophe. Roman political sentiment would not tolerate the permanent loss of a *colonia* under such circumstances and the foundation of a successor town was not long delayed. This is clear from the archaeological evidence: the upper surface of the daub of the Boudican destruction horizon at Colchester often has a fresh and unweathered appearance; nor is there any perceptible gap in the pottery sequence consistent with a protracted break in the occupation of the town. Like those of its predecessor, the citizens of the new *colonia* will have been discharged legionaries from the army in Britain. A fragment of the tombstone of such a veteran was found just outside the town. The soldier (his name has not survived) was a centurion from Legion XX. He had been born in Nicaea, a town in what is now Turkey. It is not recorded when the new *colonia* was founded, but a coin of Nero issued in AD 64 had been incorporated in the metalling of one of the roads, suggesting it took place in the AD 63-9 governorship of Trebellius Maximus. The name of the *colonia* sacked by Boudica is unknown, but an inscription tells

30. The town walls of Roman Colchester, built in the aftermath of the Boudican revolt *c.*AD 65-80. (Copyright Colchester Archaeological Trust.)

us that this new city was called *Colonia Victricensis*, 'the colony of the victorious'.

The Romans knew how to learn from their mistakes. It had not gone unnoticed that the town destroyed by Boudica had no defences, so *Colonia Victricensis* was provided with a masonry wall, the earliest in Roman Britain. Pottery dates it *c.*AD 65-80 and shows it was erected in the aftermath of the Boudican revolt. The wall itself rests on a foundation a metre or so deep. Above ground, the outer faces of the wall consist of neat courses of brick and septaria. It ran for some 3000 metres and enclosed an area of 44 hectares; half the length of the wall is still visible, standing 4 metres high in places (figure 30). These town walls are the most striking field monument of the Boudican revolt and testify to the impact the destruction of Colchester made on the Roman administration.

London

The appeal of the colonists at Colchester to Catus Decianus for military help on the eve of the revolt shows that the procurator was based elsewhere, presumably at London. It is clear from the discovery of the tombstone of Classicianus that the new procurator had his office there as well. Such a major government department in the town kept London alive through the 60s AD. Tree-ring analysis of excavated timbers from two sites shows the wood came from trees felled in AD 62 and 63, but most of the sites destroyed by Boudica remained derelict for at least a decade. Pottery also confirms the fact of continued occupation of the city, but the quantities involved are modest and the dearth of imported fine wares reflects the disruption of trade that followed in the wake of the revolt.

Real recovery did not begin until the early 70s AD when the emperor Vespasian decided to resume the conquest of the island, and it was clear that Britain was to remain a province of Rome. Then building work began anew at London. A timber amphitheatre for gladiatorial contests and wild beast fights was built at Guildhall *c.*AD 70. On Cornhill a large forum with flanking offices and buildings was under construction in the 70s and 80s. Its basilica (town hall) was added at the turn of the century. At Cannon Street station an impressive complex centred on a courtyard with an ornamental pool may have been the palace of the provincial governor himself. A large public bath-house was erected *c.*AD 80 at Huggin Hill. Across the river, Southwark was not left out of this rebirth. There a large stone building was sited on piles made from timber felled in AD 72, 73 and 74. It had a central courtyard and may have been a *mansio*, an hotel for government officials.

London was also provided with a major new quay along a 620 metre stretch of the Thames. Tree-ring dating fixes its construction in the 70s and 80s. Timber revetment walls were built up to 15 metres out on the foreshore; the earth dumped behind them came from terracing of the ground inland. Many of the timbers had been perfectly preserved through waterlogging (figure 31). The wood used was oak, taken from trees several hundred years old. Other parts of the quayside consisted of jetties and openwork timber structures resting in the water; behind the quay was a series of warehouses. Port installations of this magnitude are unknown elsewhere in Britain.

Reconstruction at London after the revolt took place on such a scale that private enterprise alone cannot account for it. This massive programme of public building must have been carried out by the state as an act of policy when it was clear that the geographical advantages of London marked it out as the capital of the province.

Verulamium

Verulamium was the last of the three towns sacked by Boudica to recover. Until *c.*AD 75 the only activity on the site of the devastated

31. Massive oak timbers from a quayside of the late first century AD at London, preserved through waterlogging. (Copyright the Museum of London.)

shops in Insula XIV was the occasional pit, presumably dug to extract salvage from the Boudican destruction horizon. One such subrectangular pit was 4 metres deep and may have been a well. This level of activity falls far short of urban life and amounts to little more than squatters in the immediate vicinity.

Urban renewal worthy of the name is first proclaimed on a Purbeck marble inscription cut when Cn. Julius Agricola was the governor of Britain. It was found at the entrance to the forum and basilica complex and is represented by only five fragments of what was originally a large and imposing text. It is evident from the text that the forum and basilica were completed in the last six months of AD 79. Bearing in mind the scale of work involved, construction must have been underway for at least some years. In his biography of Agricola, Tacitus records how in the winter of AD 79-80 the governor devoted himself to promoting the adoption of Roman town life by the Britons. Individuals were en-couraged to build forums, temples and town houses; whole communities that wanted to do the same were given state assistance. The Verulamium inscription is dramatic evidence of that policy and provides archaeological corroboration of the account in Tacitus.

Otherwise the first sign of resurrection comes from activity dated *c.*AD 70 alongside the Silchester road at King Harry Lane. But elsewhere in the town the rebuilding of private houses and shops did not begin until between fifteen and twenty years after the revolt. Sometimes the burnt daub of the Boudican destruction horizon was used to provide flooring for new houses. The post-Boudican town was defended by the 1955 ditch (so-called because that was the year of its discovery), dug in the decades after the revolt. This fortification consisted of a single rampart and ditch enclosing 47.6 hectares, an area much larger than the town destroyed by Boudica. It ran round the entire town, except for the east, where the marshes along the river Ver were thought to give adequate protection. Although recovery was slow, the new Verulamium went on to become one of the largest cities of Roman Britain.

East Anglia

The revolt against Rome was an unqualified disaster for the Iceni. Such was the scale of casualties inflicted on the tribe that it may have taken centuries for the population to return to its former levels. After the revolt a tribal capital was founded at Caistor St Edmund (also known as Caistor-by-Norwich), south of Norwich. It is difficult to describe the early history of Caistor with confidence because our knowledge of the town is heavily dependent on unsatisfactory excavations there before the Second World War. Pottery kilns discovered then are now realised to have been in production in the late Neronian and early Flavian periods, supplying a military market in the immediate vicinity. They must predate the foundation of Caistor as kilns were seldom found in towns because of the fire risk. Clearly the traditional foundation date of *c.*AD 70 for the town must be abandoned; reassessment of the site suggests that town life was not underway until perhaps thirty years later. This would explain why the forum and basilica were not built until the second century. When the town walls were erected, they enclosed only 14 hectares, to make Caistor one of the smallest walled towns in the province. Its modest size reflects the devastating impact of the Boudican revolt on the tribal economy and the morale of its aristocracy.

To begin with, the countryside tells much the same story. Samian ware of the first century AD date is rare on rural sites in Icenian territory (very different from pre-Boudican London, where 20-25 per cent of all pots were samian) and few villas developed in the region. Some of the countryside seems to have been imperial estates, land owned directly by the emperor and farmed by tenants or slaves. But wealth was eventually regenerated; it is most striking in the dazzling gold, silver and jewellery treasures found in the hoards buried at Snettisham, Mildenhall, Thetford and Hoxne between the second and early fifth centuries. Two of them – Snettisham and Thetford – were buried in the immediate vicinity of major pre-Boudican religious sites and it is an ironic commentary on the nature of archaeological evidence that even amongst these thoroughly Roman treasures there seems to be an implicit acknowledgement of the ancient sacred places of the Iceni.

8
Museums and sites to visit

Museums

Intending visitors are advised to find out the times of opening before making a special journey.

British Museum, Great Russell Street, London WC1B 3DG. Telephone: 0207 636 1555. Website: www.british-museum.ac.uk On display are selected terrets and horse gear from the Westhall hoard, Icenian coins, the reconstructed tombstone of Classicianus, the Hockwold hoard of Roman silver cups, and the treasures from Snettisham, Mildenhall, Hoxne and Thetford.

Cambridge University Museum of Archaeology and Anthropology, Downing Street, Cambridge CB2 3DZ. Telephone: 01223 333516. Website: cumaa.archanth.cam.ac.uk On display is the Santon scrap metalwork hoard.

Castle Museum, Norwich Castle, Norwich, Norfolk NR1 3JU. Telephone: 01603 223624. On display are Icenian coins, including the Honingham hoard and its container pot, the coin mould fragment from Needham, the fragment of bronze sculpture from Ashill, the Saham Toney hoard of horse fittings, and the hoard of drinking utensils from Crownthorpe.

Colchester Museum, Colchester Castle, Castle Park, Colchester, Essex CO1 1TJ. Telephone: 01206 282932. On display are two of the skulls of executed Britons, and finds from the Stanway cemetery. Material illustrating the sack of the town includes scorched samian ware, a burnt wall, carbonised foodstuffs, and the bones of a casualty of the revolt. The tombstones of Facilis, Longinus and the Nicaea centurion are also on view.

Moyse's Hall Museum, Cornhill, Bury St Edmunds, Suffolk IP33 1DX. Telephone: 01284 757488. Website: www.stedmundsbury.gov.uk On display is the Brandon hoard with its cauldron and drinking utensils.

Museum of London, 150 London Wall, London EC2Y 5HN. Telephone: 0207 600 3699. Website: www.museumoflondon.org.uk On display are the King William Street coin hoard, the Eastcheap intaglios, and three of the Walbrook skulls.

Verulamium Museum, St Michaels, St Albans, Hertfordshire AL3 4SW. Telephone: 01727 751810. Website: www.stalbans.gov.uk On display are burnt daub from the sack of the town by Boudica, and the reconstructed Agricola forum inscription.

Sites

Caistor St Edmund, Norfolk: the site of the Icenian capital in the Roman period is now farmland and offers pleasant walks; parts of the defences are still visible. There is a car park and the site is provided with interpretation panels for visitors. The site is centred on National Grid Reference TG 230035.

Colchester Castle, Essex: below the Norman castle are the vaults of the temple of Claudius. Access is through guided tours provided by Colchester Museum.

Colchester Town Walls, Essex: much survives and is readily accessible to the public. A must for the archaeological rambler, with public houses and restaurants actually built into the fabric of the wall.

Stonea Camp, Cambridgeshire: this major Icenian fort in the Fens is now open to the public. Partial reinstatement of the earth ramparts gives some idea of its original size and appearance. There are information boards to help interested visitors. The site is centred on National Grid Reference TL 448931.

9
Further reading

Roman and Greek documentary sources

The most important account of Boudica will be found in Tacitus, the greatest Roman historian. He describes her revolt in full in his *Annals*; there is a shorter account in the *Agricola*, a biography of the historian's father-in-law. Tacitus composed his historical works *c.*AD 95-120. Both are readily available in translation in the Penguin Classics. Another account of the Boudican revolt features in a history of the Roman world by the Greek writer Cassius Dio. His account was written later than Tacitus, *c.*AD 210-30. There is a translation in the Loeb Classical Text series (Dio's *Roman History*, volume 8).

Modern accounts of the revolt

Dudley, D.R., and Webster, G.A. *The Rebellion of Boudicca.* Routledge & Kegan Paul, 1962. Still useful, not least because it has an important account of Boudica in British culture.

Fraser, A. *Boadicea's Chariot: the Warrior Queens.* Weidenfeld & Nicolson, 1988. A stimulating account of Boudica from a feminist viewpoint.

Webster, G.A. *Boudica: the British Revolt against Rome AD 60.* B.T. Batsford, revised edition 1993. The standard history of the revolt.

Wood, M. *In Search of the Dark Ages.* Penguin Books, revised edition 1987. The Boudican revolt is described on pages 1-27.

Major studies of the background and context of the revolt

Cunliffe, B.W. *Iron Age Communities in Britain.* Routledge, third edition 1991.

Frere, S.S. *Britannia: a History of Roman Britain.* Routledge & Kegan Paul, third edition 1987.

Salway, P. *Roman Britain* (The Oxford History of England). Oxford University Press, second impression 1982.

Colchester, London and Verulamium

Crummy, P.J. *Excavations at Lion Walk, Balkerne Lane, and Middleborough, Colchester, Essex* (Colchester Archaeological Report number 3). Colchester Archaeological Trust, 1984.

Crummy, P.J. *Excavations at Culver Street, Gilberd School and Other Sites in Colchester* (Colchester Archaeological Report number 6). Colchester Archaeological Trust, 1992.

Crummy, P.J. *City of Victory: the Story of Colchester – Britain's First Roman Town*. Colchester Archaeological Trust, 1997.

Frere, S.S. *Verulamium Excavations* volume 1 (Reports of the Research Committee of the Society of Antiquaries of London number 28). 1972.

Frere, S.S. *Verulamium Excavations* volume 2 (Reports of the Research Committee of the Society of Antiquaries of London number 41). 1983.

Marsh, G.D., and West, B.A. 'Skullduggery in Roman London?', *Transactions of the London and Middlesex Archaeological Society* 32 (1981), pages 86-102.

Merrifield, R. *London: City of the Romans*. B.T. Batsford, 1983.

Millett, M.J. 'Boudicca, the First Colchester Potters' Shop, and the Dating of Neronian Samian', *Britannia* 18 (1987), pages 93-123.

Niblett, B.R.K. 'Verulamium since the Wheelers' in S.J. Greep (editor), *Roman Towns: the Wheeler Inheritance* (Council for British Archaeology Research Report number 93), 78-92. CBA, 1993.

Perring, D. *Roman London*. B.A. Seaby, 1991.

Icenian coinage

Allen, D.F. 'The Coins of the Iceni', *Britannia* 1 (1970), pages 1-33.

de Jersey, P. *Celtic Coinage in Britain*. Shire, 1996.

Hobbs, R. *British Iron Age Coins in the British Museum*. British Museum Press, 1996.

The archaeology of the Iceni

Davies, J.A. 'Where Eagles Dare: the Iron Age of Norfolk', *Proceedings of the Prehistoric Society* 62 (1996), pages 63-92.

Davies, J.A., and Williamson, T.M. (editors). *Land of the Iceni: the Iron Age in Northern East Anglia*. Centre of East Anglian Studies, 1999.

Gregory, A.K. *Excavations in Thetford, 1980-1982, Fison Way* (East Anglian Archaeology Report number 53). Norfolk Museums Service, 1991.

Jackson, R.P.J., and Potter, T.W. *Excavations at Stonea, Cambridgeshire, 1980-85*. British Museum Press, 1996.

Johns, C.M. 'The Roman Silver Cups from Hockwold, Norfolk', *Archaeologia* 108 (1986), pages 1-13.

Martin, E.A. *Burgh: Iron Age and Roman Enclosure* (East Anglian Archaeology Report number 40). Suffolk County Planning Department, 1988.

West, S.E. *West Stow, Suffolk: the Prehistoric and Romano-British Occupations* (East Anglian Archaeology Report number 48). Suffolk County Planning Department, 1990.

Index